WINNING THE INTEREST RATE GAME

A Guide to Debt Options

Edited by
Frank J. Fabozzi

Walter E. Hanson/Peat, Marwick, Mitchell
Professor of Business and Finance
Lafayette College
and
Managing Editor, The Journal of
Portfolio Management

Probus Publishing Company
118 North Clinton
Chicago, Illinois 60606

Library of Congress Cataloging in Publication Data

Winning the interest rate game.

Includes index.
1. Interest rate futures—Addresses, essays, lectures.
2. Put and call transactions—Addresses, essays, lectures.
I. Fabozzi, Frank J.   II. Title: Debt options.
HG6024.5.W56   1985   332.8′2   84–11473

ISBN   0–917253–01–9

Library of Congress Catalog Card No. 84–11473

Printed in the United States of America

1 2 3 4 5 6 7 8 9 0

Dedicated to Barbara and Peter Bernstein

CONTENTS

SECTION III
Regulation and Taxes   261

CONTRIBUTORS

Andrew G. Balbus, Associate, Paul, Weiss, Rifkind, Wharton & Garrison

John McLean Ezell, Vice President and Manager of Fixed Income Hedge Products, Merrill Lynch Capital Markets

Laurie S. Goodman, Vice President, Capital Markets Group, Citibank, N.A.

David P. Jacob, Senior Research Analyst, Morgan Stanley & Co., Inc.

Frank J. Jones, Vice President, Kidder, Peabody & Co.

Robert W. Kopprasch, Vice President, Salomon Brothers Inc

Mark Landau, Assistant Vice President, Citicorp Futures Corp.

Gary D. Latainer, Senior Research Analyst, Morgan Stanley & Co., Inc.

Mark Pitts, Vice President, Lehman Brothers

Robert B. Platt, Principal and Manager of Fixed Income Research, Morgan Stanley & Co., Inc.

Stephen F. Selig, Senior Partner, Baer Marks & Upham

James A. Tilley, Vice President, Morgan Stanley & Co., Inc.

Benjamin Wolkowitz, Vice President, Citicorp Futures Corp.

PREFACE

Winning the Interest Rate Game: A Guide to Debt Options provides the fundamentals for understanding debt options and the strategies that can be employed in order to capitalize on the new opportunities involving these contracts.

The book is intended for both the individual investor and the professional money manager. It will provide invaluable information to help investors and money managers become proficient and successful participants in these new and exciting investment opportunities.

To be effective, any investment book should offer a broad perspective. Information from a wide range of experts is more useful than just a single author's viewpoint. I have chosen some of the finest financial minds to write for this book. Each contributor is a recognized expert in the area of debt options.

Overview of the Book

Section I of this book provides the background for understanding the strategies that are discussed in Section II. In Chapter 1, Laurie Goodman explains what an option is and the various types of debt options—options on fixed income securities, options on interest rate futures contracts, and interest rate agreements. A general description of hedging, the advantages of over-the-counter debt options over exchange-traded debt options, the advantages of employing debt options over interest rates futures, and the ability to hedge asymmetric risk are also explained in Chapter 1.

In Chapter 2, Benjamin Wolkowitz describes the instruments underlying exchange-traded debt options—Treasury securities and Treasury bond futures. To capitalize on the strategies employing debt options that are described in this book requires an understanding of how debt options are priced. Mark Pitts provides an introduction to the valuation of options on fixed income securities and options on interest rate futures in Chapter 3.

The applications of debt options are discussed in the six chapters of Section II. In Chapter 4, Bob Kopprasch provides an overview of how debt options can be used not only by investors, but also by (1) issuers of fixed income securities, particularly when any option feature may be granted as part of an obligation (for example, callable and putable bonds) and (2) financial institutions in which options may arise from products (for example, guaranteed investment contracts and whole life policies by life insurance companies) and services (for example, mortgage origination) that are sold. The strategies involving debt options that are available to asset and liability managers that are discussed in Chapter 4 include: (1) capitalizing on or defending against market expectations, (2) gauging of value of product options, (3) buying options to offset those granted in products or investments, (4) combining with other options to alter the risk profile, and (5) buying or selling volatility.

Trading and arbitrage strategies using debt options are illustrated by Mark Landau in Chapter 5. Frank Jones describes covered call writing strategies in Chapter 6. The two chapters that follow explain how two types of financial institutions can utilize debt options. John Ezell explains how they can be used by commercial banks and thrifts. James Tilley and David Jacob demonstrate how debt options can be used by life insurance companies and point out the limitations of exchange-traded options in actual applications.

In Chapter 9, Robert Platt and Gary Latainer describe a technique for achieving the benefits of option-type portfolio strategies without using an actual option. The strategy, referred to as a *synthetic option*, provides downside protection by a dynamic process of asset allocation between a particular risky asset and a riskless asset. The advantages of employing a synthetic strategy rather than exchange-traded or OTC options to achieve downside protection are explained in Chapter 9.

Regulation of financial institutions that are potential users of debt options and the federal income tax treatment of debt options are set forth in the two chapters in Section III. In Chapter 10, Stephen Selig summarizes the extent to which regulators permit the use of debt options by pension plans, commercial banks, savings and loan associations, credit unions, insurance companies and common investment trusts such as mutual funds. The chapter on taxation, Chapter 11, by Andrew Balbus includes the changes in the tax treatment as set forth in the Tax Reform Act of 1984.

A topic that is not covered in the book is that of the accounting treatment for debt options. Until such time as generally accepted accounting principles are firmly established by the Financial Accounting Standards Board for options transactions, it is suggested that option users consult with their accountants as to the appropriate principles to be followed.

Down the Road

The exchange-traded debt options described in this book are those that are traded as of August 1984. Several exchanges have sought regulatory approval for new debt option contracts. For example, the Chicago Board Options Exchange (CBOE) in mid-1984 planned to seek approval from the Securities and Exchange Commission for the right to trade an interest rate option index. Although the exact composition of the interest rate option index was not known at the time of this writing, it is expected to be based on a basket of interest rate Treasury obligations. Unlike the exchange-traded options that are currently traded, the interest rate option index would be a cash settlement option. That is, no underlying instrument would be delivered upon exercise. Instead, only cash will be exchanged between the two parties to the contract.

The International Monetary Market plans to trade options on Eurodollar futures by the end of 1984. This will be the first exchange-traded option on an interest rate futures contract in which the underlying security for the futures is a short-term instrument. Currently, only options on Treasury bond futures are traded.

The principles and strategies described in this book are applicable to both interest rate index options and options on Eurodollar futures.

Acknowledgments

I would like to express my deep personal appreciation to the contributors. I also wish to thank David C. Fisher of Arthur Andersen & Co. who kept me abreast of the developments of the accounting treatment of debt options. Michael Jeffers, Vice President of Probus Publishing, encouraged this project and provided support at every stage. I am grateful for both his guidance in this project and his friendship.

Frank J. Fabozzi
New Hope, PA

SECTION I

Background

CHAPTER 1

Introduction to Debt Options

Laurie S. Goodman, Ph.D.
Vice President
Capital Markets Group, Citibank, N.A.

Interest rates have been very volatile in recent years. This has subjected holders of fixed income securities to larger movements in prices than they had ever before experienced. It has also subjected holders of floating rate loans and issuers of short-term liabilities to unprecedented payment fluctuations on these instruments. Consequently, interest rate variability has increased the demand on the part of market participants for instruments designed to shift interest rate risk to those better able or more willing to bear it.

This environment has fostered the development of new financial products which give market participants greater flexibility in their risk-return profile. These new instruments include interest rate swaps, products involving financial futures, and debt options.

Interest rate swaps allow debtors with floating rate liabilities to obtain fixed rate liabilities and vice versa. The increased use of hedging with interest rate futures is evidenced by the growth of these markets; moreover, they have been used extensively in financial packages, such as synthetic fixed rate loans in which a variable rate loan is extended and covered via a futures contract.

The development of markets in interest rate options is one more manifestation of a financial market innovation which allows investors to reallocate risk in a more desirable manner. This chapter provides an introduction to interest rate options, including a survey of the available markets and a comparison of their relative strengths.

OPTIONS AND THEIR RISK-RETURN CHARACTERISTICS[1]

An option is an agreement between two parties in which one party grants the other the *right* to buy or sell an asset under specified conditions, while the counter party assumes an obligation to sell or buy that asset. The party who must decide whether to exercise the option is termed the option buyer, since he must pay for the privilege. The party granting the right to buy or sell an asset is called the option seller or writer of the option. There are two basic types of options: puts and calls.

A *call option* gives the buyer the right to purchase or "call away," a specified amount of the underlying security at a specified price, up to a specified date. The price at which the security may be bought is the *exercise price* or the *strike price*. The last date on which the option may be exercised is called the *expiration date* or the *maturity date*. The price of this option contract is its *premium*.

A call option can best be described by means of a simple example.[2] A six-month call option on the 11⅞ Treasury note,

---

[1] Readers familiar with equity options can skip most of this section, as the terminology used in stock options are applicable to debt options.

[2] In this example, the quotation used is the over-the-counter quote of a major government securities dealer, and is based on the most actively traded 10-year security.

due on 11/15/93, with an exercise price of 95, gives the holder of the option the right to purchase $100,000 par value of the specified Treasury notes at the price of $95,000 on or before the expiration date. The price of these notes on March 27, 1984, was $96,000. The price of the call option on this date was $2\frac{11}{32}$ or $2.34375 per $100. The total premium on the option, or $2,343.75, is paid at the outset. If interest rates fall and the market value of $100,000 of Treasury notes is greater than $95,000 on the expiration date, the option will be exercised. The intuition is that, even if the buyer does not want to hold the bonds, they can be resold at the market price. If the market value of the Treasury notes is less than $95,000 at expiration, the option will not be exercised, because the buyer can purchase the notes at a lower cost in the market. The profit profile for the buyer and seller of the call option at expiration are shown in Exhibit 1. Note that the break-even point for the option buyer and writer is $97,345.75; as the buyer must pay the cost of the option, while the writer earns this fee.

The price of an option consists of two components—the *intrinsic value* and the *time value*. The value of an option, if exercised immediately, is the *intrinsic value*. This is the maximum of either zero, or the market price minus the exercise price. In the example above, the intrinsic value of the option is the $96,000 market price, less the $95,000 exercise price or $1,000. If the market price of the securities was $94,000 and the exercise price of the options was $95,000 as before, the option would have zero intrinsic value. An option must always sell for at least its intrinsic value or there will be arbitrage opportunities. Stated differently, if an option sells for less than its intrinsic value, one could buy the option and exercise immediately, risklessly earning a profit. Market practitioners refer to options with positive intrinsic value as an "in-the-money" option. An option whose current price equals the strike price is known as an "at-the-money" option. A call option whose strike price is greater than the current price is referred to as an "out-of-the money" option.

The *time value* of an option is the difference between the premium on the option and its intrinsic value. It is the

EXHIBIT 1

CALL OPTION PROFIT PROFILE AT EXPIRATION

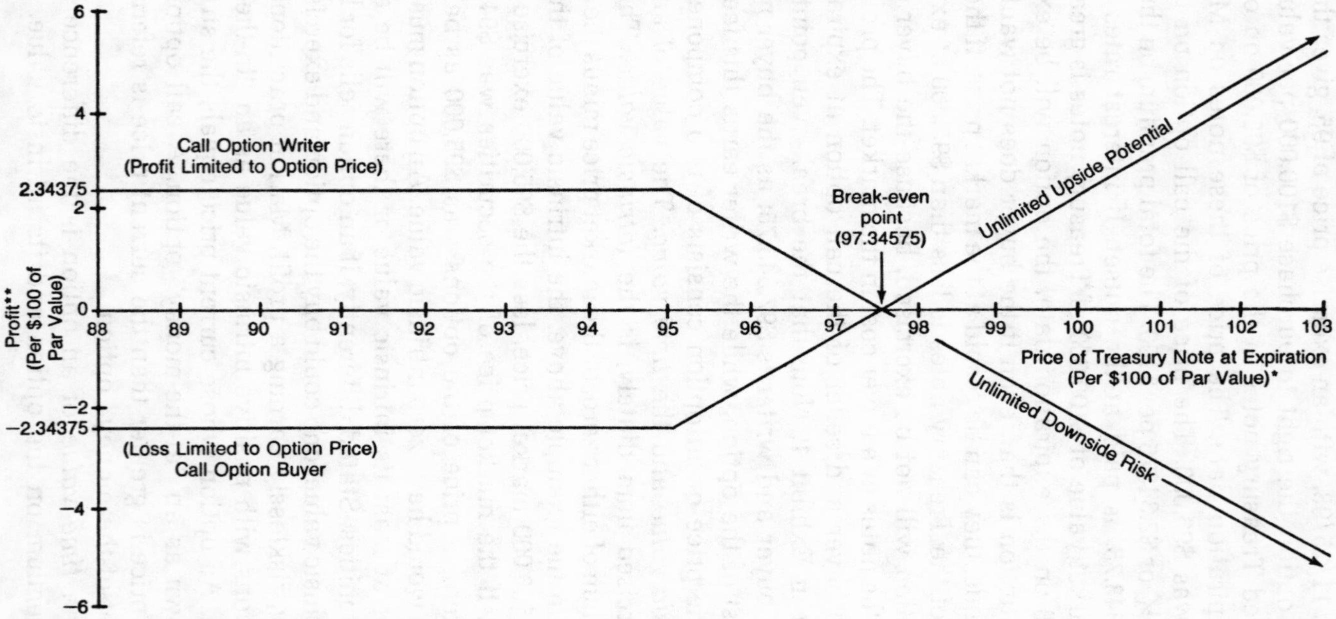

Profit**
(Per $100 of Par Value)
6
4
2.34375
2
0
-2
-2.34375
-4
-6
88
89
90
91
92
93
94
95
96
97
98
99
100
101
102
103
Call Option Writer
(Profit Limited to Option Price)
(Loss Limited to Option Price)
Call Option Buyer
Break-even point (97.34575)
Unlimited Upside Potential
Unlimited Downside Risk
Price of Treasury Note at Expiration
(Per $100 of Par Value)*

* Price per $100,000 of par value is price on axis times 1,000.
** Profit per $100,000 of par value is profit on axis times 1,000.

seller's compensation for the possibility that the option will be worth more at the end of its life than if exercised immediately. In the example referred to above, the cost of the option was $2,343.75. Since the market price of the securities was $96,000 and the strike price on the option was $95,000, the intrinsic value of the option was $1,000. The time value of the option is the difference between the total price and the intrinsic value, or $1,343.75.

A *put option* is the right to sell, or "put to" the writer of the option, a given amount of the underlying security at a given price on or before a specific date. Thus, a six-month put option on the 11⅞ Treasury note, due on 11/15/93, with an exercise price of 96, gives the holder of the option the right to sell $100,000 par value ($96,000 market value) of Treasury notes at a price of $96,000 on or before the expiration date. The price of this put option on March 27, 1984, was 2^{30}_{32} or 2.9375 per $100.[3] If interest rates fall and the market value of the Treasury notes is greater than $96,000, the buyer will not exercise the option, as the bonds can be sold on the open market at a higher price. If interest rates rise and the market value of the notes is less than $96,000, the right to sell the bonds at that price is valuable. Note that the put option has positive intrinsic value or is in the money when the current price is below the exercise price. The profit profile for a buyer and writer of a put option at expiration are shown in Exhibit 2. The break-even point is $93,062.50, as the buyer must pay the cost of the option.

Options on debt instruments are essentially options on interest rate changes. Since price and interest rates move inversely, those who are used to thinking about equity options need to be careful. A *call*, which has value if the *price* of the security *rises*, makes the holder a profit if *interest rates fall*. A *put*, which has value if the *price falls*, makes the holder a profit if *interest rates rise*. Thus, someone who wants to

---

[3] The quotation used is an over-the-counter quote of a major government securities dealer, and is based on the most actively traded 10-year note.

EXHIBIT 2
PUT OPTION PROFIT PROFILE AT EXPIRATION

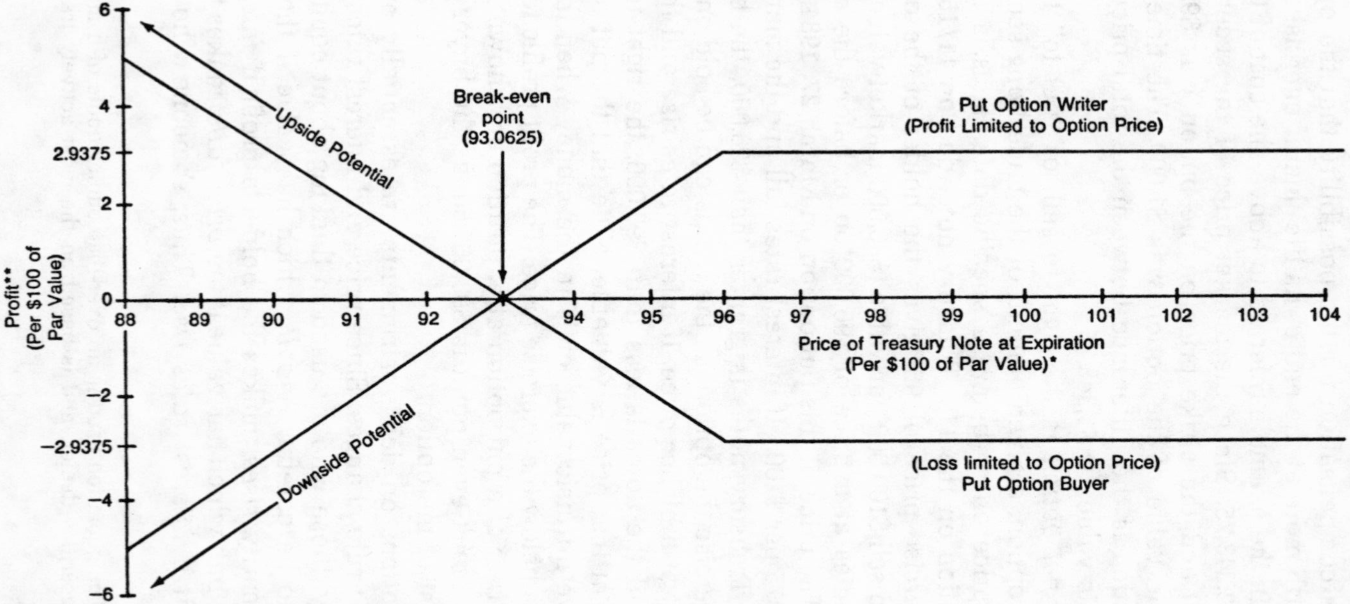

Put Option Writer
(Profit Limited to Option Price)

(Loss limited to Option Price)
Put Option Buyer

Price of Treasury Note at Expiration
(Per $100 of Par Value)*

Break-even
point
(93.0625)

Upside Potential

Downside Potential

Profit**
(Per $100 of
Par Value)

* Price per $100,000 of par value is price on axis times 1,000.
** Profit per $100,000 of par value is profit on axis times 1,000.

take a position that profits if interest rates fall will buy a
call, whereas someone who wants to take a position that profits if interest rates rise will buy a *put*.

HEDGING USES OF OPTIONS MARKETS

Market participants purchase options to hedge their position,
because they feel the protection they are receiving against
adverse interest rate movements is worth more to them than
the option premium. Thus, in the case of the call example
above, the buyer of the option felt that the protection of bond
prices rising above $95,000 was worth more than the $2^{11}\!/_{32}$ pre-
mium. In the case of the put example, the buyer is willing to
pay $2^{30}\!/_{32}$ to guard against the price of the bonds dropping below
$96,000.

As mentioned earlier, investors adversely affected by falling interest rates, would tend to buy call options as a hedge.
Examples of this would include: investors considering the purchase of long bonds in a month or a corporate treasurer with
sinking fund requirements to meet. Both of these actors might
also consider using the futures market. They face symmetric
risk, that is, they are adversely affected if rates fall and favorably affected if they rise. In a futures hedge, losses (gains)
on the underlying position would be offset by gains (losses)
on the futures position. In contrast, an option allows the investor to preserve upside potential if rates rise.

Some positions which cannot be hedged with futures can
be hedged with options—situations which involve asymmetric
risk. Consider, for example, a corporation which has issued
a warrant to purchase its debt at a given price. This actor
doesn't gain if rates rise, but loses if rates fall. This type of
risk is asymmetric. If a futures hedge is issued, and rates rise,
losses on the futures position cannot be offset. Essentially,
the corporation has written a call option, and the only way
to undo it is to buy a call option.

Investors adversely affected by rising interest rates would
buy put options as a hedge. Examples of this include: investors
who hold a bond portfolio, a corporation which plans to issue

bonds in a month, and a bank or savings and loan which has funded long-term fixed rate assets with short-term liabilities. These actors might also consider using futures, as they are favorably affected if rates fall. A futures hedge would not allow these parties to preserve their upside potential, should rates fall.

Investors who face asymmetric risk with respect to rising rates—for example, a financial institution which has made fixed rate loan commitments—cannot use the futures market. If rates move down, they will lose on their futures position and have no offsetting gain or cash position. The financial institution with a loan commitment has essentially written a put option. It can offset this only by purchasing a put option. Other implicit put options written, include: mortgage bankers who have made fixed rate mortgage commitments and life insurance companies who have rules allowing individuals to borrow against their policies at prespecified rates of interest.

Why do investors write options? Their gain is limited to the premium, while their potential loss is much larger. Option writers believe the premium is adequate compensation for the potential loss. In fact, the premium is the price which adjusts to equate the quantity of options supplied with the quantity of options demanded. If the option premium was too low to compensate the writer for the risk, there would be more buyers than sellers, forcing the premium to rise.

It is important to realize that option writing need not be speculative. An investor who writes call options on a bond he owns, may perceive himself as hedging. The option increases his return (by the amount of the premium) in periods in which the price of the bond is falling or remaining relatively stable; and reduces it in periods in which the price of the bond is going up. Similarly, if a bank which has liabilities with a shorter repricing period than its assets writes a call option on a bond or bond future, it is actually reducing its interest rate sensitivity. If interest rates rise, the option cushions the portfolio loss as the bank receives the option premium. If interest rates fall, the bank receives the premium but trades away most of the potential gain.

A summary of hedging strategies is shown below:

Direction of disadvantage	Symmetric risk	Asymmetric risk
Adversely affected by rising interest rates	Buy a put *or* Write a call	Buy a put
Adversely affected by falling interest rates	Buy a call *or* Write a put	Buy a call

TYPES OF DEBT OPTIONS

Options on debt instruments take three basic forms:

- Options on so-called physicals (i.e., actual securities)
- Options on futures contracts
- Interest rate agreements

Options on Physicals

Options on physical securities are traded on two organized exchanges. Options on U.S. Treasury notes and bills are traded on the American Stock Exchange (the AMEX) in New York. The note contracts are for $100,000 principal value and the bill contracts are for $1 million principal value. Options on U.S. Treasury bonds are traded on the Chicago Board Options Exchange (CBOE). These options are offered in denominations of $100,000 principal value and $20,000 principal value. These markets started in the fourth quarter of 1982. At the time of this writing, trading on the AMEX averages 0–100 contracts per day, with open interest[4] on puts and calls, each between 500–1,000. Trading on the CBOE is generally between 50–1,000 contracts, with option interest on both puts and calls close to 7,000 contracts. These markets are generally not sufficiently liquid to execute large transactions.

---

[4] Open interest is the number of contracts outstanding at a given moment.

Consequently, investors who wish to buy or write options on actual securities usually do this on an over-the-counter basis. Many of the large government securities dealerships maintain continuous bid-ask option quotations on several actively traded issues of notes and bonds. These markets are maintained for both puts and calls.

These Over-the-Counter (OTC) markets have two advantages over the limited trading being done on the organized exchanges. First, since quotes are maintained on a variety of notes and bonds, investors can buy or write the option on the most prevalent bonds in their portfolio. This eliminates the so-called basis risk—that is, the risk that the price changes on bonds held by an investor will not be offset by the price changes on the option. The second advantage to OTC markets is that the dealer generally stands ready to do a fairly large volume at a given quote. On the AMEX or CBOE, even a relatively small volume can move the price substantially.

GNMA dealers usually make a market in put options on GNMAs for the convenience of their mortgage-banking clients. These put options are meant to hedge the mortgage banker between the commitment date and the pooling of closed mortgages. Mortgage bankers are very sensitive to interest rates during this period—if rates rise, the percentage of mortgage commitments used will rise, and when the mortgages are pooled, the security will immediately sell at a loss. If the mortgage banker is willing to lock in his yield, he can do this via a forward sale or by using bond futures contracts. If the mortgage banker wants to be guaranteed a minimum price for the GNMA, but wishes to be able to take advantage of falling interest rates (rising prices), this can be done via the purchase of a put option.

Options on Bond Futures

Options on Treasury bond futures are traded on the Chicago Board of Trade. This market started in the fourth quarter of 1982, and it has been an immediate success. Contracts are traded on a broad range of strike prices, including: out-of-the-money, at-the-money, and in-the-money. Strike prices are spaced two points apart. The most actively traded contracts are those nearest the money. Options can be bought and sold on the nearest three futures contracts. Thus, in April 1984, when futures contracts were offered between 64½–65½, options contracts could be written on strike prices between 62 and 80. Options can be written on March, June, September, and December futures.

The volume of trading in a given day is approximately one-third of that on the underlying Treasury bond futures contracts. The open interest on option contracts is approximately as large or even larger than that on the Treasury bond futures contracts. For example, on April 25, 1984, volume of calls traded was 18,724 contracts and the volume of puts was 13,645. Open interest in calls was 165,373, while open interest in puts was 64,281. By contrast, in the futures market, volume was 113,071, while open interest was 176,874. This is because trading portfolios tend to concentrate on futures rather than options on futures.

One very interesting question is why have the exchange-traded options on bond futures contracts done substantially better than the exchange-traded options on bond physicals. Many market participants believe the contract design of options on Treasury bond futures is slightly superior for three reasons. For one, options on futures have no coupon or dividend payments; in contrast, with an options contract on a bond or note, the buyer of a call or the seller of a put must compensate the other party for accrued interest when exercise occurs.

Furthermore, options on bond futures are also believed to be "cleaner instruments," because of the reduced possibility of delivery squeezes. Options on bonds are written on particular issues; since the supply of any particular issue is fixed after the date of issuance, there is always the chance of a squeeze developing that could artificially raise the price of the bond. This is less of a worry with OTC options, as the volume in each bond is not likely to be large. Options on bond futures are written on the underlying futures contract, which, in turn, is written not on a particular bond issue, but rather on a bond with particular characteristics. One bond (usually the bond with the highest implied interest rate in a cash-and-carry transaction) will always be the cheapest to deliver against the futures contract. But, if there were a squeeze on this bond, other deliverable bonds would be available; consequently, the deliverable supply of Treasury bond futures will always provide more than adequately.

Third, it is easier to learn the price of an underlying bond future, rather than the price of the bond itself. For option pricing purposes, it is crucial to know the price of the underlying security. The price of the last bond futures trade is easily accessible, as bond futures and options on bond futures are traded on the same floor. This saves the investor the trouble of canvassing dealers to obtain a price on the security itself. This argument may also help explain the relative success of OTC physicals. The dealer makes a continuous market in the underlying government notes and bonds with a very slim spread (bid-ask spreads are generally $\frac{1}{16}$ or $\frac{1}{8}$ of a point). This continuous market allows dealers to price options more carefully than they could be done on an exchange-traded basis.

Interest Rate Agreements

Interest rate agreements are long-term arrangements which reduce interest rate sensitivity for entities issuing floating rate liabilities. These agreements take two forms: ceiling rate agreements and floor-ceiling agreements.

Ceiling rate agreements specify that if rates go above a certain level ("the ceiling"), the financial institution providing the agreement will compensate the buyer for the difference between the actual rate and the ceiling rate. This is equivalent to a put option in which the financial institution providing the agreement is the option writer. For example, let us assume a corporation took out a prime-based loan at 11½ percent. The corporation wants to place a ceiling rate of 13 percent on the loan. The corporation pays an upfront fee, say 1 percent per annum, to the writer of the option. If the average daily rate during the quarter exceeds the ceiling, then the writer of the option compensates the buyer for the difference.

A floor-ceiling product is a slight variation of this, in which an entity brackets his borrowing costs. If rates go above the ceiling, the financial institution providing the agreement pays its customer the difference between the actual rate and the ceiling rate. If rates go below the floor, the customer pays the financial institution the difference between the actual rate and the floor rate. In this arrangement, which is also known as a "collar," a financial institution has essentially written a put option and purchased an out-of-the-money call option. The fee in this arrangement is less than in a straight ceiling product, as the client is giving up part of his gain if rates fall.

MARKET MECHANICS

Margins

All exchange-traded options have margin requirements which apply only to the option writer or seller. The buyer, of course, pays the entire premium up front and is not subject to margin calls. The seller of an uncovered option is subject to an initial margin requirement; if the price moves against him, he is also subject to additional or variation margin. A specific example of margin requirements on options and their calculations are given in Exhibit 3.

For options on bond futures contracts, it is customary to hold interest-bearing assets in margin accounts; consequently, initial margin requirements do not usually represent foregone interest for these contracts. For options on physicals, initial margin requirements must be posted in cash. Variation margin must in all cases be posted in cash.

In the case in which an individual is writing a covered

EXHIBIT 3
Calculation of Margin Requirements

Margin requirements on options can best be illustrated by an example. Let us consider an investor who wishes to write a call option on thirteen-week Treasury bills on the American Stock Exchange (AMEX). Margin requirements are governed by three rules:*

(1) If the option is in the money, the writer must hold a margin equal to the premium plus a fixed amount. In the case of calls on the AMEX, the fixed amount is $3,500.

Example: A customer writes an uncovered thirteen-week T-bill call option with a strike price of 88. This means the bill is at a 12 percent discount (i.e., the strike price for $1,000,000 face value of the bill is roughly $970,000). The market price of the bill is 90, that is, the bill is at a 10 percent discount ($975,000 for $1,000,000 face value of the bill). Thus, the margin requirement is:

Option premium	$6,250
Plus fixed amount	$3,500
Total	$9,750

(2) If the option is out of the money, the writer must hold a margin equal to the premium plus a fixed amount less the amount the option is out of the money.

(3) The minimum margin requirement is the option premium plus $500 per contract.

Example: In the example above, suppose the market price of the T-bill call option falls to 85 and the option is selling for $1,500. Thus, the margin requirement is:

Option premium	$1,500
Plus fixed amount	$3,500
Total	$5,000
minus out-of-the-money amount	−$7,500
Total	−$2,500

However, the minimum margin requirement is the option premium plus $500 per contract. In this example, we have:

$1,500 option premium + $500 or $2,000.

Thus, the maintenance margin requirement is $2,000.

* Additionally, the initial deposit in a new margin account must total at least $2,000.

call on a debt security, no margin is necessary.[5] While variation margin is, in principal, required on all bond futures contracts, it will never pose a problem for options on bond futures.
If the individual has written a covered call on an option on
bond futures and prices move against the option, it means
the value of the futures has increased. Since options generally
move less than the underlying instrument, a rise in prices
would release more margin than the option writer would need
to contribute. These margin requirements are necessary protection for clearinghouse members.

On securities exchanges, the clearinghouse assumes any
credit risk in an exchange-trade. On a commodities exchange,
the clearinghouse member that handles the writer's account
assumes the credit risk. Thus, the buyer of an exchange-traded
option does not have to pass judgment on the creditworthiness
of the seller. The clearinghouse or clearinghouse member pro-
tects itself against the credit risk by marking the options contract to market on a daily basis and assessing additional margin requirements as required by price movements. If the margin
calls are not met, the clearinghouse can move quickly to liquidate the contracts.

Over-the-counter options and interest rate agreements are
not subject to margin requirements. Large government securities dealers who maintain bid-ask option quotations are sufficiently well capitalized, so that default risk on the options
they have written is not perceived as a problem. These dealers
will allow customers to buy options without a credit check.
Before a customer is allowed to write an option, a rigorous
credit check is performed, as the dealer bears the credit risk.
These credit checks are generally fairly easy for the government securities dealers to perform, as the dealer often has
other business relationships with the client (i.e., loan agreements in the case of a dealer bank, debt underwriting in the

---

[5] Covered call rules apply for margin purposes, if the individual has
written a call option and has in the account either a long position in the
underlying security, or a long call which has at least as long to run as the
short call, and has an exercise price less than or equal to the exercise
price on the short call.

case of a securities house). Moreover, other dealer type activities such as forward contracts also involve credit checks.

Delivery Provisions

Options on bond futures contracts require delivery of the underlying futures contract. It is interesting to note that the options contract actually expires one month before the futures contract. Thus, the September 1984 option on bond futures contracts expires August 17. The underlying futures contract requires delivery during the month of September. Given the current upward sloping yield curve environment of the time of this writing, delivery on the futures contract will occur toward the end of September.

Options on cash debt instruments present an interesting deliverability problem which arises due to the limited life of the underlying security. Other options on physicals (equities, stock indices, foreign exchange) have an infinite life. Thus, the instruments are not directly affected by the passage of time. Debt instruments get closer to maturity as the options get closer to expiration. This unique feature of debt instruments requires that they take one of two forms: fixed deliverable or variable deliverable.

Fixed deliverable options require that a debt instrument with specified characteristics be delivered when the option is exercised. For example, a three-month call option on a six-month Treasury bill would require that a Treasury bill with six months remaining to maturity be delivered. Contracts for fixed delivery allow for the possibility that the optioned security could have a shorter lifetime than the option itself. That is, a nine-month option on a three-month Treasury bill is possible, as when the option is exercised, a three-month bill is delivered. Treasury bills on the AMEX are traded on a fixed deliverable basis.

A variable deliverable option prescribes the existing debt issue that is deliverable against the exercise. This has been adopted for both exchange-traded and OTC Treasury notes and bonds. For example, a one-year option on a ten-year bond spells out the specific ten-year bond to be delivered. At the expiration of the option, the bond will have nine years to maturity. Thus, the maturity date of the bond must be greater than the option expiration date for variable deliverable options.[6]

Settlement features on interest rate agreements (ceiling agreements and floor-ceiling agreements) are done either quarterly or semiannually over the life of the agreement. On a prime-based ceiling agreement, settlement is usually made on a quarterly basis, by comparing the ceiling rate with the actual average rate of the published indicator. If the average daily rate exceeds the ceiling rate, the customer would be compensated for the difference through a cash settlement. Let us assume a corporation takes out a $50 million prime-based loan and enters into a ceiling agreement with a major financial institution, and the ceiling is set at 13.6 percent. If the average prime rate over the quarter was 15 percent, the financial institution would pay the corporation (.15 − .136) × $50 million × ¼ year or $75,000. Since the corporation would have to pay 15 percent on its $50 million prime-based debt, its cost would be .15 × $50 million × ¼ year or $1.875 million. Its net cost is $1.875 million minus the $75,000 received from the financial institution or $1.7 million. This amounts to an effective interest cost of 13.6 percent. Thus the ceiling provides a cap on the effective rate.

Cash settlement need not be on a quarterly average basis. It may be based on the average rate for the final few days of the quarter or six-month period. This is usually done for agreements based on the London Interbank Offer Rate (LIBOR).

In a floor-ceiling agreement, the corporation would pay the provider of the agreement if rates fall below the floor. For example, if the prime-based floor was 11.5 percent and

---

[6] This was pointed out in Walter L. Eckardt, Jr. "An Analysis of Treasury Bond and Treasury Bill Options Premiums," paper presented at the second annual options colloquium sponsored by the American Stock Exchange, New York, N.Y. March 25–26, 1982.

the quarterly average prime rate was 10.5 percent, the corporation would have to pay the agreement provider the rate difference between the floor rate and the market rate on the amount
of the agreement. This would be (.115 − .105) × $50 million
× ¼ year or $125,000. Thus, funds change hands if the indica-
tive rate is above or below the floor.

Choosing a Hedging Instrument

If an entity sees debt options as an integral part of their hedging
activities, it is particularly important to focus on the strengths
and weaknesses of various hedging vehicles. There are currently three realistic hedging alternatives: options on futures,
OTC options on physicals, and interest rate agreements. The
markets for exchange-traded options on physicals is too illiq-
uid to be a legitimate hedging vehicle.

Exchange-traded options on futures eliminate the ¼ point
dealers bid-ask spread. Since the equilibrium price in an auction market would be expected to be within the dealer's band,
exchange-traded options are usually a cheaper vehicle for purchasing options on standard contracts. Moreover, writers on
standard contracts can obtain larger fees. OTC options are
customized products and as such, they enable the hedger to
avoid the basis risk between the bond or bonds that the hedge
is designed for and the cheapest to deliver. The price of the
option on the bond futures is based on the underlying bond
futures. This price in turn is based on the bond that market
participants believe will be the cheapest to deliver. The basis
risk between bonds with different coupons can, at times, be
substantial. An OTC option also allows the customer (either
a buyer or writer) to customize the strike price. If someone
has a definite yield or price level in mind which they would
like to serve as the exercise price, the two point differential
in strike prices offered on the Chicago Board of Trade (CBT)
may seem too wide. An experienced hedger can, however,
come close to producing an option at the desired strike price
by purchasing the correct number of contracts on either side
of the desired price.

An exchange-traded option offers flexibility in timing, in that it can be resold at any time. By contrast, an OTC option is for a specific period of time. If the buyer wants to sell the option back and recontract for a different maturity, transactions costs will be fairly large. Thus, if an investor wants to purchase a put option because he anticipates a tightening in Federal Reserve Policy in the near future, but does not know exactly when the tightening will occur, he would be better off with an exchange-traded option. With an OTC option, he would probably contract for a longer maturity than he anticipates needing, just to "be sure." With an exchange-traded option he can employ a hedging strategy known as a *delta hedge* with no penalty.

Delta hedging refers to a technique by which hedgers not planning to hold options to expiration can compute out how many option contracts to purchase. The *delta* of an option is the change in the price of the option for a small change in price of the underlying instrument. An at-the-money option will usually have a delta of about .5. That is, a $1 change in value of the security will result in a $.50 change in the value of the option. Intuitively, if the option expires in-the-money, the terminal value of the option has been raised by $1. There is roughly a 50 percent chance it will expire in-the-money. The further out-of-the-money the option, the lower the delta. If the option is very far out-of-the-money, its delta will be near zero. If the option is in-the-money, its delta will generally be larger than .5. A deep-in-the-money option will have a delta close to one, as an option buyer will most likely end up with the long or short security position at expiration.

Delta hedging using options on futures requires dividing the number of futures contracts that would be required to hedge a position by the delta of the option. Intuitively, a portfolio manager who wants to buy an at-the-money put option on his portfolio for a short time—say two to three weeks, would have to sell the options back in the market before expiration. Consequently, since each option moves approximately $.50 for each $1 change in the futures price, he must buy twice as many options as he would purchase of futures. A detailed

example of a delta hedge is shown in Exhibit 4. The ability
to delta hedge an uncertain holding period makes exchange-
traded options on a futures contract a very useful hedging
tool in many instances.

OTC options are very useful in two specific instances.
The first situation is one in which a hedger needs an option
for a long maturity (more than nine months). CBT options are

EXHIBIT 4
Delta Hedging

Delta hedging using options on Treasury bond futures can best be illustrated
by a simple example. A bond portfolio manager holds $100 million face
value of 11⅞ bonds of 2003. He wants to protect himself against rising
interest rates, beginning March 13, 1984, for a few weeks. He anticipates
a series of prime rate changes during this period and wants to take off
the hedge after the changes have occurred.

A delta hedge is used when the option is not going to be held until
maturity. The portfolio manager buys a put one day and will sell it back
on another. The price difference is his gain or loss. To set up the hedge,
three steps are necessary:

1. Figure out the hedge ratio for futures contracts.
2. Figure out the delta of an at-the-money option.
3. Compute the number of needed contracts by dividing the hedge
   ratio for futures by the delta.

When the hedge is removed the portfolio manager will want to:

4. Evaluate the hedge.

1. *Figure out the hedge ratio for futures*

The hedge ratio or factor for the cheapest to deliver bond (the 8¾ of 2008) =
1.0726 for September '84 contract. These factors can be obtained from the
Chicago Board of Trade. The hedge ratio for another bond (for example
the 11⅞ of 2003) can be derived as follows:

$$\text{Hedge Ratio for } 11\tfrac{7}{8} = \text{Factor } 8\tfrac{3}{4} \times \frac{\text{yield value of } \tfrac{1}{32} \text{ on } 8\tfrac{3}{4}}{\text{yield value of } \tfrac{1}{32} \text{ on } 11\tfrac{7}{8}}$$

$$= 1.07826 \times \frac{.0054}{.0044}$$

$$= 1.316$$

Thus, the portfolio manager needs 1.316 futures contracts for each $100,000
face of the 11⅞. He would need 1,316 contracts to hedge $100 million of
face value with futures.

EXHIBIT 4 (Continued)

2. *Figure out the delta of the hedge**

An at-the-money option is used because market liquidity is greatest at or near the money. If we are looking at the September put option with a strike price of 68, we want to know for the past few days what the price change in options was in relation to the change in price on the underlying futures. If we found the following configuration

	Day 1	Day 2	Day 3	Δ Price Between Day 1 and Day 2	Δ Price Between Day 2 and Day 3
Sept. 68 option	2–20	2–35	2–21	15/64	14/64
Sept. 68 Future	65–00	65–12	65–00	12/32	12/32

$$\text{Delta} = \frac{\Delta \text{ Options Price}}{\Delta \text{ Futures Price}}$$

= .625 for Day 1

= .583 for Day 2

Note: Options prices are quoted in 64ths. Futures prices are quoted in 32nds.

We would assume the delta of the option is approximately .6. One needs to use enough recent data such that one is fairly confident of the delta estimate. One day with a great deal of movement on both the option and the underlying security may be sufficient. Alternatively, three or four quiet days may be necessary to give the hedge designed the same amount of confidence.

3. *Compute the number of needed contracts*

1,316/.6 = 2,193

4. *Evaluate the hedge*

The hedge in this example is closed as on 3/23/84 after the prime rate changes have occurred. The results are as follows:

Cash price on 3/23/84	95.1475 (yield 12.59)
Option price on 3/23/84	2 60/64
Cash price on 3/12/84	96.3125
Option price on 3/12/84	2 27/64
Loss on cash	1,165,000
Gain on option	1,130,765 (2193 × 33/64)
Net result	−34,235

* The delta of the hedge can also be derived from the Black-Scholes option pricing formula.

traded for only the three nearest futures contracts. One long term strategy is to stack enough option contracts, such that the present value of the changes in the object to be hedged are equated to the change in value of the options position. As options mature, they are rolled over into new contracts. Options are, however, very risky to roll as one cannot hedge against changes in volatility. The second situation in which OTC options and interest rate agreements are very useful is one in which the instrument to be hedged is not a bond. For example, interest rate agreements are ideal for hedging loans. If one were to hedge a floating rate loan with options, it would involve the basis risk between the short term rate and the long term rate, which can be substantial, as well as the problem with rolling options described above.

SUMMARY

In this chapter, we have examined the risk-return profile of option instruments. The hedging uses of these markets have also been discussed. Since option markets afford participants the ability to significantly alter the distribution of returns on their portfolio, and such choice is desired in the current environment, these markets can be expected to grow in importance.

CHAPTER 2

Description of the Instruments Underlying Exchange-Traded Debt Options

Benjamin Wolkowitz, Ph.D.
Vice President
Citicorp Futures Corp.

Debt options, whether over-the-counter or exchange-traded, are most often based on U.S. Government securities. The interest rates on these securities issued by the U.S. Department of the Treasury are generally accepted as the benchmark interest rates in the U.S. economy and, typically, in the world. Treasury securities have achieved this degree of importance in part because of their volume. There are more Treasury securities outstanding than any other securities in the world and the Treasury issues securities of every maturity spectrum on a regular basis. Moreover, these securities have virtually no credit risk.

The purpose of this chapter is to describe the U.S. Treasury securities market and the derivative futures market. Since options are based on these instruments, it is essential to understand them in order to understand the associated debt options markets. The following discussion is divided into two sections: the first section contains a discussion of the cash market, and the second section contains a discussion of the futures market.

THE CASH MARKET FOR U.S. GOVERNMENT SECURITIES

The primary purpose behind the issuance of government securities is the funding of budget deficits. As indicated in Exhibit 1, the value of Treasury securities outstanding has increased with the recent growth in the size of the deficit.

There are two categories of government securities—discount and coupon securities. The fundamental difference between these two types of securities is the form in which the holder receives interest and, as a result, the prices for which they are issued.

On coupon securities, explicit interest payments are periodically (usually every six months) made by the Treasury during the life of the securities. Alternatively, on discount securities, there is no explicit payment of interest by the Treasury to the holders from the time of issue until the maturity day when the principal is repaid. This difference in the method of paying interest results in a difference in issue prices between the two different types of securities.

According to current Treasury practices, all Treasury securities with maturities of one year or less are issued as discount securities; and all securities with maturities of more than one year are issued as coupon securities. Treasury discount securities are called *bills*. Treasury coupon securities with maturities between one and 10 years are called *notes*, and with maturities of greater than 10 years are called *bonds*.

On coupon securities, the annual coupon is specified before the issue, and an amount equal to half the annual coupon is paid to the holder every six months. For example, if a Treasury security is issued with a 12 percent coupon, a $60 payment is made every six months per maturity or par value of $1,000.

The issue prices of discount and coupon securities are related to the maturity or par value of the security, which is the amount paid by the Treasury to the holder of the security on the maturity date of the security. Since the coupon payment of the coupon securities represents the payment of interest during the time the security is outstanding, the initial issue

EXHIBIT 1
Outstanding Treasury Securities ($ millions)

End of Fiscal Year of Month	Amount Outstanding			Securities Held by					
				Government Accounts			The Public		
	Total	Public Debt Securities	Agency Securities	Total	Public Debt Securities	Agency Securities	Total	Public Debt Securities	Agency Securities
1973	468,426*	457,317*	11,109	125,381	123,385	1,996	343,045	333,932	9,113
1974	486,247	474,235	12,012	140,194	138,206	1,988	346,053	336,029	10,024
1975	544,131	533,188	10,943	147,225	145,283	1,942	396,906	387,905	9,001
1976	631,866	620,432	11,433	151,566	149,611	1,955	480,300	470,821	9,478
1977	709,138	698,840	10,298	157,295	155,490	1,805	551,843	543,350	8,493
1978	780,425	771,544	8,881	169,477	167,973	1,504	610,948	603,571	7,377
1979	833,751	826,519	7,232	189,162	187,683	1,478	644,589	638,836	5,754
1980	914,317	907,701	6,616	199,212	197,743	1,469	715,105	709,958	5,147
1981	1,003,941	997,855	6,086	209,507	208,056	1,450	794,434	789,799	4,636
1982	1,201,898	1,197,074	4,824	210,506	209,355	1,151	991,392	987,719	3,672
1983	1,415,343	1,410,702	4,641	237,395	236,277	1,118			

* Excludes

rice of a Treasury coupon security is approximately the same
s its maturity value. Thus, Treasury coupon securities are
ssued at about par. If interest rates subsequently increase,
he coupons of newly issued bonds will be higher; and thus
he price of the bonds previously issued at lower coupons
vill sell at a price below its maturity value, that is, "at a
liscount" to par. If interest rates subsequently decrease, the
:oupons of newly issued bonds will be lower than the coupons
)f the previously issued bonds; and thus the price of the bonds
previously issued at higher coupons will sell at a price above
its maturity value, that is, at a premium to par.

Because no explicit interest is paid on a discount security,
the security must be issued at a price that is a discount to
its maturity value, such that the difference between the initial
discount price and the final maturity price represents the return
to the holder of the security. For example, if a one-year Treasury bill with a maturity value of $1,000 is sold "at a discount"
of $900, the $100 difference is the interest payment and it is
equivalent to a 10 percent rate of interest.

The Primary Market

Government securities are initially issued into the primary
government securities market. These securities are typically
issued on an auction basis by the Treasury with the assistance
of the Federal Reserve System.

The Treasury has found that it can reduce the interest
cost of its debt, particularly when issuing substantial amounts
to fund large budget deficits, by issuing Treasury securities
on a regular basis (i.e., by having a stable schedule for auction-
ing securities with specific maturities). This scheduling provides the purchasers of Treasury debt with certainty regarding
the timing of issuances of the various types of Treasury securities. The schedule of the Treasury funding process has developed so that there are now several regular cycles on which
the Treasury auctions and issues specific maturities of debt.
A description of these cycles is provided in Exhibit 2.

As indicated in Exhibit 2 there are three discount security

(Treasury bill) cycles. Every Monday the Treasury auctions 91-day Treasury bills. These bills are issued on the following Thursday and mature on the Thursday 13-weeks (91 days) later. On the same cycle, every Monday the Treasury also auctions 182-day bills, which are issued on the following Thursday and mature on the Thursday 26 weeks, or 182 days, after their issue date. The third Treasury bill cycle is the "year

EXHIBIT 2
Treasury Auction Cycles

Discount securities:

Three-month (91-day) Treasury bills	Auctioned every Monday; issued on the following Thursday.
Six-month (182-day) Treasury bills	Same auction and issue cycle as for three-month Treasury bills. Thus, 182-day Treasury bills eventually trade in consonance with 91-day Treasury bills.
Fifty-two week (364-day) Treasury bills	Auctioned every fourth Thursday; issued the following Thursday. Thus 364-day Treasury bills eventually trade in consonance with 182-day and then 91-day Treasury bills.

Coupon securities:

(2)	Two-year Treasury notes: Every month, normally near the end of the month (although often substantially before or after the end of the month), a two-year note is auctioned and issued that matures at the end of the month 24 months hence.
(4)	Four-year Treasury notes: Four-year Treasury notes are auctioned and issued during the last weeks of March/June/September/December quarterly cycle months for maturity on the last day of these months four years hence. These notes eventually become two-year notes and thereafter trade in consonance with newly issued two-year notes.

EXHIBIT 2 (continued)

Coupon securities:

(5/15) five-year/15-year	Typically, on the January, April, July, October quarterly cycle, the Treasury auctions and issues, during alternate quarters, five-year notes and 15-year bonds. These bonds are dated to mature on the 15th day of the February/May/August/November quarterly cycle months (and thus the long-term notes and bonds issued on the refunding cycle eventually trade in consonance with these issues—see below). This cycle, however, has not followed this pattern without exception.
(R) Refunding cycle	The refunding cycle is based on the quarterly February/May/August/November cycle months. Refunding cycle notes and bonds are issued on the 15th day of the February/May/August/November months and are auctioned on different days during the two weeks prior to the issue. Each refunding issue has typically contained three issues: (1) an anchor issue note in the 3- to 3½-year range, (2) a longer-term note, typically between seven and 10 years, and (3) a long-term bond, typically between 20 and 30 years. The issues in the refunding cycle are subject to some variations, however.

bill" cycle. On this cycle, every fourth Thursday the Treasury auctions a 52-week Treasury bill, which is issued on the following Thursday and matures on the Thursday 52 weeks, or 364 days, later.

The initial 91-day and 182-day Treasury bills mature every Thursday, and the initial 364-day Treasury bills mature every fourth Thursday. Note also that during the last 91 days of its maturity, an initial 182-day Treasury bill is indistinguishable from an initial 91-day Treasury bill issued 91 days after it. Also, during the last 182 days of its maturity, a 364-day Treasury bill is indistinguishable from an initial 182-day Treasury bill issued 182 days after it.

As indicated in Exhibit 2, there are several auction cycles for Treasury coupon issues. Although none of these cycles is immutable, the auction cycles for the two-year and four-year Treasury notes and the refunding cycle have been fairly stable. In addition, there have been five-year and 20-year auction cycles.

The refunding cycle is most important, since it contains the Treasury long bond, which typically has 30 years to maturity. The Treasury refunding cycle involves the issue of three coupon securities, typically a short note, a long note, and a long bond, during the February, May, August, and November quarterly cycle months. The securities to be auctioned and issued on the Treasury refunding cycle are usually announced late in the month prior to the auction. The three securities are auctioned on different days early in the refunding month and issued on the 15th day of the month.

Both Treasury bills and Treasury coupon issues are sold on an auction basis. Treasury bills are auctioned on a price basis. Bids are taken by the Treasury and securities allocated from the high price to the low price, until the Treasury has allocated the total amount of the announced issue. The successful bids are awarded at their actual bid price. Those who have bid at the lower price are not allocated bills. Treasury coupon issues are auctioned on a yield basis. The Treasury then allocates the securities, beginning with the lowest yield bid to the highest yield, until the announced amount is fully subscribed. The average yield of those receiving an allocation is used to determine the coupon of the newly issued bonds. The coupon is usually set slightly less than the average yield, so that the new bonds are issued at a slight discount to par.

If the current yield on an outstanding bond of approximately the same maturity as that which the Treasury plans to auction is approximately the same as the coupon on the outstanding issue (i.e., the issue is trading at about par), the Treasury may announce the reissue of this outstanding security. In such a case, since the coupon is predetermined, the auction is done on a price basis rather than a yield basis.

The Secondary Market

The secondary market for Treasury securities is the most liquid financial market in the world. This market is made by a group of U.S. government securities dealers who continually provide bids and offers on outstanding Treasuries.

Dealers continuously provide bids and offers on specific outstanding government securities, buying for, and selling from, their inventories. Dealers' earnings are derived from three sources. First, dealers profit from their market making through the difference in their bid-ask quotes, "the spread." The bid-ask spread is a measure of the liquidity of the market for the issue, as discussed below. Second, to the extent that dealers hold inventories, they also profit from price appreciation of their inventories (or price depreciation of securities they have shorted), but experience a loss from their inventory positions if prices decline. Finally, dealers may profit on the basis of carry, the difference between the interest return on the securities they hold and the financing costs of these securities. Dealers, typically, do not have sufficient capital to own outright the securities they hold in their inventory, so their inventories are financed. When the interest return on the securities they hold is greater than the financing cost, a positive carry exists, and thus a profit results from this differential. In the opposite case of negative carry, dealers experience a loss from carrying their inventory.

Since dealer financing is of a very short maturity, and the securities held in inventory are almost always of a longer maturity, the carry is positive when long-term interest rates are higher than short-term interest rates and negative when short-term interest rates are higher than long-term interest rates. Obviously, when carry is negative, the dealers generate a loss on carrying their inventories and attempt to minimize the size of their inventory for this reason.

The typical mechanism for financing Treasury securities is the *repurchase agreement*, or *repo*, which is basically a collateralized loan wherein the Treasury securities owned by the dealer are used as collateral to the lender on the loan to the dealer. Repurchase agreements are typically of very short maturity, commonly one day. Longer repurchase agreements are called *term repos*. The market for term repos becomes quite thin as the maturity lengthens.

The secondary market for Treasury securities also includes brokers who intermediate between dealers. However, brokers, unlike dealers, do not buy and sell for their own inventories, but simply arrange trades between dealers for a commission. The dealers pay the brokers a commission for arranging trades between themselves and others.

Bids and offers in the dealer market for Treasury bills are made on a discount basis, not a price basis, in basis points. (A basis point is 1/100th of 1 percent in discount return; for example, the difference between 10.00 percent and 10.01 percent is one basis point.) Thus, a bid-offer quote may be 11.63 percent/11.61 percent.

On the other hand, bids and offers for coupon instruments are made on the basis of price to $\frac{1}{32}$ of 1 percent of par, which is taken to be $100. For example, a quote of 97–19 refers to a price of 97 and $^{19}\!/_{32}$. Thus, on the basis of $100,000 par value, a change in a price of 1 percent is consistent with $1,000 and $\frac{1}{32}$ with $31.25.

The government securities dealers work closely with the Federal Reserve System and the Treasury in several ways. First and most importantly, the Federal Reserve Bank of New York (FRBNY), on behalf of the Board of Governors of the Federal Reserve System, conducts its open-market operations and its repo and reverse repo transactions through the primary dealers. Such activities are conducted by the FRBNY among the dealers on an auction basis in a matter of minutes. Second, as an input into its conduct of monetary policy, the FRBNY frequently gets information from the primary dealers about the condition of the financial markets. Finally, although primary dealers do not underwrite Treasury issues in the same way corporate bonds are underwritten by investment banks, the dealers to a large extent provide the same function. To provide this function, dealers frequently bid actively at the auctions and subsequently redistribute the bonds they are allocated to their customers. Of course, if the prices decline before they are redistributed, the dealers experience underwriting losses.

There are two other components of secondary markets, in addition to the market for the spot buying and selling of Treasury securities and the repo market, that are closely associated with the Treasury spot market. The first of these is the market for shorting specific government securities. In this market, a dealer or other institution sells a security it does not own, that is, shorts the security with an agreement that the security will be returned at some future date. The short accomplishes this by borrowing a security from another dealer or institution. Of course, the interest foregone by the lender must be paid by the borrower. There is a fairly active short market for actively traded government securities, but it is confined mainly to government security dealers.

The second component is the "when-issued market," or "W/I market," wherein Treasury securities are traded prior to the time they are issued by the Treasury. The when-issued trading for both Treasury bills and Treasury coupon issues extends from the day the auction is announced until the issue day. All deliveries on when-issued trades occur on the issue day of the Treasury security traded.

FINANCIAL FUTURES MARKET FOR U.S. GOVERNMENT SECURITIES

Futures markets had their start in agriculture, where they provided a method of insulating farmers, distributors, and processors of agricultural produce from the risk of unanticipated price changes. Farmers were seeking a way to secure a price that would yield a spread over their costs early in the harvest cycle, while processors and distributors were interested in guaranteeing an adequate supply of produce at a price that would ensure them a profit. Enabling farmers to contract with distributors and processors to make delivery at a prearranged price, well in advance of the actual delivery date, would satisfy the needs of both farmers and their direct customers. The economic need for such contracts was sufficiently strong that, prior to the introduction of exchange-traded agriculture-based futures, off-exchange substitutes, which were in effect forward contracts (also known as "to arrive contracts"), had already developed.

In some ways these off-exchange contracts served the same purpose as futures contracts. They were an inferior substitute, however, and the inadequacies inherent in forward contracts contributed to the development of futures contracts. One of the key problems with forward contracts was that they carried no assurance of reliability or performance. They were essentially a customized transaction between two parties operating on the basis of trust. If one party to the contract reneged, the other party had no way of being compensated for attendant losses, except to take the matter to litigation; obviously, this would have been an unsatisfactory climax to a transaction initiated as a method of minimizing exposure to price risk. In addition, each forward contract had its own method of determining payment and price. Since price information was not generally available, the participants to a contract could never be certain of receiving the best terms. Besides lack of standardization of payment, there was no standardization of the quality of the commodities to be delivered. Consequently, there was no method of easily reselling a contract, even though various potential applications of forward delivery-type contracts do not actually require the delivery of the commodity. For example, speculators interested in profiting from price movements certainly do not need to make or take delivery of the underlying commodity; nor, in fact, do many types of hedgers.

In spite of the shortcomings of forward contracts, until the latter part of the 19th century, they were the only available method of arranging for the future delivery of an agricultural commodity. When the Chicago Board of Trade, the first commodity exchange in the United States, was organized in 1848, the objective was largely to locate the forward contracting activity in one central place. Not until 1865 were the first standardized futures contracts in the United States traded at the Chicago Board of Trade. Their introduction revolutionized the process of arranging for forward delivery of a commodity.

The obvious advantages of futures trading compared with off-exchange forward arrangements were apparent, ensuring the success of the concept. Throughout the latter part of the 19th century, a number of exchanges that are still active today were developed.

The development of competitive exchanges and the growth of interest in futures contracts encouraged the proliferation of different types of futures contracts. These ultimately spanned a range of "commodities" extending from the original Chicago Board of Trade grain contracts to the recent stock index futures contracts.

U.S. Government securities are represented by three contracts based on the three major categories of securities—bills, notes, and bonds. They are standardized exchange-traded vehicles which are all marked-to-market and margined daily. The *mark-to-the-market* convention is often identified as a strength of these instruments. Each day, all positions are valued at that day's settlement price. Those whose positions have appreciated receive funds in their accounts, and those whose positions have depreciated are debited funds within the framework of margin.

Margin in futures is considered a good faith deposit and not a payment against borrowings as it is in the equity markets. Consequently, required margin tends to be very low. Futures positions can be initiated for a level of margin typically less than 5 percent of the par value of the contract. This first payment of required margin is called *initial margin*. For each contract, margin must be maintained at a level known as *main-*

tenance, which is approximately 80 percent of the level of initial margin. If a position depreciates reducing the equity on account below the maintenance level, the holder of the position is required to add cash to the account to raise it to the initial margin level or forfeit the position. Since this margin activity is conducted daily, it is difficult for a position to get much behind without being liquidated. It is for this reason that daily marking-to-the-market is considered a discipline which is fundamental to the financial integrity of these markets.

Futures contracts are traded in a way that to the casual observer probably suggests anything but a disciplined market. Trading goes on in rings or pits through open outcry. That is, bids and offers are presented verbally in these trading pits and contracts are exchanged at mutually agreed on prices. Actually, this face-to-face trading method appears to operate more efficiently, as reflected in the bid-ask spreads, than the cash market methods described in the preceding section. Futures contracts trade with narrower bid-ask spreads than the cash market.

The efficiency of these markets is also in part due to the diversity of participants represented in the trading pits. Many of those people are actually trading their own account, attempting to profit from intraday price moves in the market. Other participants are brokers who are executing orders received from outside the pits. (Some brokers also trade their own account.) These outside orders can be from speculators that are either large institutional participants or individuals who have a view of the market. Alternatively, they can be hedgers, usually institutions that are using futures to offset the risk exposure associated with a cash position they are maintaining. Frequently primary government dealers use interest rate futures to hedge the risk from their portfolio of government securities. The other major class of participants is arbitragers who are trading the price discrepancies either between futures contracts or between cash and futures positions.

The integrity of these markets, combined with their usefulness to a diverse group of participants, and the degree of leverage inherent to these contracts, have contributed to their rapid growth. In 1975, when interest rate futures were introduced, approximately 240,000 contracts were traded. By 1983 the number of interest rate futures contracts had surpassed 40 million. Moreover, the daily trading volume for most interest rate futures contracts is at least as great, and in many cases, surpasses the daily cash market volume. Significantly the single largest futures contract measured by annual trading volume is the U.S. Treasury bond futures contract. Following is a brief summary of the salient features of the U.S. Treasury bond futures contract which is the basis for a successful exchange-traded option.

U.S. Treasury Bond Futures Contract

This contract traded on the Chicago Board of Trade is based on a hypothetical $100,000 par value Treasury bond with an 8 percent coupon and a maturity of 20 years (with a call date of at least 15 years from the date of delivery). Although there are no outstanding U.S. Treasury bonds with these precise specifications, the price of all Treasury bonds with the appropriate minimum maturity can be adjusted for their actual coupon and maturity so that they correspond to the contract price. Thus, a basket of deliverable bonds are all priced in relationship to the price of the hypothetical contract that is used as the basis for the contract. If the futures price settled at 62.00, to find the settlement price of a delivery bond requires multiplying 62.00 by the appropriate conversion factor (provided by the exchange). For example, the 12⅜ of 2,004 has a conversion factor of approximately 1.42. (Conversion factors are listed to five decimal points and are variable over time). The resultant price is 88–04 (i.e., 88 and 4/32nds) which is 62.00 times 1.42. If this bond were actually delivered, the invoice price for $100,000 par value would be $88,125, plus the accrued interest. The settlement and invoice prices for all deliverable bonds can be calculated in a comparable fashion.

Futures contracts trade for delivery in designated months. All interest rate futures, including the U.S. Treasury bond contract, trade on the March quarterly cycle, that is, March, June,

September, and December. Delivery is initiated by the seller of the contract, that is, the short, who has the option of making delivery at any time during the delivery month.

The contract trades on the same price basis as the underlying instrument, that is, in 32nds. To facilitate trading in futures, the dollar value of a 32nd is set at a constant value of $31.25, which is correct for a bond with precisely 20 years to maturity and an 8 percent coupon. In fact, the dollar value of a 32nd is a variable dependent on maturity and coupon. Consequently, hedges and trades are often weighted so that the futures and cash positions have equivalent dollar value changes.

Unlike the cash market, a constraint is imposed on the maximum daily change in the price of a futures contract. For the bond contract, the limit is two points (i.e., 64/32nds) above and below the previous day's settlement price. Trading will continue when a limit price is reached; however, a contract cannot be bought or sold at a price outside the limits. For example, using the price of 62.00 considered above, the next day's price limits would be 60.00 to 64.00. No trade can settle outside this price range. Provision is made for expanding this limit under particular circumstances, to ensure that the market clears. Obviously the intent behind limits is to dampen down wide price swings and indeed they are an effective tool for that purpose.

As previously mentioned, the bond contract has become established as the number one futures contract in terms of annual trading volume. Moreover, this contract routinely trades a larger daily volume than the underlying cash market. As a result, it has proven to be an effective hedge vehicle for all investors allowing government dealers as well as smaller investors to easily lay off their risk exposure associated with long-term U.S. Government securities and other instruments that behave in a manner closely correlated to this instrument.

SUMMARY

This chapter has provided a brief overview of the cash U.S. Government securities and derivative futures contracts which either are the basis for debt options, or may in the future become the basis for such options. For ease of exposition and for heuristic purposes, this chapter has separated the discussions of the cash and the futures markets. In practice, though, these markets are frequently viewed as two facets of the same market. Hedgers, by implication, are involved with both cash and futures, and traders will always consult both markets even if they are involved in only one. Only the most limited or specialized market participants will focus on just one of these markets.

Debt options, because of their newness, are often viewed as a derivative and separate marketplace. This perception is probably akin to the way financial futures were viewed in the mid-1970's. Over time, however, as debt options mature, they will become another integrated facet of the established U.S. Government securities market in the same way futures have.

CHAPTER 3

An Introduction to the Pricing of Options on Debt Instruments

Mark Pitts, Ph.D.
Vice President
Lehman Brothers

INTRODUCTION

Although equity options have been trading for some time, exchange traded options on fixed income securities are relatively new financial instruments. Aside from the call provision attached to most long bonds, the fixed income investor has, until recently, had little reason to concern himself with options of any kind. The advent of exchange traded options on fixed income securities and exchange traded options on futures contracts on fixed income securities provides investors with many new opportunities. However, to capitalize on these opportunities, market participants must acquire new skills.

The subject of this chapter is the valuation of options on fixed income securities and options on futures contracts on fixed income securities. We examine the value of the options at expiration, as well as prior to expiration. To obtain option values prior to expiration, we use a well-known technique known as the *riskless hedge*. There is, however, less agreement on the best approach for valuing options on fixed income securities prior to expiration than there is on the valuation of options on equities prior to expiration; consequently, the riskless hedge technique is not the only valuation method that one may wish to consider.

The analysis is divided into two major sections. The first section treats the valuation of options on actual (or spot) fixed income securities. This includes the value of the option at expiration, and the *relative* value of put and call options prior to expiration. Using the riskless hedge technique, we then examine the *absolute* value of call (or put) options prior to expiration. In the second section, the valuation of options on futures on fixed income securities is examined in essentially the same order.

OPTIONS ON ACTUAL DEBT SECURITIES

The Contract

Like a stock option, an option on a fixed income security is a contract that gives the buyer the right (but not the obligation) to buy or sell the underlying security. In the case of a *European option*, the buyer has this right only on the option *expiration date*. For *American options*, the buyer can exercise his right on any day, up to and including the expiration date. In the case of a *call option*, the option buyer has the right to purchase the underlying security at the *strike (or exercise) price*. Alternatively, the buyer of a *put option* has the right to sell the underlying security at the predetermined strike price. Should the option buyer decide to exercise his option, the option seller is obligated by contract to sell the underlying security (in the case of a call) or buy the underlying security (in the case of a put) at the strike price.

Since the option buyer retains all the rights of sale or purchase, and will only exercise those rights when it is to his advantage (and, as it turns out, to the option seller's disadvantage), the option buyer must pay the seller to enter into such an agreement. This payment is known as the option *premium,* or simply, the *price* of the option.

The Value of the Option at Expiration

The Basic Concepts

Any understanding of the value of a put or call option begins with a clear grasp of the value of the option on the day it expires. For simplicity, let us work with options with a strike price of $100. At expiration, the call option buyer will exercise his right to purchase the underlying security if, and only if, the market value of the security is above $100. Thus, the holder of the call option will purchase the security for $100 and, if there is no desire to own the security, resell it in the market at a price greater than $100. Similarly, the holder of a call option will never exercise his option if the market value of the security is below $100, even if he believes the security is worth more than $100. If he wants to own the security, he will purchase it in the open market at a price lower than the $100 he would have to pay if the option were exercised. For the put option, the situation is reversed. If the market price at expiration is above the $100 exercise price, the option will not be exercised. If, however, the market price is below $100, the owner of the option will "put" the security to the option seller for $100.

Thus, the value of owning an option on the day it expires is completely determined by the strike price and the price of the security. These values for the put option and the call option, each with an exercise price of $100, are shown in Exhibit 1. Since the holder of an option has rights, but no obligations, the value of an option cannot be negative and can never become a liability. In the case of the call option, the option value at expiration is zero for all prices of the underlying security up to the strike price. At the strike price, the call option starts to acquire value; in fact, for prices above strike, the value of the option at expiration increases dollar for dollar with increases in the price of the underlying security. The situation

EXHIBIT 1
Value at Expiration of Long Positions in Options

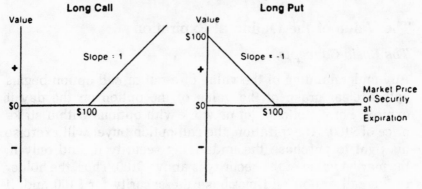

is reversed for the put option. The put has no value at expiration if the price of the underlying security is above the strike price. However, for prices below the strike price, the value of the put increases dollar for dollar with *decreases* in the value of the underlying security. The maximum value for the put is the strike price, since, of course, the value of the underlying security cannot fall below zero.

The *intrinsic value* of a call option (either before or at expiration) is defined as the market price minus the strike price, or zero, whichever is greater. For the put, the intrinsic value is the strike price minus the market price, or zero, whichever is greater.

Profit for those with a *short* position in either a put or a call option (i.e., the sellers) is the negative of that shown in Exhibit 1. This is evident in Exhibit 2.

If we know the premium that was paid for the option, we can easily calculate the purchaser's net profit at expiration of the option. Net profit is simply the option's value at expiration minus the premium paid (ignoring, for now, the time value of money). For example, assume that a buyer paid a $4 premium for the option with a strike price of $100. To show profit as a function of the market price of the underlying security at expiration, we shift the graphs in Exhibit 1 down by $4 (see Exhibit 3). From this diagram, it is evident that the option

EXHIBIT 2
Value at Expiration of Short Positions in Options

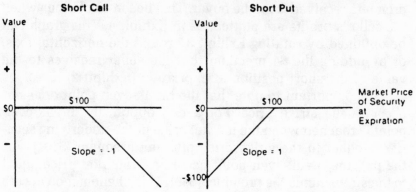

buyer will lose money if the price of the security moves against him; however, the maximum loss is $4. On the other hand, profit could be as high as $96 for the put buyer, and, conceptually, there is no limit to the profit that the call buyer could obtain. The potential for a limited loss but a large, or unlimited, profit appeals to many option buyers.

The potential profit for the seller, or *writer*, of options is the other side of the coin. Since options are a *zero-sum game*, any profit to the buyer corresponds to a loss of equal

EXHIBIT 3
Profit at Expiration for a Long Position in Options
(Excluding Financing Costs)

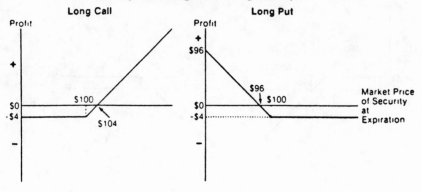

magnitude for the seller. Thus, option sellers can experience very large losses, but, at best, reap a profit equal to the option premium received from the buyer. This becomes obvious when the seller's profits are plotted, as in Exhibit 4. This graph can be obtained by rotating Exhibit 3 around the horizontal axis, or by adding the $4 premium that the seller receives to the value of the short position at expiration (Exhibit 2).

It is important to note that the break-even point does not occur at the strike price. For a call option, the break-even point is reached when the market price of the underlying security is equal to the strike price plus the premium ($104). For the put, the break-even point occurs at a market price equal to the strike minus the premium ($96). This phenomenon occurs because the seller effectively has a cushion equal to the premium, but the buyer bears the initial cost of the premium which he must retrieve before breaking even on the trade.

When the time value of money is included, the preceding results are somewhat altered. The option seller has the advantage of being able to invest the premium until expiration, but the option buyer loses this opportunity. Consider our previous example (strike = $100 and premium = $4) for a six-month option when the short-term interest rate is 10 percent. The

EXHIBIT 4
Profit at Expiration for a Short Position in Options
(Excluding Financing Costs)

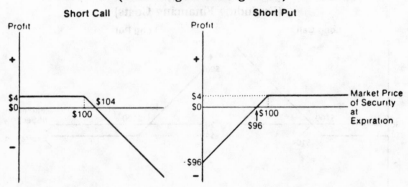

EXHIBIT 5
Profit at Expiration for a Long Position in Options
(Including Financing Costs)

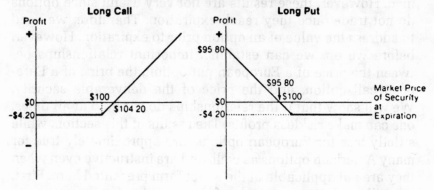

option seller in this case earns $0.20 in interest on the premium during the life of the option. The buyer loses a like amount in opportunity cost. In order to break even then, the buyer needs to earn even more ($4.20) at option expiration; likewise, the seller can lose more at expiration and still break even. In light of these considerations, in Exhibits 5 and 6 we have redrawn Exhibits 3 and 4 to account for the time value of money on the profits of the buyers and sellers of options.

EXHIBIT 6
Profit at Expiration for a Short Position in Options
(Including Financing Costs)

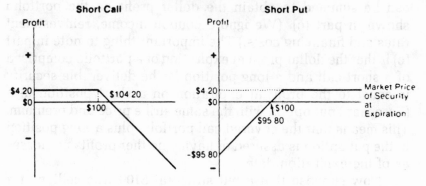

Conversions and Reversals

So far, only the option's value at expiration has been examined. However, these results are not very useful since options do not trade once they reach expiration. Therefore, we need to address the value of an option prior to expiration. However, before we do, we can establish important relationships between the price of a European put option, the price of a European call option, and the price of the deliverable security. We will show that if the relationships do not hold at all times, one can make riskless profits. The results of this section, while strictly true for European options, are approximately true for many American options as well, and are instructive even when they are not applicable in the exact form presented here. First, we will present an example of a conversion for European options.

In the previous section, we plotted the profit earned on put and call options as a function of the price of the deliverable security at expiration (Exhibits 3 and 4, when the time value of money is ignored). We can expand the usefulness of these graphs by using the fact that we can plot the profit of a portfolio merely by summing the profits of the parts. For instance, we might be interested in the profit on a *covered call* position (i.e., a portfolio that is short a call option and long the deliverable security). In the example in Exhibit 7, we assume for simplicity that the security is purchased at $100, the strike price is $100, and the premium is $4. Parts (a) and (b) of Exhibit 7 can be summed to obtain the dollar profit on the portfolio shown in part (c). (We ignore coupon income, reinvestment rates and financing costs.) The important thing to note in part (c) is that the dollar profit at expiration of a portfolio comprised of a short call and a long position in the deliverable security is equal to the profit at expiration on a short position in a (European) put option with the same strike price and premium. This means that the covered call portfolio plus a *long* position in the put option is assured of having neither profits nor losses as of the expiration date.

Now suppose that a put struck at $100 was selling at a

EXHIBIT 7
Profit on a Covered Call (Strike Price = Purchase Price—Excluding Financing Costs and Coupon Income)

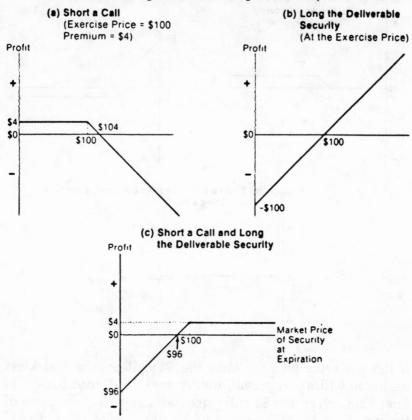

(a) Short a Call
(Exercise Price = $100
Premium = $4)

(b) Long the Deliverable Security
(At the Exercise Price)

(c) Short a Call and Long the Deliverable Security

premium less than that of the call, say $3. Combining the covered call position and a long position in the put, we derive the result illustrated in part (c) of Exhibit 8. From the graph, it is evident that whatever the value of the deliverable security at expiration, the holder is assured of a $1 profit. Obviously, arbitrageurs will not permit this situation to prevail for long; these cannot be equilibrium prices. Proceeding in this manner, we could prove that *any* price for the put below $4 cannot be an equilibrium price. Furthermore, it can be shown that

EXHIBIT 8
The Conversion (Excluding Financing Costs and Coupon Income)

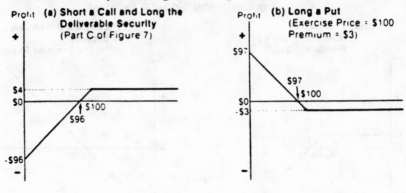

(a) Short a Call and Long the Deliverable Security (Part C of Figure 7)

(b) Long a Put (Exercise Price = $100 Premium = $3)

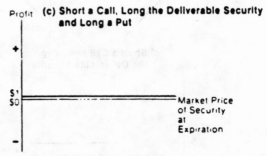

(c) Short a Call, Long the Deliverable Security and Long a Put

if the put price is *more than* the $4 call premium, riskless arbitrage will again prevail until prices are forced back into line. Thus, given the $4 call price, we know that the price of the put *must* be $4, or one could make profits without risk. (When financing, coupons, and reinvestment incomes are considered, this is no longer true. We consider this more complicated situation in the next section.) We assumed in this example that the exercise price on the call equals the purchase price of the underlying security. However, this is not necessary for deriving parity conditions with the put. In Exhibit 9, we show that if the premium on a call option is $2, and the strike $106, then, at expiration, the profit on a covered call portfolio is equivalent to a short position in a put with a strike of $106 and an $8 premium (when the purchase price of the security is $100).

EXHIBIT 9

Profit on a Covered Call (Strike Price ≠ Purchase Price—Excluding Financing Costs and Coupon Income)

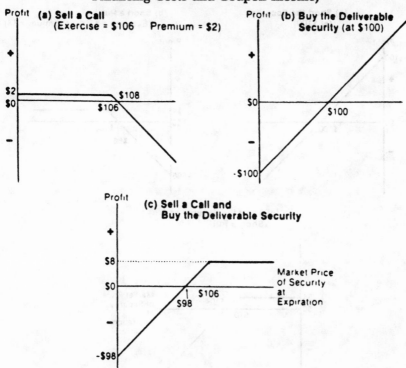

Constructing a covered call position along with a long put is known as a *conversion* and is one of many portfolios that can be established in order to take advantage of prices that are not in line. Another well-known method, the *reversal,* makes use of the fact that a short position in the deliverable security, plus a short position in a put option on that security, exhibits a profit pattern like a short position in the call on the security. This is indicated in Exhibit 10. Thus, if one shorts the security, shorts a put on the security, and goes *long* a call (with the appropriate exercise price), the profit is guaranteed to be zero on expiration if equilibrium prices prevail. As before, if the premiums on the options are not "correct," riskless profits are available. (Recall that we are still excluding

EXHIBIT 10
Profit for a Short Position in the Security and a Short Position in a Put (Excluding Financing Costs and Coupon Payments)

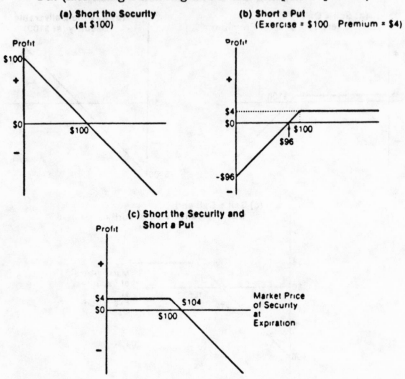

coupon income, reinvestment income, and financing costs.)

Conversions and reversals are not the only relationships that must exist between the prices of the deliverable security and the prices of the put and call options on that security; many more exist. Some of the more interesting equivalent portfolios are displayed in Exhibit 11. Some of these relationships might seem confusing at first, but they can all be derived by rearranging and transposing the terms in the simple conversion relationship.

Coupon Income and Financing Costs

In the previous section, we disregarded several factors that play a major role in determining which portfolios are truly

EXHIBIT 11
Equivalent Portfolios

Long the Security[a] (The Conversion)	+ Short Call	= Short Put
Short the Security (The Reversal)	+ Short Put	= Short Call
Long the Security	+ Long Put	= Long Call
Short the Security	+ Long Call	= Long Put
Long Call	+ Short Put	= Long the Security
Long Put	+ Short Call	= Short the Security

[a] In each case, "the security" is the security that underlies each of the options.

equivalent. To start with, we ignored the fact that in order to establish a position in the underlying security, one must either finance the position or incur the opportunity cost of establishing the position. Furthermore, in the case of coupon-bearing securities, the holder of the security receives the coupon income and the reinvestment income on the coupons. These factors may significantly alter the equilibrium relationships between the price of the security, the put, and the call that were described in the previous section.

To illustrate how one includes these complicating factors, consider again the covered call portfolio—a long position and a short call on the same security. We assume the underlying security is a 12 percent bond selling at $95 and that the short-term borrowing and lending rate is 14 percent. Consider a one-year call option with a strike of $100 selling for $4 on a coupon date. Regardless of the price of the bond on the expiration date of the option, the bond holder will have received $12.42 from the coupons and coupon reinvestment ($6 × 1.07 + $6). However, the price of the bond net of the income from the option must be financed at a cost (or carried for an opportunity loss) of $12.74 [i.e., .14 × ($95 − $4)]. Thus, the net cost of carrying the bond and call is $0.32.

The profits for the call, the bond, and financing and investment income are shown respectively in Exhibit 12, parts (a), (b), and (c). From their sum shown in part (d), it is clear that

EXHIBIT 12
The Conversion (Including Financing Costs and Coupon Income)

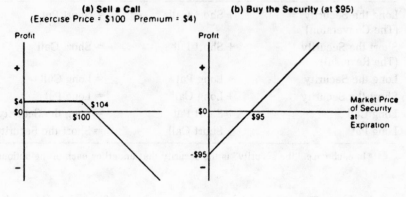

(a) Sell a Call
(Exercise Price = $100   Premium = $4)

(b) Buy the Security (at $95)

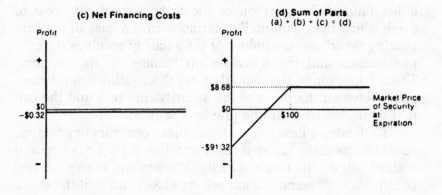

(c) Net Financing Costs

(d) Sum of Parts
(a) + (b) + (c) = (d)

the profits on the portfolio are still very much like that of a short position in a put option. When investment income is considered on such a short put position, the profit on the foregoing portfolio is exactly the same as that of a European put with a strike of $100 and a premium of $7.61.

A Theory of Option Valuation: Riskless Hedge Valuation Models

In the previous sections, we established parity conditions for call options and put options. Given the price of the underlying security and the price of one type of option, we can establish the equilibrium price of the other type of option. But how do we ascertain the price of the first option? Finding the fair value of the first option is the problem that we now address.

The most widely accepted method for valuing options prior to their expiration uses an important principle known as the *riskless hedge*. Such a hedge makes use of the fact that, whatever the value the option, it is bound to respond to changes in the price of the underlying security. In the case of a call, the option's value will move in the same direction as the price of the underlying security; for a put, the two values move inversely. This does not mean that a $1 move in the price of the security will cause the option price to move by $1; in fact, it can be shown that the change in the option value will nearly always be less than the change in the price of the underlying security.

Assumptions that Underlie the Riskless Hedge Valuation Models

Keep in mind that in the riskless hedge valuation models, as in any model, we obtain results only at a cost—we will have to make simplifying assumptions that do not precisely conform to reality. Stated loosely, the assumptions that underlie most riskless hedge valuation models for fixed income securities are as follows:

- Yields may change rapidly but cannot "jump." (To say this in another way, we could draw the graph of yields over time without lifting the pencil from the page.) It is assumed that one can take market action in response to a change in prices, no matter how small.
- There is a risk-free rate of interest for borrowing and lending from the current period until the expiration date of the option. It is assumed in most riskless hedge valuation models that this rate is constant throughout the life of the option.
- For simplicity, taxes can be ignored. (Taxes are ever-present, but their effect on prices "at the margin" may be small.)

- Market participants can sell securities short and make use of all proceeds from the sale. Transactions costs are small enough to be disregarded in the valuation procedure.

Obviously, the real world does not work according to these assumptions. However, it is generally believed that these assumptions are not so unrealistic as to destroy the validity of the model. In any case, many of the results of the model (such as how each input affects the option price) can be enlightening, even when the precise option value given by the model is off the mark.

The Binomial Pricing Model

To illustrate riskless hedge valuation, we use a special example, the binomial model, to value a European call option on a noncoupon-bearing security. The binomial model is one of several ways to use the riskless hedge framework for valuing options. The Black-Scholes model, which is widely used for equity option valuation, also uses the riskless hedge. The mathematics of the Black-Scholes formulation, however, prohibit most market participants from understanding the valuation process. In contrast, the binomial model is straightforward, yet powerful in terms of the problems it can handle. In the pages that follow, we will show how the binomial model can be used to understand the essentials of option valuation.

We will examine a simplified form of the binomial model: we assume that given a starting price, the price of the underlying security in each successive period will move either up or down by $1. A three-period example for a security with a starting price of $95 is shown schematically for monthly periods in Exhibit 13. Suppose that at the beginning of the first month, when the price of the underlying security is $95, we want to value a European call option with a strike of $94 that expires two periods later, at the beginning of the third month. What is a fair price to pay for this option?

To begin with, for any given price of the security at expiration, we know the value of the option at expiration. The option value will be the price of the underlying security minus the

EXHIBIT 13
Network of Possible Prices: Step 1

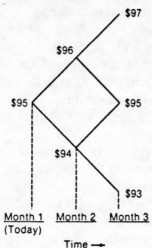

strike price, or zero, if the former is negative. Thus, we can repeat Exhibit 13 with some option values included. This is shown in Exhibit 14 where the option values at expiration are shown in parentheses.

EXHIBIT 14
Network of Possible Prices: Step 2

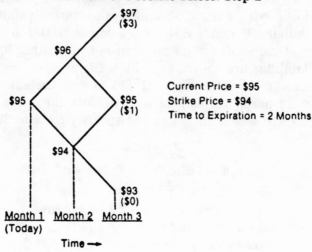

Our objective is to work back from month 3 to get option values for month 2. The method that is used to make these backward steps is the riskless hedge.

The riskless hedge can be illustrated as follows. First, we want to determine the price of the option at the beginning of month 2, *given that* the price of the security turns out to be $96 at the beginning of month 2. With the price of the security at $96, let us construct a portfolio that is long $100 par amount of the security and short one call option on the security.

A period later (at the beginning of month 3) the price of the security could rise to $97 or fall to $95. Since the strike on the call is $94, the short option is equivalent to a $3 liability if the price goes up to $97, and it is equivalent to a $1 liability if the price goes down to $95.

If it is not clear why the short option position is equivalent to a liability, consider the obligations of the writer. If he does nothing, the security will be called, and he will be paid $94. Since the security will be worth more than $94, the option writer will effectively have a loss of $1 (if the price goes to $95) or a loss of $3 (if the price goes to $97). Alternatively, the option writer can purchase an option of the same strike and expiration, offsetting his short position with a long position, thereby ending up with no net position in options. Since the cost of buying the option will be the market value of the option (either $95 minus $94, or $97 minus $94), the cost, or liability, of the short option position is again either $1 or $3. These liabilities are shown in Exhibit 15.

Since the value of the portfolio is just the sum of the value of its parts, we can easily calculate the value of the portfolio for the case in which the security rises to $97, and

Exhibit 15
Option Liabilities at Expiration
(Strike = $94)

Case	Option Liability
Security Rises to $97	($3)
Security Declines to $95	($1)

for the case in which it falls to $95. This is shown in Exhibit 16.

As Exhibit 16 shows, the value of the portfolio after one month will be $94, whether the security price moves up or down. Therefore, there is no risk in this portfolio. We have created a riskless hedge using the underlying security and the call on the security.

Since the portfolio is risk-free over the one-month period, we know that it cannot have a rate of return greater than the risk-free (i.e., Treasury) rate. (If it were greater, no one would buy Treasury securities; they would invest in our risk-free portfolio instead.) It can also be shown that the rate of return on the risk-free portfolio cannot be less than the risk-free rate; otherwise arbitrageurs could make profits with no risk. Thus, the rate of return on the risk-free portfolio must equal the risk-free rate. In this example, we'll let the risk-free rate be 0.5 percent per month.

With these facts in mind we can calculate a price for the option at the beginning of the second month *given that* the price of the security at that time is $96. We have shown that the value of the riskless portfolio one period later must be $94. If the portfolio earns the risk-free rate of return over this one-month period, its initial value, or cost, must be $93.5323 (i.e., $94/1.005). But we also know that the cost of buying the portfolio is $96 (the price of the underlying security), minus the premium received on the option that was sold. By equating these costs, we can prove that the premium must be $2.4677. This is illustrated in Exhibit 17. If the option premium were not $2.4677, the portfolio would not cost exactly $93.5323, and any other cost would imply that the risk-free portfolio would earn something other than the risk-free rate.

EXHIBIT 16
Portfolio Values (Portfolio is Long the Security and Short One Call)

Case	Value of Security	− Option Liability	Value of = Portfolio
Security Rises to $97	$97	($3)	$94
Security Declines to $95	$95	($1)	$94

EXHIBIT 17
Portfolio Costs and Option Value at the Beginning of Month 2
(Security Price = $96)

To Earn Risk-Free Rate: Cost of Portfolio = $94/1.005
                                          = $93.5323

By Construction: Cost of Portfolio = Cost of Security − Revenue
                                             from Selling 1 Option
                                          = $96 − Market Price of 1 Option

Set Costs Equal: $93.5323 = $96 − Market Price of 1 Option

Solve for Market
Price of Option: Option Price = $96 − $93.5323
                                       = $2.47

Thus, the value of the option at the beginning of month 2 must be about $2.47 (given that the price of the underlying security is $96 at that time).

We have now used the riskless hedge to solve for one value of the option prior to expiration. Applying this same method, we can solve for the value of the option at the beginning of month 2 *given that* the price of the underlying security at that time turns out to be $94. In this case, if one constructs a portfolio consisting of $100 par amount of the underlying security and *two* short calls,[1] the value of the portfolio one period later (the beginning of the third month) will be $93 regardless of whether the security price goes up to $95 or down to $93. This is shown in Exhibits 18 and 19. Since the portfolio is riskless, it must earn the risk-free rate of return, and so the cost of establishing the portfolio must be $92.5373 ($93/1.005). Therefore, as shown in Exhibit 20, only if each of the two options are priced at $0.7314, will the risk-free portfolio earn the risk-free rate of return. In Exhibit 21, we use these results and add two new option values in parentheses.

---

[1] Each time we use riskless hedge to work back one period, the number of calls in the riskless portfolio will be different. To find the correct number, we ask the question: how many calls are needed to make the value of the portfolio the same whether the price of the security moves up or down? For example, in the present case, if x is the number of calls in the portfolio, we want $95 − x($1) = $93 − x($0). Solving for x tells us that we need two (short) calls to make the portfolio riskless.

EXHIBIT 18
Option Liabilities at Expiration
(Strike = $94)

Case	Option Liability
Security Rises to $95	($1)
Security Declines to $93	($0)

EXHIBIT 19
Portfolio Values (Portfolio is Long the Security and Short Two Calls)

Case	Value of Security −	Liability of Two Calls Short =	Value of Portfolio
Security Rises to $95	$95	($2)	$93
Security Declines to $93	$93	($0)	$93

EXHIBIT 20
Portfolio Costs and Option Value at the Beginning of Month 2 (Security Price = $94)

To Earn Risk-Free Rate:	Cost of Portfolio = $93/1.005
	= $92.5373
By Construction:	Cost of Portfolio = Cost of Security − Revenue from Selling 2 Options
	= $94 − Market Price of 2 Options
Set Costs Equal:	$92.5373 = $94 − Market Price of 2 Options
Solve for Market Price of Option:	Market Price of Each Option = $.7314

To get the option value at the beginning of month 1, that is, the value of the option today, we use the riskless hedge to take one more backward step. We know that given today's price of $95, the price of the underlying security will either go up to $96 or down to $94, and from our previous calculations we know that the respective option prices will be $2.47 and $0.73 (see Exhibit 22). Now suppose that we construct a portfolio that is long one unit of the underlying security and short

EXHIBIT 21
Network of Possible Prices: Step 3

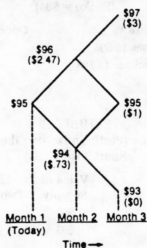

1.15 call options. In Exhibit 23, we show that if the price of the security goes up to $96, the value of the portfolio will be $93.16, and if the price of the security goes down to $94, the portfolio will still be worth $93.16. A riskless hedge has been created. Proceeding as before, we require that the return on this risk-free portfolio be the risk-free rate. This means that

EXHIBIT 22
Option Liabilities at Beginning of Month 2

Case	Option Liability
Security Rises to $96	($2.47)
Security Declines to $94	($0.73)

EXHIBIT 23
Portfolio Values (Portfolio is Long the Security and Short 1.15 Calls)

Case	Value of Security	−	Liability of 1.15 Calls Short	=	Value of Portfolio
Security Rises to $96	$96		($2.84)		$93.16
Security Declines to $94	$94		($0.84)		$93.16

the cost of the portfolio at the beginning of month 1 must be $92.70 (i.e., $93.16/1.005). But also, the cost of the portfolio is $95 minus the revenue from selling 1.15 calls. This means that the calls must sell for $2.00. These calculations are shown in detail in Exhibits 23 and 24.

We have finally answered our original question—what is a fair price to pay for the option today if the security is selling for $95. We have shown that $2.00 is the only possible answer, given the risk-free rate of interest and the set of possible future prices. Thus, starting at expiration, we have used the riskless hedge to find the value of the option today, two periods before the option expires. To solve for the fair value for longer-term options, all we need is a bigger set of possible prices, and we can use the same techniques for finding the current fair price of the option.

At this point, the reader may be thinking that we have presented a few tricks, but have not solved any problems found in the real world. After all, prices fluctuate almost continuously, not just once a month. To make matters worse, when prices change, they can move to any one of many new values, not just two, as we have assumed in our example. However, if the reader is willing to accept the assumptions for the riskless hedge valuation models outlined in the previous section, these objections can be overcome by suitably modifying the binomial model. To construct a binomial model that conforms

EXHIBIT 24
Portfolio Costs and Option Value at the Beginning of
Month 1 (Security Price = $95)

To Earn Risk-Free Rate: Cost of Portfolio = $93.16/1.005
                               = $92.70

By Construction: Cost of Portfolio = Cost of Security − Revenue
                                    from Selling 1.15 Options
                               = $95 − Market Price of 1.15
                                 Options

Set Cost Equal: $92.70 = $95 − Market Price of 1.15 Options

Solve for Market
Price of Option: Market Price of Each Option = $2.00

more closely to the real world, we would let the price shift much more frequently than once a month. By letting the price move more frequently, we end up with a continuum of possible option prices at expiration, rather than just three possible values, as in our example. Other modifications account for the possibility of early exercise. A more complicated network of prices can be used to account for the fact that the volatility of prices depends upon interest rate levels.[2]

Options on Coupon-Bearing Securities

The binomial valuation model can be modified for options on coupon-paying securities. To do this, we let Exhibit 13 depict the flat prices for the security (i.e., the price before accrued interest has been added on), and let the strike price be $94 plus accured. Again, we start by filling in the option values at expiration. Continuing as before, we would want to find the option value at the beginning of the second month, *given that* the flat price of the underlying security turns out to be $96 at the beginning of month 2. We let the security have a 12 percent coupon and, for simplicity, assume monthly coupon payments. As in the previous example, a portfolio that consists of $100 par amount of the bond, and a short position in one call option, will be riskless. Only this time, the portfolio will be worth $95 immediately after the coupon payment ($94 plus $1 coupon), regardless of the final value of the bond. This is shown in Exhibit 25.

Accordingly, the cost or value of the portfolio must be $94.5274 (i.e., $95/1.005) at the beginning of month 2. This means that if the price of the security turns out to be $96 at the beginning of month 2, then the price of the option must be $1.4726 at that time (see Exhibit 26). (Note that the difference between $1.4726 and the value of the option derived in Exhibit

---

[2] These complications are explained in more detail in Mark Pitts, "The Pricing of Options on Debt Securities," *The Journal of Portfolio Management* (forthcoming Winter 1985).

EXHIBIT 25
Portfolio Values (Portfolio is Long the Security and Short One Call)

Case	Value of Security	Option − Liability[a]	Coupon + Income	Value of = Portfolio
Security Rises to $97	$97	($3)	$1	$95
Security Declines to $95	$95	($1)	$1	$95

[a] See Exhibit 15.

17 is just the discounted value of the foregone coupon. That is, $2.4677 − $1.4726 = $1/1.005.) Any other value would mean that the riskless portfolio would have a rate of return not equal to the risk-free rate. To complete the process, one would calculate an option value for the beginning of month 2, should the price of the underlying security be $94 at that time. Given both the option values for the beginning of month 2, the current value of the option may be obtained by using the riskless hedge to work back to the beginning. This example shows that the inclusion of coupons does not pose any problems in the valuation process. Furthermore, the effect of coupons is unambiguously clear; when other factors are held constant, the greater the coupon, the lower the value of the call option. This is apparent when one considers that in order to receive

EXHIBIT 26
Portfolio Costs and Option Value at the Beginning of Month 2 for Coupon-Bearing Security
(Price of Security = $96)

To Earn Risk-Free Rate: Cost of Portfolio = $95/1.005
                                         = $94.5274

By Construction: Cost of Portfolio = Cost of Security − Revenue from Selling 1 Option
                                      = $96 − Market Price of 1 Option

Set Costs Equal: $94.5274 = $96 − Market Price of 1 Option

Solve for Market Price of Option: Option Price = $1.4726

the riskless return (and no more), the holder of the riskless portfolio must receive less for the call option(s) when he receives more in coupon income.

Riskless Hedge Valuation Models

As stated earlier, the binomial model is just one of a large family of models that employs the riskless hedge to value put and call options. The first such model, the Black-Scholes valuation model, is widely used in equity option valuation. Fortunately, given the same assumptions and the same inputs, all option valuation models that use the riskless hedge will "converge" upon the same value for a given option. (However, there are many reasonable price patterns for which there is only one known riskless hedge solution procedure. In these cases the binomial model will generally not be applicable.)

A surprising aspect of the riskless hedge valuation models is that it is not necessary to specify the probabilities that the price of the underlying security will increase or decrease. This occurs, in part, because the model only derives the fair price of the option in terms of the current price of the underlying security. We have completely ignored the question of whether the underlying security is selling at a fair price.

Factors that Affect the Option's Value

To use the riskless hedge valuation model for an option on a fixed income security, one needs six inputs, most of which are readily available. These are:

- The current price of the underlying security
- The strike price
- The short-term risk-free interest rate (assumed constant)
- The time to option expiration
- The coupon (if any)
- The volatility of yields

Although the first five factors are easily obtained, the sixth, yield volatility during the life of the option, is not directly observable. A perfect estimate of this volatility would require the ability to foretell the future; clearly this is the most difficult factor needed for pricing options. One can use historical yield volatilities to estimate future volatility, but as recent years have shown, this method is unreliable.

In the following sections, we discuss how each input affects the option's value. The effects of some of these variables on the option's price are illustrated in the binomial example of the previous sections. The reader may want to refer back to "The Binomial Pricing Model" section.

The Price of the Underlying Security

As the price of the underlying security increases, the value of a call option rises; but the value of the put option falls. This is because the holder of a call option tends to benefit from high prices of the underlying security, but the put holder tends to benefit from low prices of the underlying security.

The relationship between the value of a call with a strike price of $100 and the price of a noncoupon-bearing security may look something like Exhibit 27. In this graph the price of the underlying security is on the horizontal axis and the value of the option is on the vertical axis. The dashed line that projects diagonally from the horizontal axis is a plot of the price of the underlying security minus the strike price. Thus, the intrinsic value of the option is denoted by the dashed line in Exhibit 27.

Several significant points about calls are illustrated in this graph. First, the option price can never exceed the price of the underlying security. If this were not the case, buying the security itself would always be preferable to buying a call on the security. Thus, if the value of the security is zero (for instance, in the case of total bankruptcy if the call is on a corporate security), the call option must be worthless. Also, as shown in Exhibit 27, the value of the option on a noncoupon-bearing security can never be less than the market price minus the strike price. Since the owner of an American call can exercise his right to purchase at any time, the truth of this statement is obvious for the American calls. It turns out, however, that

EXHIBIT 27
Value of a Call Option Prior to Expiration

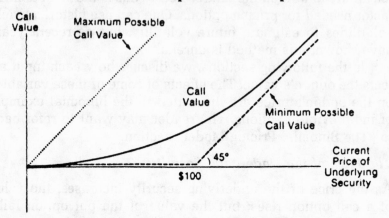

this is equally true for European options on noncoupon-bearing securities. For either coupon-bearing or noncoupon-bearing securities, American options will never sell for less than their intrinsic value.

Exhibit 27 also reveals some important properties of the volatility of option prices compared with the volatility of the price of the underlying security. The change in the price of the option relative to a change in the price of the security is represented by the slope of the curved line in Exhibit 27. When the line is steep, there is a large response in the option price to a change in the price of the underlying security. When the line is almost level, there is very little response. However, since the line is never steeper than 45°, the dollar change in the price of the option is never more than the dollar change in the price of underlying security. (*Proportional* changes, however, are always larger for the option.) The ratio of the change in the price of the option to the change in the price of the underlying security is known as the *hedge ratio*. This ratio is critical in option valuation since it determines the mix of options and underlying security that is needed to create the riskless portfolio.

Typical price patterns for a European put option on a noncoupon-bearing security with a $100 strike are shown in

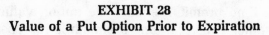

EXHIBIT 28
Value of a Put Option Prior to Expiration

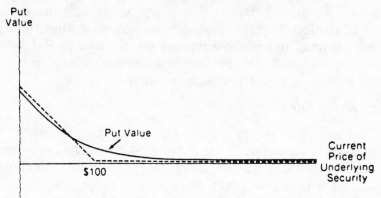

Exhibit 28. The pattern for puts can be thought of as the opposite of that for calls. Unlike American options and European call options on noncoupon-bearing securities, option values for European puts on noncoupon-bearing securities can be less than their intrinsic value.[3]

As in the case of calls, the dollar price change in the put option is always less than the price change in the underlying security. Of course, for the put, the moves are in opposite directions.

Finally, Exhibits 27 and 28 clearly illustrate the two components of the value of the option. The first component is the intrinsic value. This is simply the value that would be received if one could exercise the option immediately. The other component of value is the *time premium* and constitutes all the value of the option above its intrinsic value. For a call on a noncoupon-bearing security (Exhibit 27) whose price is below the strike price, the entire value of the call is the time premium (since intrinsic value is zero). At prices above

---

[3] For example, suppose that the price of an American put option just reaches the point where one would want to exercise early. The price of the American put would then be its intrinsic value. But, since the European put cannot be exercised early, it must have a lower price than the American option which is selling for intrinsic value.

strike, the time premium equals the option value minus the intrinsic value. Thus, the time premium is represented by the vertical distance between the option value and the dashed line in Exhibit 27. One should note, however, that the time premium need not be positive. As we showed in Exhibit 28, some options can sell for less than their intrinsic value. In such a case, the time premium is negative.

The Strike Price

If two call options are identical in every respect except the strike price, the one with the lower strike will always be more valuable. This is apparent when one considers that the holder of a call with a low strike price would never prefer to own a call with a higher strike price. The situation is reversed for puts: the higher the strike price the more valuable the option.

The relationship between the value of a call and the strike price is presented in Exhibit 29 where we superimpose the graphs for call options with strikes of $100 and $90. As the graph shows, the difference between the price of the two calls is greatest when the price of the underlying security is high.

EXHIBIT 29
The Effect of the Strike Price on the Value of a Call
Prior to Expiration

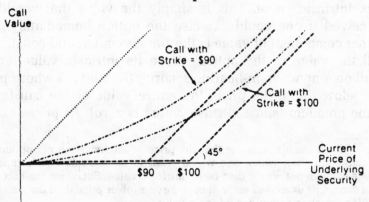

The Short-Term Interest Rate

In the riskless hedge valuation models, we usually assume that current and future interest rates for very short-term borrowing (such as the overnight repurchase rates) are known with certainty for all periods up until the option expires.[4] It is frequently assumed that one such rate will be in effect during the entire period.

When the short-term rate of interest increases, the value of a call option will rise if all other factors are held constant. This occurs primarily through the effect of the interest rate on the cost of carry of the underlying bond and on the present value of the strike price. If the short-term interest rate rises, the forward price of the bond increases and the net effect is very much like a higher current price—the call becomes more valuable. However, as we showed in the prior section, when bond prices increase, a put becomes less valuable. Thus, when the short-term interest rate increases, and the forward price increases, the value of a put option falls. (Alternatively, consider what happens in the binomial model when the short-term rate increases. The cost of the risk-free portfolio must go down. Since the price of the underlying security is unaffected, this implies that the revenue received from selling a given number of calls must increase. Similar logic can be used to show that put prices must decline when the short-term interest rate rises.)

At this point, a clarifying note is in order. As we have shown, when the yield on the underlying security rises and the price falls, the call option becomes *less* valuable if other factors are held constant. Yet, we say that if the short-term interest rate rises, the call option becomes *more* valuable, if other factors are held constant. These are not contradictory statements, however, since we are referring to two distinctly different rates. In the first instance, we are referring to the rate on the underlying security. In the latter, we are referring

---

[4] More precisely, the riskless hedge models are applicable as long as the very short-term rate of interest (at any point in time) is a function of time and the yield on the underlying security.

to the rate in effect for very short-term borrowing and lending from today until the option's expiration date.

The reader may also wonder why we assume that the short-term rates are known, yet allow the rate on the underlying security to vary randomly. Unarguably, the short-term rates in the real world are not known for future periods. These objections are valid, but fortunately can be overcome in a more sophisticated model for option valuation. Such a model allows for variable short-term rates and allows changes in the short-term rates to be correlated with changes in the yield on the underlying security. Unfortunately, the more sophisticated pricing model is considerably more involved than the model with known short-term rates. Thus, for simplicity, we have assumed that the short-term interest rates are known with certainty.

The Time to Option Expiration

For American options, the effect of time to expiration is apparent. With other factors held constant, the longer the time to expiration, the more valuable the option. This is true for puts as well as calls and options on coupon-bearing and noncoupon-bearing securities. If the reader has any doubts concerning the truth of the foregoing, he need only consider the fact that the holder of a long-term American option has every privilege, and more, than the holder of a shorter American option. If the shorter American option sold for more than the longer American option, it would have no buyers.[5] A typical set of price patterns for an American call option on a noncoupon-bearing security is shown in Exhibit 30. As expiration approaches, option prices tend to move down and to the right until, at expiration, the option value is just the intrinsic value. In other words, as the American option approaches expiration, the time premium decreases until, at expiration, there is no time premium and the value of the option is merely its intrinsic value.

---

[5] This same argument can be used to prove that with other factors held constant, American options never sell for less than their European counterparts.

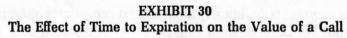

EXHIBIT 30
The Effect of Time to Expiration on the Value of a Call

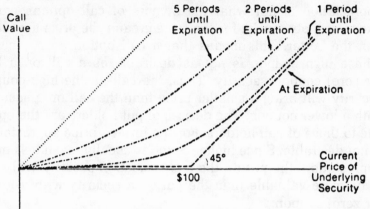

For European options, the situation is not so straightforward. One cannot make blanket statements about the effects of time to expiration on the option's value. For European options, one must proceed on a case-by-case basis, considering whether the option is a put or a call, whether the underlying security has coupons, as well as what the values of the other inputs are in the valuation process.

The Coupon

Coupons tend to decrease the value of call options. This was clear in the binomial model where coupon income "replaced" income from the sale of options in the riskless portfolio. This implies that, with other factors held constant, a call option on a coupon-bearing security will sell for less than a call option on a noncoupon-bearing security. (For an example, compare Exhibits 25 and 26 with Exhibits 16 and 17.) As one might expect, the situation is reversed for puts. Higher coupons tend to boost the value of the put option.

If these statements are not clear, consider the following. A fixed income security can provide the holder return in two ways: it can increase in price, or it can make coupon payments. If we fix the rate of return over a given period, an increase in the payments (coupons) implies that the price appreciation will not be as large as it otherwise would be. Smaller price appreciation is not what the owners of call options would like to see; obviously, for them the greater the price appreciation the better. This means that a call option on a security with a high coupon is not as desirable as a call on a low (or zero) coupon security. Thus, the call on the high-coupon security will bring a smaller price than the call on a security with a lower coupon. The desires of put holders are the opposite to those of call holders. For the former, price appreciation is not desirable. Since higher coupons usually mean less price appreciation, the put on the higher coupon security will tend to be more valuable than the put on a security with a lower (or zero) coupon.

The Volatility of Yields

The volatility of yields (and therefore, prices) increases the value of both puts and calls. To see this, consider first the holder of a call option. Highly volatile yields mean that there is a wide dispersion of possible prices for the underlying security. High prices are in his favor, but low prices are not. Unlike the owner of the underlying security, if the security price is far below the strike price at expiration the call holder's position is no worse (or better) than if the security price is only slightly below the strike at expiration. In contrast, on the upside, the call holder always benefits from increases in the security's price above strike. Therefore, a wide dispersion of final prices is beneficial to the call owner: there is no limit to the amount he can gain from high prices, but there is a limit to his losses from low prices. The most he can lose is the premium he paid for the option. This asymmetry in the effects of the price of the underlying security make the call option more valuable if the underlying security is more volatile.

The situation is similar for put options. Like the call, the effects of the price of the underlying security on the value of the option are asymmetric. High prices for the underlying security can, at worse, cost the option holder his premium. But low prices are not so limited in their benefit; in the most

EXHIBIT 31
Price Effects on Call and Put Options

Increase in	Affect on Call Price[a]	Affect on Put Price[a]
Current price of underlying	Increase	Decrease
Strike Price	Decrease	Increase
Short-Term, Risk-Free Rate[b]	Increase	Decrease
Time to Expiration (for American Options)	Increase	Increase
Coupon	Decrease	Increase
Volatility	Increase	Increase

[a] With all other variables held constant.
[b] For borrowing and lending over the life of the option.

favorable situation, the option at expiration will be worth the entire strike price. Thus, both put and call option holders benefit from higher volatility and prices for both options rise with increasing volatility.

Exhibit 31 summarizes how each of the six inputs in the valuation process affects the value of a put or call option.

In the next section we proceed to options on futures on fixed income securities. As the reader will quickly discover, many of the principles that have been established in the foregoing pages also apply to options on futures.

OPTIONS ON FUTURES ON DEBT SECURITIES

The Contract

As with options on actual (or spot) fixed income securities, both put and call options are available on fixed income futures. The buyer of a call has the right to buy the underlying security at a fixed price. The buyer of a put has the right to sell the underlying security at a fixed price. The option seller (or writer) is obligated to sell the security (in the case of the call) or buy the security (in the case of the put), if the buyer chooses to exercise the option.

An option on a futures contract differs from the more traditional options in only one essential way: The underlying security is not a spot security, but a futures contract on the security. Thus, for instance, if an option buyer exercises his call, he acquires a long position in futures instead of a long position in a cash security. The corresponding seller of the call will be assigned a short position in the same futures contract. For put options, the situation is reversed. If an option buyer exercises his put, he acquires a short position in futures, and the seller of the put is assigned a long position in futures. The resulting long and short futures positions are like any other futures positions and are subject to daily marking to market.

Whenever one acquires a position in futures, he does so at the current futures price. However, if the strike price on the option does not equal the futures price at the time of exercise, the option seller must compensate the option buyer for the discrepancy. Thus, when a call option is exercised, the seller of the call must pay the buyer the current futures price minus the strike price. On the other hand, the seller of the put must pay the buyer the strike price minus the current futures price. (These transactions are actually accomplished by establishing the futures positions at the strike price, then immediately marking to market.) Note that, unlike options on spot securities, the amount of money that changes hands at exercise is only the difference between the strike price and the current futures price. Of course, the option need not be exercised for the owner to reap a profit. In many situations, it will be advisable for the owner of an in-the-money option to close out his position by selling the option instead of exercising it.

Conversions and Reversals with Options on Futures

Profit at Option Expiration

For options on futures held until expiration, the profit on the put or call is determined by the option premium and the price of the futures on the day the option expires. For purposes of

EXHIBIT 32
Profit at Expiration for Long Positions in Options

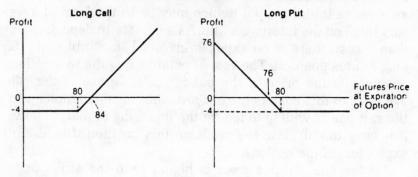

illustration, assume that the option in question is an option on a long Treasury bond future with a strike price of 80. (Futures prices, like spot prices, are quoted in percentage points of par.) If the premium is four points, the profit to the option buyer (ignoring the opportunity loss of interest on the premium) is shown in Exhibit 32. The profit that the option buyer realizes is a loss to the seller. Similarly, the seller's profit is a loss for the buyer (see Exhibit 33).

The Conversion and the Reversal

Suppose one constructs a portfolio comprising a long futures contract, a short call option, and a long put option with the

EXHIBIT 33
Profit at Expiration for Short Positions in Options

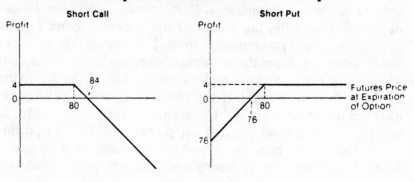

same strike price and expiration date as the call. As indicated earlier, construction of such a portfolio is known as a *conversion*. Since initial margin (which may be in the form of Treasury bills) on the futures constitutes a good faith deposit rather than a cost, there is no expense involved in establishing the long futures position. The cost of establishing the two options positions is the price of the put minus the price of the call. We refer to this cost as the *net premium* for the options positions. If one is willing to ignore the financing of margin flows, it is easy to calculate the profit on this position if held until expiration of the options.

If the final futures price is higher than the strike price, the call option will be exercised, and the sale price will equal the strike. If the final futures price is less than the strike, the put will be exercised and the futures will be sold at the strike. Whatever the price of the futures contract on the day the option expires, it will be sold at the strike price stipulated in the option contracts. Thus, there is no risk surrounding the sale price for the futures contract; it is known in advance.

To make the point more concrete, suppose one buys a Treasury bond futures contract at 76 and simultaneously sells a call option and buys a put option, both with a strike price of 70. If the position is held until the options expire, the futures contract will undoubtedly be closed out at 70. If the final futures price is below 70, the investor will exercise the put, and the futures will be sold at 70. On the other hand, if the final futures price is above 70, the call will be exercised. Either way, the futures contract that was purchased at 76 will be sold at 70 for a six-point loss. Furthermore, unlike the holder of the spot security, the holder of the Treasury bond futures contract receives no coupon inflows. If, however, the call provides exactly six points in income over and above the cost of the put, the investor breaks even (ignoring the financing of the option premiums). If the revenue from the call option exceeds the price of the put by more than six points, the trade will provide sure profits, and it will pay to establish this portfolio or "do the conversion." However, consider what happens when the net premium provides less than six points in income.

Obviously, no one will do the conversion; to do so would lock in a sure loss. Instead, it will be profitable to do the *reversal*. To do the reversal, one takes a short position in the futures contract, a long position in the call option and a short position in the put. In this case, the futures contract will be sold at 76 and repurchased at 70, providing a six-point gain. Therefore, if it costs less than six points to establish the put and call positions, the reversal will be profitable, regardless of the price of the futures contract on the day the option expires.

From this example, it should be clear that, whatever the price of the put, the equilibrium price of the call must differ by exactly six points. Any other price would lead to risk-free arbitrage by either the conversion or the reversal. Furthermore, since we are dealing with options on futures rather than options on actual securities, we need not explicitly recognize the cost of carry associated with the Treasury bonds that underlie the futures contract. (However, the cost of carry on the underlying cash bond will undoubtedly be one of the primary determinants of the futures price.)

The previous analysis applies equally well to any strike price. If, for example, the strike on both the options is 80, then the difference between the put and call price must be four points (80 minus 76). However, in this case, the price of the put should be greater than the price of the call. If it is not, either the conversion or reversal would provide riskless profits.

We have, then, a simple rule for put and call options on futures contracts if we ignore early exercise, the financing of margin, and the financing of the net option premium: The price difference between a put and a call with the same strike on the same futures contract should equal the difference between the current futures price and the strike price. If the strike is less than the current futures price, the call will cost more than the put; if the strike is more than the current futures price, the put will cost more than the call. If this relationship does not hold, there are riskless profitable arbitrage opportunities. This rule can be restated as a formula:

Strike Price − Current Futures Price = Put Price − Call Price

As the formula shows, at-the-money puts and calls will sell for the same price.

Incorporating Financing Costs

Because the margin flows on the futures contract and the corresponding financing costs or revenues are not known in advance, it is usually impossible to totally assess the effect financing will have on the conversion or the reversal. However, it may not be unreasonable to assume that, over the long run, margin flows on the futures contracts will be zero, and thus, financing of the margin flows will also be approximately zero on average.[6] One may thus choose to ignore the financing on the margin flows and be content to amend the formula to include only the financing of the net option premium:

$$\text{Strike Price} - \text{Current Futures Price} =$$
$$(\text{Put Price} - \text{Call Price}) \times (1 + r)^t$$

In this formula, r is the rate at which the net option premium will be financed, and t is the time until option expiration.

It is important to remember that we are still assuming that the futures and options positions in the conversion or the reversal can and will be held until the options expire. One cannot, however, count on this. Since both the conversion and the reversal involve a short position in one of the options, there is no guarantee that the buyer of the option will not exercise before expiration (or that one will not want to exercise the long option positions before expiration).

Valuation of Options on Futures

In this section, we explore the valuation of options on futures and show how their valuation differs from options on cash securities. As with options on actual debt securities, we again

---

[6] If the interest rate for financing margin flows is known, more sophisticated techniques can be used to hedge out the risk associated with the financing of margin flows.

use a *riskless portfolio* comprised of an option and the security that underlies the option (i.e., the futures contract). This portfolio is continuously adjusted to ensure that the futures contract and the option are held in just the right proportions, so that risk is eliminated. Since, in equilibrium, riskless portfolios will return the risk-free rate of return, one can use the risk-free portfolio to solve for the theoretical value of the option on the futures contract.

To derive the value of the option on the futures contract using the riskless hedge method, we again make some idealized assumptions. For the riskless hedge valuation of options on futures on fixed income securities, the assumptions are almost identical to the assumptions that were stated in the section for options on actual fixed income securities. The necessary assumptions are:

- Yields on futures contracts change continuously, and possibly very rapidly, but cannot "jump." It is assumed that the volatility of yields is fixed and known. Also, market participants can take market action in response to any change in prices, no matter how small.
- There is a risk-free rate of interest at which one can borrow, as well as lend. It is assumed in most riskless hedge valuation models that this rate is constant throughout the life of the option.
- For simplicity, taxes and transaction costs are ignored.
- Market participants can sell securities short and make use of all proceeds from the sale.

As with options on actual debt securities, it is important to point out what has *not* been assumed. We have not made any assumptions about the preferences of market participants. No assumptions have been made about their attitudes toward risk. One need only assume that more wealth is preferred to less wealth. Also, the option can be valued without any knowledge of, or even opinion on, the price trend of the underlying futures contract. This occurs, in part, because the equilibrium value of the option is found as a function of the price of the

underlying futures contract, and the option valuation method
does not address the problem of whether the underlying contract is fairly priced.

Riskless Hedge Valuation Using the Binomial Model

The riskless hedge valuation process will again be illustrated
using the *binomial model*. To show how to solve for the value
of an option on a futures contract using the binomial pricing
model, we assume, as shown in Exhibit 34, that futures prices
can move up or down each month by exactly one point. We
assume also that the annualized monthly compounded rate
of interest for one-month loans is fixed at 12 percent. With

EXHIBIT 34
Network of Possible Futures Prices: Step 1

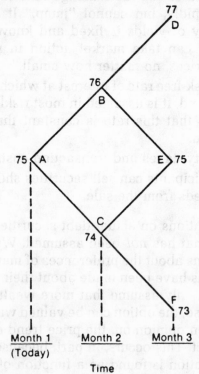

Month 1
(Today)   Month 2   Month 3

Time

a current (beginning of month 1) price on the futures contract at 75, our goal is to find the fair price of an at-the-money call option—that is, one with a strike price of 75—that expires in two months (at the beginning of month 3). To simplify matters, we assume that the option cannot or will not be exercised prior to expiration.

To start the valuation process, we calculate the value of the call option at expiration. This is always easy since the value at expiration will be the greater of zero or the futures price minus the strike price. In Exhibit 35, the option values at expiration are shown in parentheses.

The riskless hedge technique starts at expiration and works backwards in time to the current period. Assume that the futures price at the beginning of month 2 turns out to be

EXHIBIT 35
Network of Possible Prices: Step 2

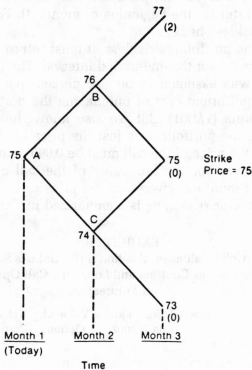

76. This corresponds to position B in Exhibits 34 and 35. In that case, consider the return over the next period to a portfolio that is short one futures contract and long one call option on the futures. Since there is no cost involved in establishing the short position in futures, the cost of this portfolio is just the cost of the call option. If the futures price falls from 76 to 75, the option expires worthless, but the decline in the futures price will lead to a one point margin inflow. If the futures price rises to 77, the option is worth two points because it gives the owner the right to establish a futures position at 75 when the market price is 77. However, the increase in futures price entails a one point margin outflow. Thus, as shown in Exhibit 36, the value of the option and futures portfolio will be one point whether the futures price moves up or down. The most important characteristic of this portfolio is that it is riskless. Regardless of whether the futures price moves up to 77 or down to 75, the portfolio will be worth one point one period later (at the beginning of month 3). We have thus created a riskless hedge.

Since the portfolio is riskless, it must return the risk-free rate of interest over the one-period interval. The risk-free rate of interest was assumed to be one percent per month, and thus, the equilibrium cost of purchasing the portfolio should be 0.990 points (1/1.01). But we also know that the cost of establishing the portfolio was just the price of the call. This means that the price of the call must be 0.990 points. We have therefore solved for the fair value of the call option at the beginning of month 2, *given that* the price turns out to be 76 at that time. Our reasoning is summarized in Exhibit 37.

EXHIBIT 36
Portfolio Values for Position B (Portfolio is Short One Futures Contract and Long One Call Option on Futures)

Futures Price	Margin Flow on Future	+	Value of Option	=	Value of Portfolio
Rises to 77	(1)		2		1
Declines to 75	1		0		1

EXHIBIT 37
Portfolio Costs and Option Value for Position B
(Futures Price is 76 at Beginning of Month 2)

By Construction	Cost of Portfolio = Price of Call Option
To Earn Risk-Free Rate	Cost of Portfolio = 1/1.01 points
	= 0.990 points
Set Costs Equal	Price of Option = 0.990 points
Therefore	Option Value = 0.990 points

Having solved for the fair price of the option at the beginning of month 2, given that the futures price is 76 at that time, we must also solve for the option value should the price of the futures turn out to be 74. This corresponds to position C in Exhibits 34 and 35. In this case, the solution is trivial. Regardless of the direction in which the futures price moves (up to 75 or down to 73), the option will expire worthless. Thus, its only fair value is zero. Now we have solved for the value of the option at each possible price of the futures contract at the beginning of month 2. These values are shown in parentheses in the network of possible prices in Exhibit 38.

We are now in a position to use the riskless hedge to value the option at the beginning of month 1—in other words, to find its current value.

To find the current value of the option, consider a portfolio constructed in the current period (position A) that is short one futures contract and long 2.02 options. As shown in Exhibit 39, the value of this portfolio will be one point at the beginning of month 2, regardless of which way futures prices move. If futures prices move down from 75 to 74, the options will have no value, but there will be a one-point inflow on the short futures position. The portfolio will therefore be worth one point. If futures prices move up from 75 to 76, there is a one-point outflow in the futures position, but, as shown earlier, each of the 2.02 options will be worth 0.990 points. Again, the net value of the portfolio is one point.

Since the portfolio of futures and options on futures is riskless, it must earn the risk-free rate of return. Thus, the initial cost of the portfolio must be 0.990 points to return the

EXHIBIT 38
Network of Possible Prices: Step 3

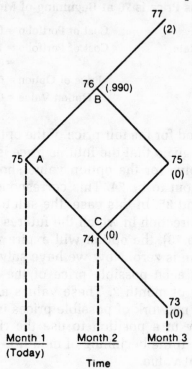

risk-free rate over the one-period interval. However, we also
know that the cost of establishing the options and futures
portfolio is the price of the 2.02 call options. Thus, the price
of each call must be 0.49 points (0.990/2.02). If the current
price of the option is not 0.49 points, prices will not be in

EXHIBIT 39
Portfolio Values for Position A (Portfolio is Short
One Futures Contract and Long 2.02 Call Options
on Futures)

Futures Price	Margin Flow on Future	+	Value of 2.02 Options	=	Value of Portfolio
Rises to 76	(1)		2		1
Declines to 74	1		0		1

EXHIBIT 40
Portfolio Costs and the Option Value for Position A

By Construction	Cost of Portfolio = Price of 2.02 Options
To Earn Risk-Free Rate	Cost of Portfolio = 1/1.01 points
	= 0.990 points
Set Costs Equal	Price of 2.02 Options = 0.990 points
Therefore	Option Value = 0.490 points

equilibrium. The derivation of the current fair price for the option is summarized in Exhibit 40.

Notice that several variables never entered the option valuation problem. Coupons were never considered because the security underlying the option—a futures contract—does not make coupon payments. Also, the price of the security underlying the futures contract does not explicitly enter the problem. Obviously, coupon payments and the price of the security underlying the futures contract affect market prices, but this information is already contained in the price of the futures contract and, thus, need not be explicitly considered for the valuation of options on futures. Recall that the option valuation process values the option *given* the price of the security underlying the option—in this case, the futures price. The valuation procedure therefore implicitly assumes that the underlying security is fairly priced.

Factors Affecting the Price of an Option on Futures

There are five variables that affect the price of an option on a futures contract:

- The current futures price
- The strike price
- The rate of interest for borrowing and lending over the life of the option
- The time to option expiration, and
- The volatility of futures yields (or prices) over the life of the option.

Usually all variables except the last are readily available. However, the volatility of yields cannot be known in advance,

EXHIBIT 41
Variables that Affect the Prices of Call and
Put Options on Futures

Increase in	Affect on Call Price[a]	Affect on Put Price[a]
Futures Price	Increase	Decrease
Strike Price	Decrease	Increase
Short-Term, Risk-Free Interest Rate[b]	Decrease	Decrease
Time to Expiration (for American Options)	Increase	Increase
Volatility	Increase	Increase

[a] With all other variables held constant.
[b] For borrowing and lending over the life of the option.

and thus it becomes one of the most significant and difficult considerations in the valuation process.

Exhibit 41 summarizes the effect of each variable on the value of the option on the futures contract. The primary difference between options on futures and options on cash securities is that an increase in the interest rate for borrowing and lending over the life of the option *decreases* the value of the call option, as well as the put option.

The magnitude of the effect of any particular variable on the value of the option is generally a complex function of all the other relevant variables. For example, while greater volatility always adds to the value of an option, a one percent increase in volatility adds more to the value of an at-the-money option than it does to a deep out-of-the-money option (all other factors being equal). These interrelationships are best described graphically; in the Appendix, we have included a number of three-dimensional graphs that will enhance one's understanding of the theoretical value of an option on a futures contract (as well as an option on actual securities), and the complex interrelationship of the variables that affect that value.

CONCLUSION

This chapter provides an introduction to the valuation of options on fixed-income securities. The model that has been presented is an adaptation of the equity option models to the fixed-income markets. The model, like all models that are currently available for valuing debt options, depends upon many simplifying assumptions. While more sophisticated models that relax some of these assumptions do exist, they are generally very complex. However, since the foregoing pages are truly only an introduction to the valuation of debt options, the reader is encouraged to become familiar with the more complex models that frequently appear in the academic literature.

APPENDIX

Theoretical Values for European Call Options on Futures

Interest Rate and Futures Price

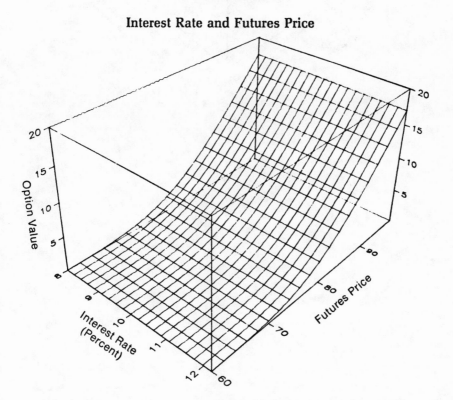

Time to Expiration and Interest Rate

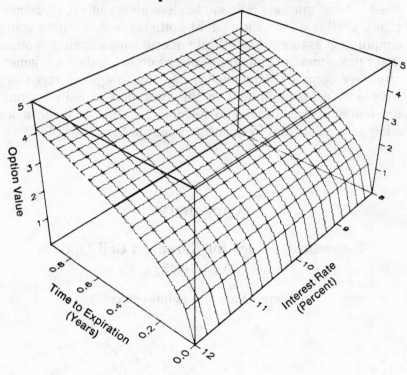

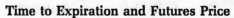

Time to Expiration and Futures Price

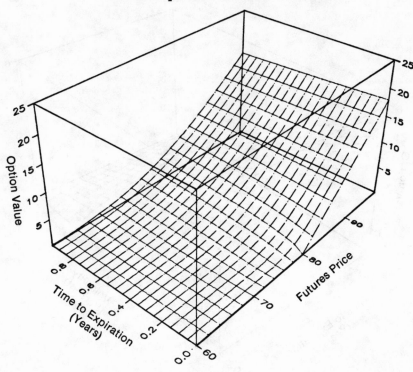

Time to Expiration and Volatility

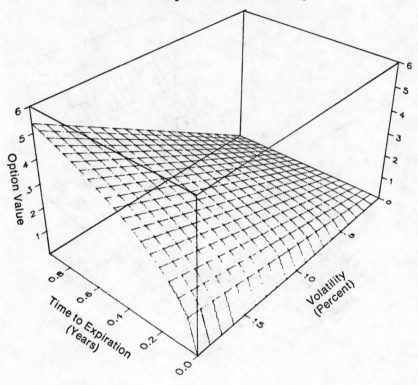

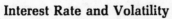

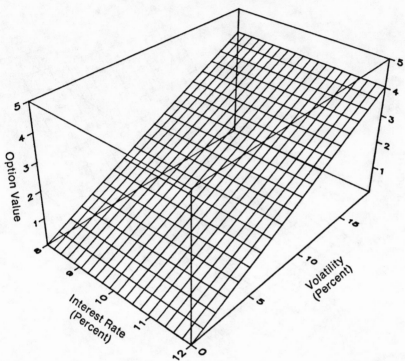

Interest Rate and Volatility

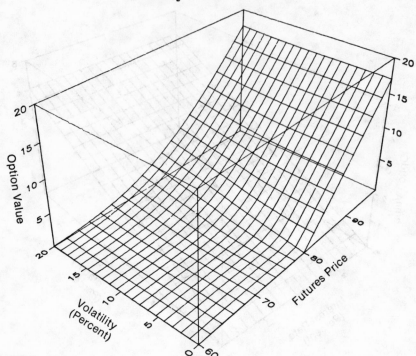

SECTION II

Applications

CHAPTER 4

Overview of the Use of Debt Options

Robert W. Kopprasch, Ph.D., CFA
Vice President
Salomon Brothers Inc

The introduction of listed option trading on debt instruments opened up a variety of new opportunities for the managers of debt portfolios. Yet the appearance of listed trading did not mark the first use of interest rate related options in the debt market. In December of 1980, the Kingdom of Sweden issued a five-year note with an attached warrant that allowed the holder to purchase another five-year note at a fixed price until June of 1981. This was the first "tradable" debt option, and a flurry of similar options (they are usually referred to as warrants) were issued in the domestic and Euro markets.[1] But even these were not the first "debt options." For many years, corporations have issued callable debt, and somewhat more recently, putable debt. While these "puts" and "calls" are usually not separable from the underlying issue, they nev-

---

[1] For more information on debt warrants, see "Contingent Takedown Options on Fixed Income Securities," Chapter 23, in Frank J. Fabozzi and Irving M. Pollack, eds. *The Handbook of Fixed Income Securities*, Dow Jones-Irwin, Homewood, Ill., 1983.

ertheless have the same profit patterns as the fixed income options shown in Chapter 1 and can be analyzed similarly.[2]

Although they are less "visible," there are a number of interest rate options that are embedded in the products or services of many financial institutions, as well as additional security-related options beyond the "vanilla" callable and putable bonds mentioned earlier. These will be described shortly, but some definition of terminology is appropriate here. First, how do we know that these are "options"? We will define as a fixed income option any feature that has some yield point analogous to a strike price, even if the holder does *not* have the choice of exercising or not. Many of the "options" described below are "automatically" exercised if it is in the best interest of the *holder* (not necessarily the investor) to do so. Because a call holder benefits as prices rise beyond the strike price (i.e., as yields drop below the strike yield), we will use the term "call" to describe an option that benefits the holder if yields decline. Similarly, we will use the term "put" to describe an option that benefits the holder if rates rise.

Callable bonds—Viewed as an asset to the investor or a liability to the corporation, the investor has in effect sold a call to the issuer. The payment is usually received in the form of a higher yield than noncallable paper.

Note the relationship here. The investor is on one side and the issuer is on the other. With the exception of warrants or convertible bonds, most options in the equity market are created when one investor sells the option to another investor. The issuer of the underlying paper plays no role.

Putable bonds—The investor has the right to put the bond back to the issuer at specified intervals. This feature can arise as a general sweetener or to make the bond eligible for purchase by specific institutions.

Adjustable Rate Preferreds—The rate on the preferred stock is pegged off the "higher of" Treasury bills, notes, and bonds. This is, in effect, an option on the yield curve. In addi-

---

[2] See "Early Redemption Options on Fixed Income Securities," Chapter 24, in *The Handbook of Fixed Income Securities.*

tion, these ARPs usually have "collars" or maximum and minimum rates. The maximum rate represents a *put* sold *by* the investor to the issuer, because the issuer is favored if rates rise; while the minimum rate represents a *call* sold *to* the investor by the issuer. These options are automatically exercised.

Mortgages—Virtually all mortgages contain a provision for the early repayment of the mortgage, either for refinancing purposes, or because the house is sold, etc. This option is a *call* sold to the homeowner/borrower by the holder of the mortgage. This option is inherent in the mortgage, and any subsequent purchaser of the mortgage (anyone who buys GNMAs, FNMAs, FHLMCs, etc.) acquires a short call position with the mortgage.

Adjustable Rate Mortgages—ARMs can have two basic options associated with them, related to the maximum rate that can be charged and to the maximum change in the rate that can take place between subsequent resets. The maximum rate constitutes a *put* sold *to* the borrower, as does the maximum upward rate move. If the rate is also "sticky" as interest rates decline, this would represent a *call* sold *by* the borrower to the investor. These "maximum change" options effectively have their strike prices reset at each new rate level.

Mortgage bankers and thrift institutions are in the business of, among other things, originating mortgages. During this origination process, a mortgage commitment is normally issued to the prospective mortgagor. (The homeowner/borrower is the "issuer" of the mortgage, the mortgage banker is the "buyer" of the mortgage.) This commitment is normally binding only on the mortgage originator, not the home buyer, who can go elsewhere for the loan if rates decline before closing. This mortgage "commitment" is, then, a *put*. If rates decline, the home buyer will go elsewhere (or demand a lower rate); while if rates increase, he will "sell" his mortgage note to the mortgage originator at "par" (less the usual points), even though it has a below market coupon.

This list is not all-encompassing, as there are many other options not mentioned. Many of these arise in products sold by life insurance companies, and will be described in a later section.

WHY STUDY OPTIONS?

It should be obvious by now that fixed income options come in many forms. Even if an organization does not have regulatory approval to trade listed options, it may frequently come in contact with options, both on the "long" side and the "short" side. The institution's products may have options embedded in them; even if they cannot be explicitly hedged in the listed market, an understanding of the risks, the pricing, and potential risk altering strategies of options can only help the asset and liability managers in the debt market. Such understanding might also help in the effort to secure approval to use options from regulators and boards. It is also important to note that debt market use of options does not parallel the equity market. This will be covered in the final sections of this chapter.

FIXED INCOME OPTION USES

There are a number of strategies available to asset and liability managers now that listed option trading on debt instruments is well established. The list that follows contains some of these possible strategies; we will examine each in later sections.

1. Capitalize on or defend against market expectations
2. Use options market as gauge of value of product options
3. Buy options to offset those granted in products or investments
4. Combine with other options to alter risk profile
5. Buy or sell volatility

Prior to explaining each of these strategies, we will digress for a moment to look at the life insurance industry's option-riddled product line to provide additional motivation and examples for the sections that follow. This will give the reader a greater appreciation of the widespread nature of non-listed fixed income options, as well as some insight into the difficulty of hedging some of these options.

The Life Insurance Company—a Bundle of Options

Life insurance companies offer many products that contain option-type features. While these products are assets to the "holders" or investors (I use the term loosely, because the products are not "securities" in the regulatory sense), they are liabilities to the insurance companies. In most whole life insurance policies, the policyholder has the right to borrow against his cash value at a fixed rate of interest. These policy loans are attractive to the policyholders when rates have increased above the fixed rate—the "strike yield" in option terminology. This provision is nothing more than a *put* granted to the policyholder, allowing him the right to sell a fixed income security (his note or promise to repay) to the insurance company at a fixed price (par—the full face amount of the loan). Naturally, as interest rates rise, many policyholders borrow, diverting funds that the insurance company would rather put into higher yielding corporate bonds into the lower yielding policy loans.

These *puts* are complex in form, first because the "underlying instrument" increases through time as the cash value grows. Second, the growth in the cash value is somewhat dependent upon the proportion of policyholders exercising their options, because this lowers the return on the portfolio. Third, we might characterize this option as a resettable American option, because it can be exercised at almost any time, and, once the loan is repaid, it can be exercised again. Yet, the insurance companies have not been subjected to the rationally expected number of exercises, because many policyholders do not borrow against their policies, even when an arbitrage profit is possible. As a result, it is more difficult to measure the impact of a move in rates on the insurance company without modelling the policyholder response.

Two additional products provide even greater risk to life insurance companies, because of their option provisions: guaranteed investment contracts (GICs) and single premium deferred annuities (SPDAs). In a GIC, the insurance company guarantees a certain rate of interest, either paid out or compounded, for the life of the contract (typically five years). There are two basic options inherent in GICs that subject the insurance company to interest rate risk. The first relates to the "investment window," often as long as a year or more. During this time, the investor can invest and receive the guaranteed rate from the investment date to the termination date of the contract, even though market rates may have declined between the inception of the contract and the ultimate investment date. While it is easy to quantify the risk to the company per dollar invested for a particular decline in rates, the investment amount is often not limited and must be estimated. Even if options are purchased to offset this risk, there is the question of how many to buy. These options, by the way, are *calls,* because they give the holder the right to buy a fixed income security (the GIC) at a fixed price (par, the invested amount). A second option often included in a GIC is a *put*—many times the investor has the right to withdraw from the contract early, with little or no penalty. A third aspect of GICs that compounds the investment problem (but which is not related to options) is that the GICs must often be bid for on a forward basis, with several months between the setting of the rate and the opening of the investment window.

SPDAs offer several option related investment challenges to the life insurance company. The rates on SPDAs are usually reset every 12 months, and investors can frequently leave the program with little or no penalty if the reset rate has declined by more than a specified amount. In order to be competitive, the rates are usually set off the longer end of the curve (in a positive yield curve). In order to earn this higher rate, the insurance company must invest in the longer maturities, but this causes problems if rates should rise. In the higher rate environment, when the insurance company has already locked in an income stream at the lower rate and now has an unrealized loss on the position, it must now offer an even higher rate to the investor. If it does not, the investor may withdraw, and the need for liquidity may cause the underlying securities to be sold at a loss, thereby affecting reserves and the ability of the company to continue writing the same level of business. For this reason, the insurance company must often offer an extremely competitive rate (read *high*), when it can least afford to do so.

These SPDA problems stem from the options inherent in the product: the option to earn a competitive rate each year or to withdraw. This is, in essence, an option on the yield curve, because the investor can essentially earn the highest point on the curve each year, without the usual principal risk that accompanies an investment that earns the long rate. (Adjustable rate preferred stock, mentioned earlier, offers a similar yield curve option to investors.)

At this point, there is no need to examine the life insurance industry's products in greater detail; that will be the subject of Chapter 8. The discussion thus far should be sufficient to convince the reader that life insurance companies offer interest rate sensitive options in a number of their products. Exhibit 1 summarizes these and other options, and classifies them as related to assets or liabilities, and whether the options are held by, or have been granted by, the insurance company.

Capitalize on or Defend against Market Expectations

Options offer an investor or issuer a way to capitalize on (correct) market expectations with limited risk. This is one of the most obvious uses of options and probably needs very little explanation. When an upturn in rates is expected, puts can be purchased and will pay off if the expectation turns out to be correct. Similarly, an expected downturn in rates can become a profitable event if calls are purchased prior to the rate decline. When this strategy is engaged, there is not necessarily a sophisticated analysis performed, and the number of options purchased is usually dependent on the maximum loss exposure that can be tolerated. More sophisticated players

EXHIBIT 1
THE 'OPTIONS' BALANCE SHEET

	ASSET SIDE	LIABILITY SIDE
HELD BY INSURANCE COMPANY	—Putable Bonds —Extendible Bonds —Bonds with Warrants —Floating Rate Preferred at 'Higher-Of' Yields	—Dividend Distribution
GRANTED BY INSURANCE COMPANY	—Issuer 'Call' —Sinking Fund Double-Up Option —Mortgage Prepayments —Implicit 'Put' Option in Forward Commitment Process	—Policy Loans —Cash Value Surrender —'SPDA' Cash-In —'Higher-Of' Guarantees —Period Rate Guarantees ("Investment Window")

will attempt to optimize the risk return trade-off by structuring the options (how many of each strike price) so as to maximize return for the expected rate change. Because "out-of-the-money" options cost less than "at-the-moneys," more out-of-the-money options can be purchased for the same cost, but they will begin to provide value only after a larger rate move.

Options can also be used defensively in a similar manner. When a position in fixed income securities must be maintained, but there is an expectation for an upturn in rates, puts can be purchased as insurance. If the expected rate increase does occur, and the price or value of the position declines, the value of the put should increase and at least partially offset the loss. A properly structured hedge would leave the investor essentially indifferent to an increase in rates. Naturally, considering only the asset position and not the entire balance sheet, the investor would still prefer a decline in rates, and an increase in the value of his securities.

Investors who expect that rates will decline before they can invest (e.g., a pension fund expecting a contribution at year end), can purchase calls. If rates decline as expected, and the funds are invested at lower rates, the call value will increase, and this can also be invested. A properly structured hedge would result in an effective investment rate that is not dependent on the level of rates (on the downside). An increase in rates will be the favored outcome, even though the investor will not collect on his insurance.

Using the Options Market to Value Product Options

Many of the options described thus far arise from the products (GICs, whole life policies) or services (mortgage origination) of financial institutions. In many cases, there is no explicit fee for the options, and their "cost" is often borne by the institution, without knowing what the true cost is. Many of these options can be valued with reference to the listed option market.

One way in which option valuation models are used to input the known parameters and estimate the unknown one (volatility) to arrive at a value. A similar approach can be used to value many product options. Another approach is to accept the current market price of an option as "correct" and solve backwards for the "implied volatility." This dual approach can also be used for product options. Once the market's implied volatilities for several points on the yield curve are known, the volatility for various product options can be estimated, and the options can be valued.

This process can be important to institutions entering new lines of business or modifying existing products. During periods of high rate volatility, it might serve as the impetus to modify the cost or return structure of the product to better reflect the risk being taken on the option position. While sales of many products (such as whole life insurance) are probably insensitive to rate level and volatility, many others (mortgage origination, GICs) will be quite responsive, and flexible pricing policies would be easier to implement with better option value information.

It is interesting to note that some institutions charge an explicit fee for some of the options that they grant, such as standby financing agreements. But even those who charge a fee often do so in a way which is biased against them. For example, in some standby agreements, in which an insurance company is liable to provide funds if the borrower cannot obtain more advantageous funding elsewhere, the fee (say, 1 percent) is charged only if the put option is *not* exercised. (The option is a *put*, because the borrower can put, at his option, a promissory note to the insurance company at the strike price of par.) This pricing policy would not work as part of a large option writing program, because the fees from all options exercised and unexercised are needed to offset the losses incurred on the options that were exercised.

Buy Options to Offset Those Granted in Products

This is the most direct hedging application of options for financial institutions. Once the options in the product have been identified as puts or calls, with fixed or resettable strike yields, the next step is to estimate the dollar impact on the institution for a particular change in rates. This can then be compared with the expected payoff on various options that are available for purchase, and a "hedge ratio" determined. Note that this is not the same hedge ratio that is output from a valuation model.

In the listed debt option market, only options on Treasury bills and options on Treasury bond futures offer sufficient liquidity that a major institution can hedge a large position. Obviously, not all product options fit neatly into this mold, and the ideal hedging options are not, therefore, always available. As a result, several large dealers offer over-the-counter debt options tailored to the needs of the individual institution. These options will be described in a later section.

Combine Options with Other Options to Alter Risk Profile

While the direct purchase of offsetting options, as described above, appears to be a direct solution to an option "problem," in many cases the purchase of the opposite option may provide the solution. In these situations, the short option position is viewed in combination with another position. As shown in Chapter 3, for example, a long position in the underlying security and a short call is equivalent to a short put position. An investor in this situation (long the underlying, short a call) could purchase a put to neutralize the risk, even though the explicit option position is a short call.

Let us examine another example (in which the author was involved) in detail. An insurance company has granted a mortgage "commitment" (actually, a standby agreement) to a commercial developer for four months. As mentioned earlier, this type of agreement is simply a put, because the borrower is not obligated to take the loan (sell his note). At first glance, then, it appears that the insurance company would have to buy a put to hedge against changes in interest rates. But as we look further into the situation, we find that there are other "linked" positions here. The insurance company has obligated itself in a GIC for which the funds will become available in four months. It expects that the income on the mortgage will be sufficient to provide the income it has guaranteed on the GIC. If rates rise, the mortgage will probably be taken down, because alternative financing will be more expensive for the developer. But if rates decline, the potential borrower will likely seek financing elsewhere, and the insurance company will be without an investment that can provide the necessary return.

The solution to the problem is the purchase of a call. It is clear that the insurance company is exposed to a decline in rates, and that is exactly when a call would become profitable. Enough calls should be purchased so that at any lower level of rates, the investment income available at the lower rate level, combined with the profit from the calls, will generate the income necessary for the GIC.

In option terminology, the insurance company was short a put, had a short position in the GIC (let's view that as the underlying security for a moment), and then purchased a call. As described in Chapter 3, this is a reverse conversion and is a risk neutral position. In this case it is not entirely risk free because of the risk of changes in spreads in the rates between mortgages, GICs, and Treasuries (the call was an OTC call on a five-year Treasury note to match the five-year balloon payment mortgage).

It should be clear that individual option positions should not be examined in a void, but must be considered in the overall portfolio context for effective hedging.

Buy or Sell Volatility

With "straight" (non-option type) securities, there are only two basic positions that can be taken: long and short. With options, one can take long or short positions in asymmetric securities that represent long or short positions. (That is, you can buy or sell calls, or buy or sell puts.) But the success or profitability of even these positions is dependent upon being correct with regard to the direction of the market. There are, however, certain option "combinations" that represent bets with regard to the volatility of the market, but not the direction per se.

The simplest of these positions is the *straddle*, which consists of a put and a call with the same strike price. If the investor believes the market is going to be more volatile than the market does as evidenced by the implied volatility, he can buy a straddle and profit if the market moves far enough in *either* direction to more than recoup his premiums (one put, one call). On the other hand, if he believes that the market is overestimating the volatility, he can sell a straddle and receive the two premiums. As long as the market does not move outside the range defined by the strike price plus or minus the premiums received, the short straddle will be profitable.

A similar position can be taken in a combination known as a *strangle*. A strangle consists of a put and a call, but the call strike price is higher than the put strike price. For example, suppose that a 68 put and a 70 call on bond futures each sell for one point. If the investor believes that the market is overestimating volatility, he would sell the strangle and receive two points in premiums. As long as the market remained between 66 and 72, the short strangle would be profitable.

Straddles and strangles are described in more detail in Chapter 5.

DEALER OPTIONS VERSUS LISTED OPTIONS

As mentioned earlier, several government securities dealers will now also quote prices on over-the-counter options. The dealer is most often a principal in the option trade, rather than an agent. In effect, the dealer will "create" an option that is tailored to the needs of the institution requesting it. Because each contract is individually negotiated, all of the terms can be adjusted as necessary. For example, the call on five-year Treasury notes mentioned earlier was just such an option, and here it was important to closely match the maturity on the underlying instrument. Additionally, the strike price and the expiration date were selected to offset as closely as possible the option that was being hedged.

It is also possible to develop specialized options in the dealer market. Salomon Brothers, for example, has offered options on the yield curve which pay off if the bill-to-bond spread exceeds (or is less than) a particular value. One category of options has guaranteed the average borrowing cost over a period of time, or the rate on each individual borrowing. Other options have been written on prime rate, spreads between corporates and Treasuries, and spreads between different coupon GNMAs. In the dealer market, it is important to trade with a large, well capitalized dealer, because there is no clearing corporation involved to take on the credit risk of the trade.

THE MOTIVATION TO USE OPTIONS: DEBT VERSUS EQUITY

Most early equity option promotion was directed at a retail audience, and stressed two appealing features of buying options: leverage and limited losses. While leverage had been available in the form of margin trading, the leverage offered by options was far greater than had been available in the equity market in a long time. In the debt market, however, leverage had been available, prior to option trading, in several forms, including futures, forward transactions, repos, and, on a retail level, margin as low as 5 to 10 percent on government bonds. Thus, leverage was not likely to be the major attraction of debt options. The limited losses argument had been made with the purchase of the underlying equity as the "bogey," but purchasing the stock was usually at the discretion of the investor, so he need take no risk at all by avoiding both the stock *and* the option. As we have seen, many debt market participants *already* have and must frequently maintain a position in the underlying (or similar) instruments, or, due to the nature of their business, offer options to customers; and the option decision is not an "either-or" choice. As a result, the use of options as substitutes for underlying debt instruments is often not a viable alternative.

Since the inception of listed trading, covered call writing has been recommended as a way to enhance the returns on equity portfolios. Because it appears to represent a lower risk approach to equity investing, many institutions were able to convince their boards and regulators that covered call writing programs should be initiated. Whether such programs are actually all that they are claimed to be or not, there is a difference in the way they work in debt and equity portfolios. In the equity portfolio, some stocks are likely to rise (and be called), while others decline or remain essentially the same. This mixture of underlying returns is common in equities except in strong bull or bear markets, when most securities tend to follow the market. In the debt market, however, the correlation of returns of different instruments is typically much higher, so a beneficial portfolio effect is less likely. The covered call writer in the debt market is likely to find his entire (optioned) portfolio called at one time, or none of it will be called. As a result, covered call writing is not as widespread in the debt market as it is in equities. Covered call writing is explained in Chapter 6.

This high correlation can also work to the advantage of the debt option user. With only a few underlying securities at different points along the yield curve, the options on those securities can be used as surrogates for options on many other securities. That is, options on long governments or futures can be used when options on corporates, or possibly even mortgages are needed. In other words, the debt market already has "options on the market" and does not need index options to provide this function.

THE MAJOR DIFFERENCES: DEBT VERSUS EQUITY USE OF OPTIONS

In the equity market, options were first created to bolster income on the futures exchange (CBT), where futures trading volume had been declining. The instruments proved popular with speculators and covered call writers, who essentially *developed strategies* to use the options. However, *options arise naturally in the course of business in many institutions in the fixed income market,* and a market to offset these obligations arose as a result.

The second major difference, and probably the most significant one, is that debt options are being used by managers of both debt asset portfolios and *liability* portfolios. In the equity market, it is investors, not issuers, who play the major role. In the debt market, the natural players fall on both sides of the balance sheet. Portfolio managers can use debt options in strategies analogous to their equity counterparts, while at the same time the issuer of long-term debt can put a ceiling on the rate on bonds yet to be issued; the borrower whose rate fluctuates as short-term rates move can "cap" his borrowing cost, and the insurance company can hedge the rate promises made to policyholders and annuity buyers. These types of uses are unique to the debt market.

In the five chapters that follow, the applications discussed in this chapter will be covered in greater depth. The regulation of potential users of debt options is explained in Chapter 10.

CHAPTER 5

Trading and Arbitrage Strategies Using Debt Options

Mark Landau
Assistant Vice President
Citicorp Futures Corp.

The development of listed debt options has added a multi-faceted trading dimension for speculators and arbitrageurs. Now, not only the stock market, but the debt markets and bond futures market have options strategies enabling traders to fully avail themselves of a myriad of trades with different risk and reward scenarios. Any interest rate outlook can have an option trade tailored to the needs of the speculator. Whether it is the expectation of a specific interest rate level or the general trade of an interest rate; whether it is low dollar risk, unlimited dollar risk but strong likelihood of a profit, or moderate profit expectations with moderate dollar risk, listed debt options will allow speculators to play out their scenarios to exactly fit their risk needs.

In this chapter, trading and arbitrage strategies for debt options are described. At the outset, it should be noted that since commissions, margin rules, financing costs, and liquidity of the particular option exchange will greatly affect options trading strategies, the current status of these factors should be checked when reviewing a strategy and before initiating any trade. This is especially the case in arbitrage strategies.

ARBITRAGE STRATEGIES

Many traders of listed debt options use arbitrage strategies to produce profits. With low commission and execution costs, they strive to make small profits on low or no-risk trades, taking advantage of temporary aberrations in the price of a particular option or underlying instrument.

Basic Arbitrage

Basic arbitrage is the most simple form of arbitrage. The trader purchases an option for less than its intrinsic value; simultaneously, he goes the opposite way with the underlying item. He then exercises the option.

This opportunity typically occurs in a deep-in-the-money option. Theoretically, such options might have no time value and are worth only their intrinsic value. Usually, trading volume and liquidity is thin. Floor traders, in making a market in such options, will bid slightly less than intrinsic value to cover their transaction costs for offsetting the purchase with the underlying instrument and exercising the option. The floor trader does this because of the lack of interest in the option and the remote chance of reselling it quickly. If the underlying security or future is thin, the trader may look to sell a different deep-in-the-money option at higher than intrinsic value and unwind the trades later.

Below is an example of a basic call arbitrage:

Buy June 64 Call	$6^{00}\!/_{64}$
Sell June T-Bond Futures	$70^{2}\!/_{32}$
Intrinsic Value of the Option	$6^{2}\!/_{64}$

In this example, the trader immediately exercises the call. The next day, his account would show no position and a profit of $^4\!/_{64}$ ($62.50 per option). The 64 call costs $6,000, but is exercised into a long June T-Bond futures position at 64. That offsets the sale of June T-Bond futures at $70\frac{2}{32}$, a profit of $6,062.50 on the futures, producing a $62.50 profit on the set of transactions.

Below is an example of a basic put arbitrage:

Buy June 70 Put	$5\frac{28}{64}$
Buy June T-Bond Futures	$64\frac{16}{32}$
Intrinsic Value of the Option	$5\frac{32}{64}$

The immediate exercise of the put would produce a profit of $\frac{4}{64}$ ($62.50), the difference between its intrinsic value and actual cost. Upon exercise, the account will show a long futures position at $64\frac{16}{32}$ and a short futures position at 70 (the exercise price), producing a profit $5,500, less the cost of the put, $5,437.50.

Boxes

A common risk-free arbitrage strategy for floor traders is the *box spread*. Buying the box is a four-legged trade consisting of: the purchase of a lower strike call, and sale of a higher strike call; and the purchase of a higher strike put, and sale of a lower strike put. Two strike prices are used and all have the same expiration.

Following is an example of buying the box:

June T-Bond Futures	$64\frac{29}{32}$	
June 64 Call	$1\frac{9}{64}$	
June 66 Call	$\frac{15}{64}$	
June 64 Put	$\frac{18}{64}$	
June 66 Put	$1\frac{23}{64}$	
Buying the June 64 Call	$1,140.63	debit
Selling the June 66 Call	234.38	credit
Selling the June 64 Put	281.25	credit
Buying the June 66 Put	1,359.38	debit
Net Cost	$1,984.38	

Difference in strike prices: 2 points = $2,000

If the trader can execute the four sides for a net cost that is less than the difference in the two strike prices, as in this example, a locked-in profit at expiration is created.

The value of a box is the difference in the two strike prices of the options employed. Therefore, *selling the box* with net proceeds over the difference in strikes produces a profit at expiration.

An example of selling the box follows:

June T-Bond Futures	$64^{29}\!/_{32}$
June 64 Call	$1\%_{64}$
June 66 Call	$^{15}\!/_{64}$
June 64 Put	$^{18}\!/_{64}$
June 66 Put	$1^{28}\!/_{64}$

Selling the June 64 Call	$1,140.63	credit
Buying the June 66 Call	234.38	debit
Buying the June 64 Put	281.25	debit
Selling the June 66 Put	1,437.50	credit
Net Proceeds	$2,062.50	

Difference in strike prices: 2 points = $2,000

Effectively, the box is made up of two vertical spreads. Long the box is buying a bull spread in calls and a bear spread in puts. Selling the box is selling a bull spread in calls and a bear spread in puts. The two spreads move to "cancel" each other out; thus, the value of the box is the difference in strikes.

Buying and selling boxes by floor traders and arbitrageurs adds much to the liquidity of outright and vertical spread trading in debt options. Since the trades are virtually riskless, the costs involved in the execution determine whether they are profitable, and opportunities rarely exist for anyone off the floor for this arbitrage situation.

Conversions

Buying a put and selling a call with the same expiration and strike, and buying the underlying security or futures contract is called a *conversion*. It is a completely matched position. Long the put and short the call produces a synthetic short position in the underlying instrument. Being long the underlying instrument at the same time, produces a matched position. If there were no carrying costs to consider, the arbitrageur would lock in a risk-free profit if the proceeds from buying the put and selling the call were more than the amount that the underlying exceeds the strike price.

The following is an example of a conversion:

Sell June T-Bond Futures	$66^{12}\!/_{32}$
Sell June 64 Call	$2^{49}\!/_{64}$
Buy June 64 Put	$^{18}\!/_{64}$

Buying a put and selling a call would produce a credit of $2^{31}\!/_{64}$ (the difference between the proceeds from selling the call and the cost of buying the put). Since the futures were $2^{12}\!/_{32}$ ($2^{24}\!/_{64}$) over the exercise price, a profit of $^{7}\!/_{64}$ would be locked in by the trader.

In reality, the trader must fully evaluate carry costs to determine if the trade will be profitable. For futures, these costs are less important than when dealing with actual debt securities and they depend heavily on margin requirements in existence at the time the trade is contemplated.

Reverse Conversions (Reversals)

A *reverse conversion* (or simply *reversal*) is an arbitrage strategy and is the exact opposite of a conversion. With this strategy, the trader buys a call and sells a put with the same exercise and expiration, and sells short the underlying future or debt security.

The long call and short put parts of the trade produce a synthetic long position of the underlying instrument. An evaluation of the synthetic long position versus the price the underlying instrument can be sold, determines whether the trade will be profitable in a basic review of the strategy.

If the proceeds of the options portion of the trade (the put sale price less the call cost) exceed the strike price minus the sale price of the underlying instrument, the trade has a locked-in profit before carry considerations. Evaluating all aspects of carry will then determine if the trade is worthwhile. An example of a reverse conversion follows:

Sell 12's of 2013 Treasury Bond	87
Buy June 88 Call	$1\frac{3}{32}$
Sell June 88 Put	$2\frac{16}{32}$

Buying a call and selling a put would produce a credit of $1\frac{13}{32}$ ($1,406.25). The strike price of the options less the sales price of the Treasury bond is one point ($1,000). Before carry considerations $\frac{13}{32}$ ($406.25) would be locked up by doing this reverse conversion.

Carry Considerations

Cost of carrying a position can turn an apparently profitable trade into a losing one. The cost of carry is dependent on the cost of money, margining rules for particular options markets, the general level of interest rates, the ability to borrow a particular security, and the difference between short-term interest rates and the yield on the debt instrument involved in the trade. The proceeds from the options portion of a transaction can earn interest for the arbitrageur if it is a credit, and may cost interest expense if it is a debit depending on exchange, clearing corporation, or regulatory body rules. In addition, the underlying instrument produces interest income or expense. If the underlying instrument is a futures contract that is marked-to-the market, the variation margin that results from the daily mark-to-the market will provide interest income or expense.

When the underlying instrument is an actual debt security, the interest expense or income can be dramatic. If the arbitrageur is long a Treasury bond as part of a conversion, he is earning interest income daily, and he must finance the security (usually via a repurchase agreement or "repo"). The difference between the coupon interest received and the financing expense is the net interest income from carry. When current yield is above the repo rate, net interest income is earned;

in an inverted yield curve environment, there is a net interest expense.

The amount can fluctuate daily depending on changes in long-term versus short-term rates. To get around this, the trader may finance the bond using a term repurchase agreement, locking in the financing rate for the term of the agreement, but losing flexibility in coming out of the arbitrage.

In a reverse conversion, the net carry to the trader will be negative (an expense) in a positive yield curve environment as he loses the difference between the coupon income and the reverse repurchase rate (the rate at which he "borrows" the security he is short). In addition, he may have difficulty borrowing the security he is short, increasing his net interest expense.

TRADING STRATEGIES

For the speculator, listed debt option trading strategies offer potential profits for the trader that can correctly anticipate the price movement or volatility of the underlying instrument. These changes do not have to occur at expiration of the option, because trading is a dynamic process where individual and market expectations must be reevaluated continuously. Many times, most of the profit potential of a strategy is achieved before expiration, and the trader may decide to liquidate the position or change it to give it further potential. The same may be true for a losing position. Though execution and commission costs and margin rules have an effect on the outcomes of trading strategies, they are usually not a determining factor in a trading decision. Potential profits per trade, as well as risks, are greater than for arbitrage strategies and they may overwhelm these other considerations.

Synthetic Calls and Puts

Synthetic Put

Buying a deep-in-the-money call and selling the underlying instrument results in a synthetic put. Although similar to basic call arbitrage, this strategy can be one of the best trading strategies around because of its low dollar loss risk. The trader is not trying to buy a call below intrinsic value, but is trying to benefit from a major price movement in the market. The call should have a great deal of time left before expiration, but little time value in the premium, because the market has been non-volatile for an extended period of time. This strategy is a bearish trade with the expectation of increasing market volatility.

To illustrate this strategy, suppose that on February 8, 1984, the following situation existed:

Buy June 66 Call	$4^{14}/_{64}$
Sell June T-Bond Futures	$70^{5}/_{32}$
Intrinsic Value of the Call	$4^{10}/_{64}$
Time Value of the Call	$^{4}/_{64}$

Potential outcomes at expiration (May 19, 1984) are shown below and in Exhibit 1.

Price of June Bond Futures at Expiration	Gain(Loss) on Futures	Gain (Loss) On Call	Net on Trade
62	$8,156.25	($4,218.75)	$3,937.75
64	6,156.25	(4,218.75)	1,937.50
66	4,156.25	(4,218.75)	(62.50)
68	2,156.25	(2,218.75)	(62.50)
70	156.25	(218.75)	(62.50)
72	(1,843.75)	1781.25	(62.50)

Potential profit for this trade was almost unlimited, while the loss could never exceed the *time* value portion of the call premium. When the trade was initiated, the market had been in a narrow trading range for several months, and volatility was consistently declining for two years. The call option that was little more than four points in-the-money had a time value

EXHIBIT 1
Potential Outcomes at Expiration for Synthetic Put
(Buy June 66 Call, Sell June T-Bond Futures with June Futures at
$70\frac{5}{32}$)

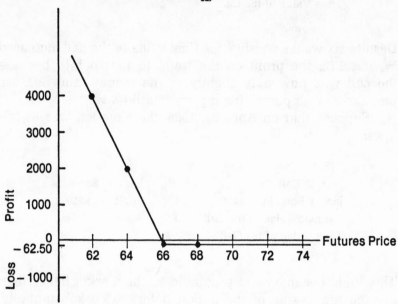

of only $\frac{4}{64}$, despite the fact it had over three months to expiration. The marketplace had perceived it almost impossible for
prices to change dramatically. In fact, the interest expense
(or opportunity lost) in paying for the call was larger than
the time value of the option.

The trader in this illustration was looking for a substantial
drop in price. If prices fell quickly, the call would have been
less in the money, and the time value portion of the premium
would have increased. The short futures position would be
accumulating profits more quickly than the call would be dete-
riorating.

Suppose that on March 21, 1984, the situation was as follows:

June 66 Call	$1\frac{7}{64}$	Loss	$3,109.38
June T-Bond Futures	$66\frac{7}{32}$	Profit	3,937.50
Intrinsic Value of the Call	$\frac{14}{64}$		
Time Value of the Call	$\frac{57}{64}$		

Despite six weeks passing, the time value of the call increased $\frac{53}{64}$ ($828.12, the profit on the trade to that point), because the call was now only slightly in the money, and because the market was perceiving higher volatility.

Suppose that on April 24, 1984, the situation was as follows:

June 66 Call	$\frac{15}{64}$	Loss	$3,984.38
June T-Bond Futures	$64\frac{29}{32}$	Profit	5,250.00
Intrinsic Value of the Call	0		
Time Value of the Call	$\frac{15}{64}$		

This trade became more profitable as the market fell further, but the time value of the option deteriorated substantially. The trader could have liquidated the trade in March, knowing that he had already benefitted from the increasing volatility and drop in futures prices that he had expected. He could also review the situation to see if selling the 66 call and moving to a deeper in-the-money call fit his expectations better.

Suppose, for example, the following on March 21:

June 66 Call	$1\frac{7}{64}$ >	cost of switching to
June 64 Call	$2\frac{31}{64}$	lower strike of $1\frac{24}{64}$
June T-Bond Future	$66\frac{7}{32}$	
Intrinsic Value of 64 Call	$2\frac{14}{64}$	
Time Value of 64 Call	$\frac{17}{64}$	

If the June 66 call was liquidated and the June 64 call purchased, the potential outcomes at expiration would be as follows:

Price of June Bond Futures at Expiration	Gain (Loss) on Futures	Gain (Loss) On Calls	Net on Trade
58	$12,156.25	($5,593.75)	$6,562.50
60	10,156.25	(5,593.75)	4,562.50
62	8,156.25	(5,593.75)	2,562.50
64	6,156.25	(5,593.75)	562.50
66	4,156.25	(3,593.75)	562.50
68	2,156.25	(1,593.75)	562.50

Switching to the lower strike calls locks in a profit for the trade of $562.50, while lowering the profit potential at each bond futures price level if the market continues to fall. The trader has a guaranteed profit, while he can still benefit from any further slump in T-bond futures prices.

Our creation of a put by purchasing a call and selling the futures contract does not appear superior to the actual purchase of a put. However, some traders or institutions may not be allowed the purchase of a put, so the synthetic is a good substitute. Also, the strike price needed on a put may not be listed. Using this synthetic put strategy allows the trader to make a play with results similar to an out-of-the-money put that does not exist when conditions are right for the strategy.

Synthetic Call

Buying a deep-in-the money put and buying the underlying instrument results in a *synthetic call*. This strategy is similar to buying deep-out-of-the-money calls, as the trader is trying to benefit from a substantial upward movement in the price of the underlying instrument, while taking small dollar risk. The best situation for instituting this trade is a sideways, quiet market, about to break out to the upside.

To illustrate this strategy, suppose that on February 8, 1984, the following existed:

Buy June 74 Put	4
Sell June T-Bond Futures	$70\frac{5}{32}$
Intrinsic Value of the Put	$3\frac{54}{64}$
Time Value of the Put	$\frac{10}{64}$

Potential outcomes at expiration (May 19, 1984), are shown below and in Exhibit 2:

Price of June Bond Futures at Expiration	Gain (Loss) on Futures	Gain (Loss) on Put	Net on Trade
66	($4,156.25)	$4,000.00	($156.25)
68	(2,156.25)	2,000.00	(156.25)
70	(156.25)	0.00	(156.25)
72	1,843.75	(2,000.00)	(156.25)
74	3,843.75	(4,000.00)	(156.25)
76	5,843.75	(4,000.00)	1,843.75
78	7,843.75	(4,000.00)	3,843.75

EXHIBIT 2
Potential Outcomes at Expiration for Synthetic Call
(Buy June 74 Put, Sell June T-Bond Futures with June Futures at 70⅝₃₂)

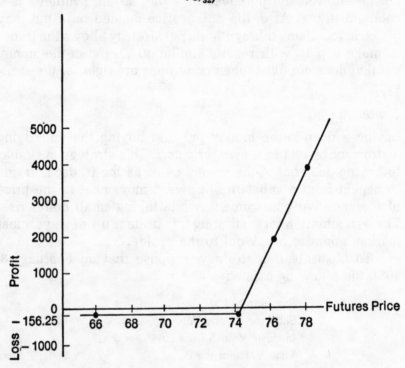

An examination of the potential outcomes indicates that the results are similar to the purchase of a 74 call. In fact, the June 74 calls were trading at %₆₄ ($125) on February 8. Like the synthetic put strategy, synthetic calls might allow an institution that is not permitted the purchase of calls, to substitute this strategy. It also permits the trader to be "long" an out-of-the-money call with a strike price that does not actually exist.

Straddles and Combinations

Strategies that involve the simultaneous purchase (or sale) of puts and calls are called *straddles* and *combinations*. They are for the most part volatility plays, but can have a bullish or bearish bias. They can be short- or long-term trades.

Straddle Purchase

The buying of a put and a call with the same strike and expiration is a *straddle purchase*. A trader initiating this position wants the market to move sharply, far from the strike price. In addition, a perceived increase in volatility will add to the options' premiums.

This strategy has limited risk as the trader cannot lose more than the cost of the straddle. The profit potential is unlimited, since an extended move in the underlying instrument will drive an option substantially higher in price, while the other will approach zero. The key to this strategy is the market changing from a low volatility to a substantially higher volatility.

For example, suppose on February 7, 1984, a trader decided that June T-bond futures have been in a quiet trading range for too long. She is not sure which way they will move, but eventually the movement will be substantial. On February 7, the prices are as follows:

June T-Bond Futures   70
Buy June 70 Call   1%₆₄ = $1,062.50
Buy June 70 Put   1%₆₄ = $1,062.50

The cost of buying a June 70 straddle is 2⅛₆₄ ($2,125). To compute the two break-even points at expiration, the cost of the straddle is subtracted from the strike, and then the cost is added to the strike producing break-evens of 67²⁸⁄₃₂ and 72⁴⁄₃₂.

Potential outcomes at expiration are as follows, and as shown in Exhibit 3:

Price of June Bond Futures at Expiration	70 Call	70 Put	Cost	Profit
64	$ 0	$6,000	$2,125	$3,875
66	0	4,000	2,125	1,875
68	0	2,000	2,125	(125)
70	0	0	2,125	(2,125)
72	2,000	0	2,125	(125)
74	4,000	0	2,125	1,875
76	6,000	0	2,125	3,875

EXHIBIT 3
Potential Outcomes at Expiration For June 70 Straddle Purchase

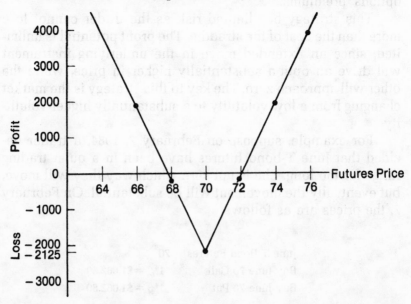

By March 20, 1984, June Treasury bond futures had dropped sharply to 66%₃₂. At that point, the position had the following results:

June 70 Call	1%₆₄ to %₆₄	Profit:	($ 953.13)	
June 70 Put	1%₆₄ to 3⁵⁰⁄₆₄		2,718.75	
			$1,765.62	

The trader was uncertain that the market would continue to fall, so she could have liquidated the straddle and accepted her profits. She also could have left the straddle on, looking for a continued decline in price of June T-bond futures, but, to give her more leeway if the market were to rally, she sold her 70 call at %₆₄ and purchased a 66 call at 1%₆₄. She moved the losing side of her straddle to a closer strike—she rolled her call down. Even though the total cost of the position increased to $3,125 (the original cost of $2,125, plus the difference between the cost of the new call and the proceeds from the sale of the original call), she now has a *locked-in profit*. The new position had to be worth a minimum of $4,000, the difference between the strikes of the options she owns, and she still has an unlimited profit potential. The minimum profit on the entire trade was $875 ($4,000 − $3,125).

Combination Purchase

A *combination purchase* strategy is a variant on the straddle purchase, the put and call having different terms. Typically, the expiration of the options is the same, but the strike prices are different. If the strike of the put is below the price of the underlying instrument, and the strike of the call is above, it is referred to as a *strangle;* as the options "strangle" the price of the security or futures contract.

Just as trading out-of-the-money options is more popular than in-the-money options, the strangle is the most popular form of straddles or combinations. Because both the put and call are out-of-the-money, the dollar cost is cheaper. At the same time, the maximum loss possible is limited to the dollar investment, while the profit potential is unlimited.

Suppose, for example, that on February 7, 1984 a trader
decided that June T-bond futures were likely to have a substantial price move, because of the state of the economy, and the
fact that it is a Presidential election year. The T-bond futures
market had been quiet for a period of time, so the purchase
of options looks cheap. The trader decided to buy a strangle.

June T-Bond Futures	70	
Buy June 68 Put	$24/64$	
Buy June 72 Call	$24/64$	
Cost of the Strangle	$48/64$	= $750

At expiration, the potential outcomes are as follows, and
as shown in Exhibit 4:

Price of June Bond Futures at Expiration	68 Put	72 Call	Cost	Profit
62	$6,000	$ 0	$750	$5,250
64	4,000	0	750	3,250
66	2,000	0	750	1,250
68	0	0	750	(750)
70	0	0	750	(750)
72	0	0	750	(750)
74	0	2,000	750	1,250
76	0	4,000	750	3,250
78	0	6,000	750	5,250

As can be seen, strangles have a substantial price range
in the underlying instrument that will produce a loss, or the
maximum loss. When compared to straddles, as shown in Exhibit 5, they are a cheaper, but a riskier strategy. It is even
more important to expect a sharp price movement to profit
from this type of trade.

A common circumstance for buying strangles is when they
are close to expiration, and the trader expects a very quick
and substantial move in the market because a key economic
statistic is to be released—for example, an important Treasury

EXHIBIT 4

Potential Outcomes at Expiration For Strangle Purchase—68 Put and 72 Call

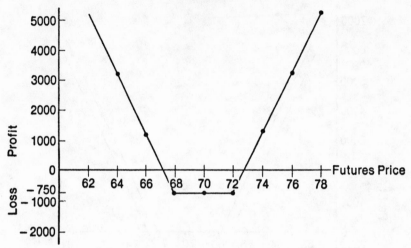

auction (or a refunding) is taking place, or a Fed action is expected (e.g., discount rate change). The strangle can be a cheap way of taking advantage of a short-term movement in the price of debt securities or futures, without taking a great deal of risk. If the event does not cause a big move or does not take place, the strangle is quickly liquidated. If it does take place and produces a sharp price movement, the strangle can be liquidated for a profit, or the losing leg may be liquidated with the hope that the other option will continue to increase in value.

Buying strangles can be done with additional risk by purchasing options further out of the money. The cost is very low, but the likelihood of profit is slim. The trader looking for a very substantial move will do this to get the most "bang for the buck." The following example illustrates this point:

June T-Bond Futures	70
June 66 Put	$\frac{7}{64}$
June 74 Call	$\frac{7}{64}$
Cost of the Strangle	$\frac{14}{64} = \$218.75$

EXHIBIT 5
Potential Outcomes at Expiration of Straddle Purchase vs Strangle Purchase

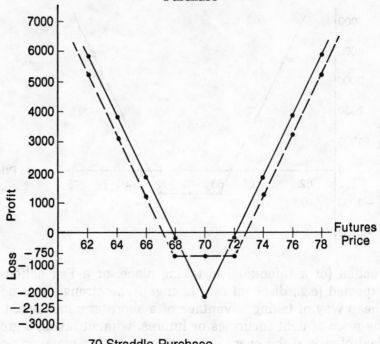

— 70 Straddle Purchase
--- Strangle Purchase—68 Put and 72 Call

Potential outcomes at expiration are shown below and in Exhibit 6:

Price of June Bond Futures at Expiration	66 Put	74 Call	Cost	Profit
60	$6,000	$ 0	$218.75	$5,781.25
62	4,000	0	218.75	3,781.25
64	2,000	0	218.75	1,781.25
66	0	0	218.75	(218.75)
68	0	0	218.75	(218.75)
70	0	0	218.75	(218.75)
72	0	0	218.75	(218.75)
74	0	0	218.75	(218.75)
76	0	2,000	218.75	1,781.25
78	0	4,000	218.75	3,781.25
80	0	6,000	218.75	5,781.25

EXHIBIT 6
Potential Outcomes at Expiration for Strangle Purchase—66 Put and 74 Call

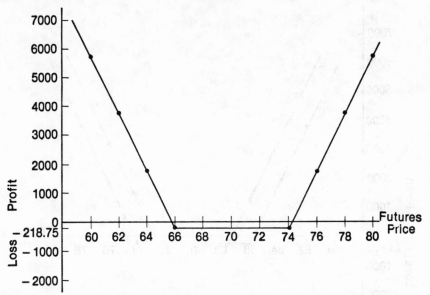

For those traders with a high risk preference, the more "bang for the buck concept" becomes quite graphic when buying strangles that are far out of the money but still keeping total dollar risk constant. This speculator might compare outcomes between the strangle purchase of a 68 put and 72 call, and the purchase of 3.43 strangles of 66 puts and 74 calls (in our example). This comparison is shown in Exhibit 7. The 3.43 amount is derived by dividing the cost of the closer-to-the-money strangle by the cost of the further-from-the-money strangle (750 ÷ 218.75 = 3.43). Since the cost of a strangle is the maximum potential loss, owning 3.43 66 put—74 call strangles has the same maximum loss potential as owning one 68 put—72 call strangle. (See Exhibit 8.)

Other Combination Strategies

Rather than purchasing the strangle form of the combination, other strategies can be quite useful. In Treasury bond futures, the price of each contract month reflects expected net cost

EXHIBIT 7
**Comparison of Potential Outcomes at Expiration for Two Strangle
Purchases**

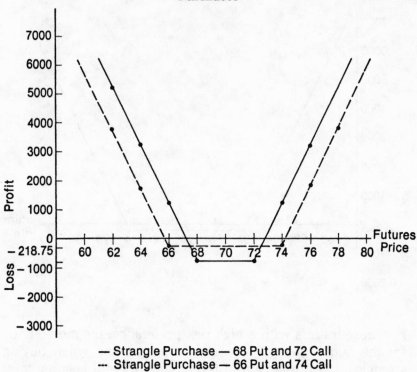

— Strangle Purchase — 68 Put and 72 Call
--- Strangle Purchase — 66 Put and 74 Call

of carry of the underlying bonds, as well as cheapest to deliver
expectations of the marketplace. Therefore, if the trader has
expectations of substantial changes in the price spreads between months of the futures contract, his combination option
buying strategy may reflect those expectations.

For example, if the trader were indifferent to the direction
of price movement, but was sure a substantial movement was
about to take place, and that the September bond future would
gain in price sharply relative to the June contract, the call
purchase portion of the combination might come in the September contract and the put purchase would be in the June contract. This would allow the trader to take advantage of movements in the price spread of T-bond futures. This strategy

EXHIBIT 8
Potential Outcomes at Expiration for Two Strangles

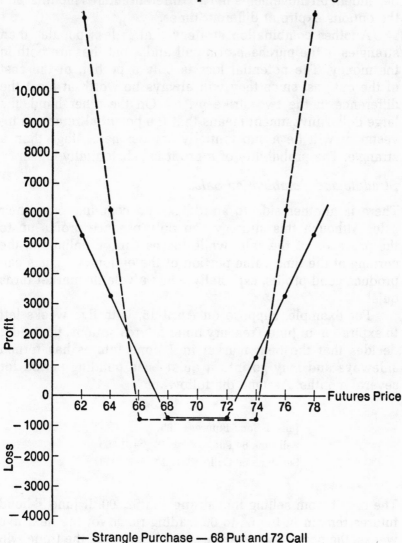

— Strangle Purchase — 68 Put and 72 Call
··· Strangle Purchase of 3.43 Options
66 Puts and 74 Calls

[Weighting Reflects Equal Dollar Risk]

becomes less clear-cut in potential outcomes, because it is dependent on movements in two different futures months, and the options expire at different times.

Another combination strategy that is less popular than strangles is the purchase of a call and a put that are both in the money. The potential loss is only a portion of the cost of the options, since they will always be worth at least the difference in the two strike prices. On the other hand, the large dollar investment means that the potential return on investment will be a substantially smaller percentage than a strangle. The probability of a profit is substantially higher.

Straddle and Combination Sales

There is another side to straddles and combinations—their sale. Although this strategy can only produce profits up to the proceeds of the sale, while losses can be unlimited, the earning of the time value portion of the option premiums can produce good profits, especially when a volatile market turns quiet.

For example, suppose on April 15, with five weeks left to expiration of June Treasury bond futures options, the trader decides that the bear market in T-bond futures has turned sideways and may go into a quiet base building period for several months. Assume the following:

June T-Bond Futures	65	
Sell June 64 Put	$1\frac{16}{64}$ =	$1,250
Sell June 66 Call	$1\frac{16}{64}$ =	$1,250

The credit from selling this strangle is $2,500. If June T-bond futures remain in the 64 to 66 trading range for the next five weeks, the options will expire worthless. If not, the trade will still make money if June T-bond futures are between 61½ and 68½ at option expiration.

Potential outcomes at expiration are as follows, and as in Exhibit 9:

Price of June Bond Futures at Expiration	64 Put	66 Call	Proceeds	Profit
58	($6,000)	$ 0	$2,500	($3,500)
60	(4,000)	0	2,500	(1,500)
62	(2,000)	0	2,500	500
64	0	0	2,500	2,500
66	0	0	2,500	2,500
68	0	(2,000)	2,500	500
70	0	(4,000)	2,500	(1,500)
72	0	(6,000)	2,500	(3,500)

The trader is not really making a market play. It is a volatility play. The market perceives high price volatility so the options appear "expensive" to the trader and he shorts the strangle, looking to earn the time value in the options. Typically, this

EXHIBIT 9
Potential Outcomes at Expiration for Strangle Sale
(64 Put, 66 Call with Futures at 65)

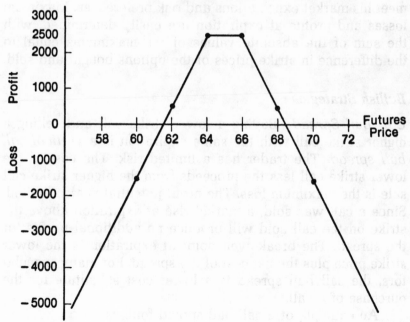

trade is popular over the last five weeks of the life of the options, when time value deteriorates rapidly. One pitfall that commonly occurs is that after periods of low volatility, traders are sometimes "lulled" into believing that the market can only remain quiet, and it is easy money to sell strangles. That type of situation can easily backfire if volatility abruptly increases. The better strategy is to evaluate where and why volatility might change before selling strangles; only doing it when finding good reason for a period of declining volatility.

Vertical Spreads

The simultaneous purchase and sale of calls (or puts) with the same expiration and different strike prices is a *vertical spread*. These spreads are less risky than outright option trading, since one part of the trade partially offsets the other part. By varying the difference in strike prices and the amount in or out of the money, the trader can produce a strategy to meet his market expectations and risk preferences. Maximum losses and profits at expiration are easily determined, with the sum of the absolute values of the maximums equal to the difference in strike prices of the options bought and sold.

Bullish Strategies

Call Bull Spread—Buying a lower strike call and selling a higher strike call with the same expiration is a *vertical call bull spread*. The trader has a limited risk. The cost of the lower strike call less the proceeds from the higher strike call sale is the maximum loss. The profit potential is also limited. Since a call was sold, a market rise at expiration above the strike on the call sold will produce no additional profits for the spread. The break-even point at expiration is the lower strike price plus the net cost of the spread. For many speculators, the call bull spread is a lower cost substitute for the purchase of a call.

An example of a call bull spread follows:

$$
\begin{array}{lll}
\text{June T-Bond Futures} & 70 & \\
\text{Buy June 70 Call} & 1\%_{64} & = \$1,062.50 \\
\text{Sell June 72 Call} & 2\%_{64} & = \$\ 375.00
\end{array}
$$

The cost of buying this spread is \$687.50 (\$1,062.50 − \$375.00). The maximum potential profit is \$1,312.50 [\$1,000 × (72 − 70) −\$687.50]. The break-even point is $70^{22}\!/_{32}$ $(70 + 1\%_{64} - 2\%_{64})$.

Potential outcomes at expiration are as follows, and as in Exhibit 10:

Price of June Bond Futures at Expiration	70 Call	72 Call	Cost	Profit
66	$ 0	$ 0	$687.50	($687.50)
68	0	0	687.50	(687.50)
70	0	0	687.50	(687.50)
72	2,000	0	687.50	1,312.50
74	4,000	(2,000)	687.50	1,312.50
76	6,000	(4,000)	687.50	1,312.50

This strategy is not a very aggressive one, because the call purchased was virtually at the money, and the call sold was the next higher strike price. Any substantial upward movement in prices would not fully reward the trader; only a moderate move is needed to reach the maximum profit potential. One can get even more conservative by using both strikes in the money. For example, consider the following strategy:

$$
\begin{array}{ll}
\text{June T-Bond Futures} & 70\%_{32} \\
\text{Buy June 68 Call} & 2^{28}\!/_{64} = \$2,437.50 \\
\text{Sell June 70 Call} & 1\%_{64}\ = \$1,062.50 \\
\text{Cost} & \$1,375.00 \\
\text{Profit Potential} & \$\ \ 625.00 \\
\text{Break-even} & 69^{12}\!/_{32}
\end{array}
$$

Potential outcomes at expiration are as follows:

Price of June Bond Futures at Expiration	68 Call	70 Call	Cost	Profit
66	$ 0	$ 0	$1,375	($1,375)
68	0	0	1,375	(1,375)
70	2,000	0	1,375	625
72	4,000	(2,000)	1,375	625
74	6,000	(4,000)	1,375	625
76	8,000	(6,000)	1,375	625

In this strategy, the profit potential is much smaller than the dollar risk, but it has a much larger likelihood of working than vertical call spreads with higher strikes. It will even be profitable if the market moves sideways to slightly lower.

To be more aggressive than the prior two examples, the spread should involve out-of-the-money calls, as illustrated below:

June T-Bond Futures	70$\frac{5}{32}$
Buy June 72 Call	$\frac{24}{64}$ = $375
Sell June 74 Call	$\frac{8}{64}$ = $125
Cost	$250
Profit Potential	$1,750
Break-even	72$\frac{8}{32}$

Potential outcomes at expiration are as follows:

Price of June Bond Futures at Expiration	72 Call	74 Call	Cost	Profit
66	$ 0	$ 0	$250	($250)
68	0	0	250	(250)
70	0	0	250	(250)
72	0	0	250	(250)
74	2,000	0	250	1,750
76	4,000	(2,000)	250	1,750

With a substantially higher break-even level than the prior two examples, this strategy is a more aggressive bullish play.

EXHIBIT 10
Comparison of Potential Outcomes at Expiration for Two Vertical Call Bull Spreads

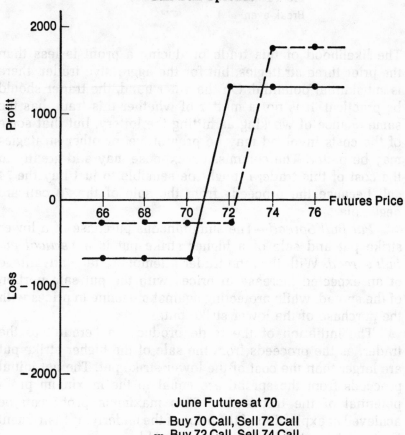

June Futures at 70
— Buy 70 Call, Sell 72 Call
··· Buy 72 Call, Sell 74 Call

It has a lesser chance of working, but if it does succeed, the profit per dollar of risk is substantial. This is shown in Exhibit 10.

To become even more aggressive, the speculator can reach to higher strikes. For example, consider the following strategy:

June T-Bond Futures 70⁵⁄₃₂
Buy June 74 Call ⁸⁄₆₄ = $125.00

Sell June 76 Call	$\frac{3}{64}$ =	$ 46.88
Cost		$ 78.12
Profit Potential		$1,921.88
Break-even		74$\frac{3}{32}$

The likelihood of this trade producing a profit is less than the prior three strategies, but for the aggressive trader, there is substantial potential. On the other hand, the trader should be practical. It is not a matter of whether this trade has the same chance of working as hitting the lottery, but that some of the costs involved may be prohibitive, or other strategies may be better. The commission expense may add greatly to the cost of this trade; it might be sensible to just buy the 74 call because the proceeds from the sale of the 76 call are negligible.

Put Bull Spread—The simultaneous purchase of a lower strike put and sale of a higher strike put is a *vertical put bull spread*. With this, the trader attempts to take advantage of an expected increase in prices with the put sale portion of the spread, while protecting against a decline in prices with the purchase of the lower strike put.

The initiation of the trade produces a "credit" to the trader, as the proceeds from the sale of the higher strike put are larger than the cost of the lower strike put. The net initial proceeds from the spread are equal to the maximum profit potential of the transaction. This maximum profit can be achieved at expiration, if the price of the underlying instrument is at or above the strike of the put sold.

To illustrate this strategy, consider the following:

June T-Bond Futures	70	
Sell June 72 Put	2$\frac{20}{64}$ =	$2,312.50
Buy June 70 Put	1$\frac{1}{64}$ =	$1,062.50
Credit from Spread	$1,250.00	

Potential outcomes at expiration are shown on page 141, and in Exhibit 11:

Price of June Bond Futures at Expiration	72 Put	70 Put	Proceeds	Profit
68	($4,000)	$2,000	$1,250	($750)
70	(2,000)	0	1,250	(750)
72	0	0	1,250	1,250
74	0	0	1,250	1,250
76	0	0	1,250	1,250

The maximum loss is the difference between the two strike prices less the initial credit from putting on the trade. This is because the short sale of the higher strike put is fully protected by the purchase of the lower strike put if a downward

EXHIBIT 11
Potential Outcomes at Expiration for Vertical Put Bull Spread
(Buy 70 Put, Sell 72 Put; June Futures at 70)

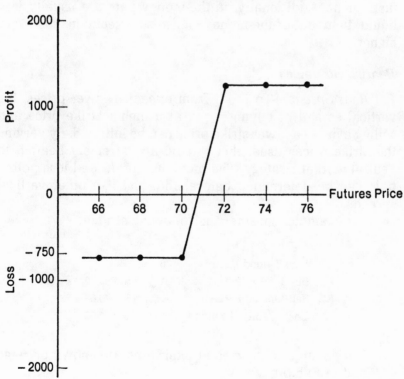

movement in prices occurs (at expiration) to or below the lower strike put. There is no protection at expiration before that lower price, except for the credit from initiating the spread. The break-even on the trade is the higher strike less the proceeds from the spread (in price points).

For a more aggressive strategy than the above example, the speculator would use higher strike prices for the spread which are less likely to be reached. A 72–74 spread might have a profit potential of $1,687.50 and a maximum loss potential of $312.50. A rally to 74 at expiration would be needed to reach the profit potential.

Vertical put bull spreads are similar in outcome to vertical call bull spreads, but less popular. Since the put spreads typically involve in-the-money puts, the trader may have early exercise of his short put, especially in debt securities options under negative cost of carry conditions in the underlying debt instrument. Additionally, in-the-money puts are usually less liquid than out-of-the-money calls, so execution costs are higher.

Bearish Strategies

Put Bear Spread—To profit from expected lower prices, the vertical spread of buying a put at a higher strike price and selling a put at a lower strike price can be initiated. By varying the strike prices used, this can be an extremely bearish to neutral market strategy. The maximum profit and loss potentials can be determined beforehand, just like other vertical spreads.

For example, consider the following strategy:

June T-Bond Futures	70	
Buy June 70 Put	$1\frac{4}{64}$	= $1,062.50
Sell June 68 Put	$\frac{24}{64}$	= $ 375.00
Cost (Debit) of Spread		$ 687.50

The potential outcomes at expiration are shown on page 143, and in Exhibit 12:

Price of June Bond Futures at Expiration	70 Put	68 Put	Cost	Profit
66	$4,000	($2,000)	$687.50	$1,312.50
68	2,000	0	687.50	1,312.50
70	0	0	687.50	(687.50)
72	0	0	687.50	(687.50)

The maximum profit potential for this spread is the difference in strike prices less the initial cost of the spread, since profits from a drop in prices are limited by the short sale of the lower strike put. The break-even point is the higher strike less the debit of the spread.

The put bear spread is the "other side" of the put bull

EXHIBIT 12
Potential Outcomes at Expiration for Vertical Put Bear Spread
(Buy 70 Put, Sell 68 Put; June Futures at 70)

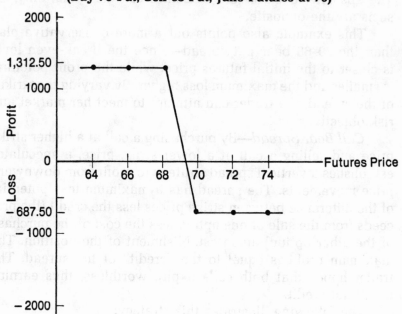

spread. This is clearly seen by comparing the following example to the put bull example previously shown.

June T-Bond Futures	70
Buy June 72 Put	$2\frac{20}{64}$ = $2,312.50
Sell June 70 Put	$1\frac{4}{64}$ = $1,062.50
Cost (Debit) of Spread	$1,250.00

The potential outcomes at expiration are as follows:

Price of June Bond Futures at Expiration	72 Put	70 Put	Cost	Profit
68	$4,000	($2,000)	$1,250	$750
70	2,000	0	1,250	750
72	0	0	1,250	(1,250)
74	0	0	1,250	(1,250)

The absolute levels of the outcomes are the same, only the signs are the opposite.

This example also points out a more conservative play than the 70–68 bear put spread—since the break-even level is closer to the initial futures price, while the profit potential is smaller and the maximum loss higher. By varying the strikes of the spread, the trader can attempt to meet her market and risk objectives.

Call Bear Spread—By purchasing a call at a higher strike price and selling a call at a lower strike price, a speculator establishes a vertical spread strategy to profit from downward price movements. The spread has a maximum loss potential of the difference between strike prices less the credit (the proceeds from the sale of one option less the cost of the purchase of the other option), upon establishment of the position. The maximum profit is equal to the "credit" of the spread. The trader hopes that both calls expire worthless, thus earning the initial credit.

The following illustrates this strategy:

June T-Bond Futures   70
Buy June 72 Call $^{24}\!/_{64}$ = $ 375.00
Sell June 70 Call $1^{2}\!/_{64}$ = $1,062.50
Proceeds (Credit) of
    the Spread $ 687.50

Below and in Exhibit 13, the potential outcomes at expiration are shown:

Price of June Bond Futures at Expiration	72 Call	70 Call	Proceeds	Profit
68	$ 0	$ 0	$687.50	$687.50
70	0	0	687.50	687.50
72	0	(2,000)	687.50	(1,312.50)
74	2,000	(4,000)	687.50	(1,312.50)

This spread is the "other side" of the call bull spread. When
compared to the call bull spread with the same strikes, the
results are identical, except profits and losses are reversed.

By using lower strike prices, the strategy becomes more
aggressive but less likely to succeed, since a substantial drop
in prices would be needed. The profit potential increases, while
the maximum loss declines.

Horizontal Spreads

The simultaneous sale of one option and purchase of another
more distant expiration option with the same strike price is
called a *horizontal spread.* It is also referred to as a *calendar*
or *time spread.* It is a neutral strategy where the trader typically wants prices to move sideways, so he can profit from
the quicker decay in the time value of the shorter option relative to the later maturity option. For listed debt options, this
strategy is trickier than for stock options. Potential changes
in the cheapest to deliver item against interest rate futures,
or changes in the yield curve or net carrying costs of the underlying instrument can greatly affect the price relationship between different months of the futures contracts or "forward"

EXHIBIT 13
Potential Outcomes at Expiration for Vertical Call Bear Spread
(Buy June 72 Call, Sell June 70 Call; June Futures at 70)

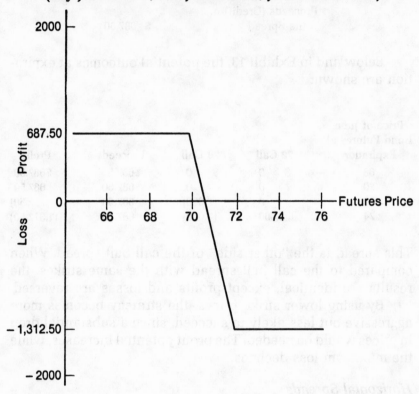

values on the underlying debt instruments, thus affecting price relationships between options of two different maturities.

A horizontal spread can be illustrated as follows:

June T-Bond Futures	70	
September T-Bond Futures	$69^{16}\!/_{32}$	
Sell June 70 Call	$1^{4}\!/_{64}$	= \$1,062.50
Buy September 70 Call	$1^{30}\!/_{64}$	= \$1,468.75
Debit	$^{26}\!/_{64}$	= \$ 406.25

The trader expects a sideways market and wishes to benefit from the fact that the time value on the June 70 call will shrink quickly over the last eight weeks of its life, much faster than the deterioration in the premium on the September call. At expiration of the June call, the situation might look like this:

June T-Bond Futures	$69^{28}\!/_{32}$
September T-Bond Futures	$69^{12}\!/_{32}$
June 70 Call	0 producing a profit of $1,062.50
September 70 Call	1 producing a loss of $ 468.75
Profit	$ 593.75

If prices moved substantially, higher or lower, a loss would be incurred on the trade because the time value on both options would quickly drop, and the longer maturity option has more time value to lose.

For debt options, there is a great deal more to consider. At the time the relationship between June and September T-bond futures remained at a constant $^{16}\!/_{32}$ premium to the June contract, but that rarely is the case. If the Treasury announced that it would be issuing a 40-year Treasury bond at its August refunding, that issue might mean a new cheapest to deliver bond for the September futures delivery. The spread between June and September futures might move to a one point premium and greatly affect the value of the calendar spread. The futures spread can also be affected by movements in net carry (the difference between financing rates and bond yields). For options on actual Treasury bonds, especially puts, changes or expected changes in the net carry will greatly alter calendar spread relationships, even if the price of the underlying bond does not move. All this must be evaluated before entering into a calendar spread.

Some traders use the calendar spread as an attempt to "finance" option positions for later on. In effect, they have expectations of a sideways market for the near term, with a bull (or bear) market down the road. The sideways market, for now, allows them to earn the nearby call (put) premium which decreases the actual cost of the long call (put) for the expected rally (decline) in the future.

This type of strategy is poor. There are really two different trading decisions being made, and too many traders miss moves or pervert their outlook in attempting to reduce the expense of an option purchase.

Reverse Calendar Spreads

The purchase of a nearby option and sale of a more distant option with the same strike price is a *reverse calendar spread*. This is the exact opposite of the calendar spread, and produces at different price levels the same results with opposite signs. Substantial price movements in the underlying instrument normally produce profits in this strategy, but just like calendar spreads, changes in net cost of carry, the slope of the yield curve, and cheapest to deliver for futures adds another dimension to evaluating such strategies. Margin rules have worked against using reverse calendar spreads for most traders, so they have used other strategies (such as combinations) to make plays on the expectation of large price movements.

SUMMARY

The advent of listed debt options is a boon for the participants in the debt market. The arbitrage and trading strategies are innumerable, allowing the astute to tailor investment strategies to their interest rate outlook and risk preferences. The strategies should never be a simple hold and wait until expiration. Instead, they should be reevaluated constantly, based on current levels of interest rates and expected changes, perceived and expected volatility of prices, and changes in the risk and reward makeup of the trade. Profits can be protected or extended, and losses cut if strategies are closely monitored.

CHAPTER 6

Covered Call Writing Strategies

Frank J. Jones, Ph.D.
Vice President
Kidder, Peabody & Co.

Options are extremely flexible hedging and investment vehicles. A wide variety of strategies that are not only bearish and bullish, but neutral, can also be constructed via options. And these strategies can be constructed with either limited or unlimited profit and loss potentials.

This chapter describes a particular type of neutral strategy, a covered call writing strategy. For over a decade, managers of equity portfolios have generated additional income on their portfolios and provided some protection against price declines by writing calls on stock options against their stock portfolios. This strategy is particularly effective during times of relatively stable stock prices.

With the advent of the Chicago Board of Trade (CBT) options on the Treasury bond futures contract during late 1982, the covered writing strategy is available to managers of bond portfolios. And, during recent periods of stable interest rates, many bond portfolio managers have been adopting this strategy.

CALL WRITING

This chapter focuses on writing calls on the options on Treasury bond futures contracts against actual Treasury bonds and other closely related bonds, such as corporate bonds and mortgage related bonds. Since the options themselves, however, are based on the Treasury bond futures contract, such covered call writing on actual bonds is an indirect strategy; options on Treasury bond futures are written against actual bonds. This complexity, the relationship between the Treasury bond futures contract underlying the option and the bond in the portfolio, is considered in the next section.

This section considers the covered call writing strategy in general as it applies against any underlying instrument, whether it be stocks, bonds, or futures contracts. The next section then considers specifically writing calls on the Treasury bond futures options against actual Treasury bonds.

Specifically, this section summarizes various types of call writing: that is, selling calls against the instrument underlying the Treasury bond futures option itself—the Treasury bond futures contract.

Naked Call Writing

Naked call writing consists of writing or selling calls without having a related offsetting position in the underlying market. Exhibit 1 shows the profit/loss profile from only selling a March 70 call at a premium of three versus the price of the futures contract *at the expiration of the option*. It is important to note that this graph and the other profit/loss graphs in this chapter apply only at the expiration of the option, when there is no time value remaining in the call premium. Assume that the price of the futures contract was 70 at the time the option was sold, that is, the call was at-the-money.

The naked call write in this example provides for a *limited profit* (of three), if the futures price remains the same or declines (since the option expires worthless and the seller collects the initial time value of the option); and for an *unlimited*

EXHIBIT 1
Naked Call Writing
(Short One Call)

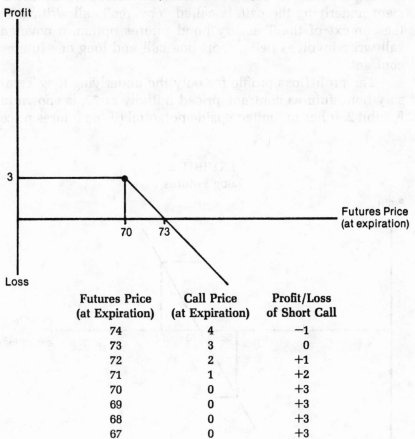

Futures Price (at Expiration)	Call Price (at Expiration)	Profit/Loss of Short Call
74	4	−1
73	3	0
72	2	+1
71	1	+2
70	0	+3
69	0	+3
68	0	+3
67	0	+3

loss if the futures price increases (since the option seller will have to "buy" a futures contract at the higher market price, and deliver it at the strike price of 70).

Writing a Treasury bond futures call without owning the underlying futures contract is called "naked" call writing. It provides for a limited profit (if the futures price remains constant or decreases) and an unlimited loss (if the futures price increases). This is, thus, either a neutral or bear strategy.

Covered Call Writing

Writing or selling a call, while owning the amount of the instrument underlying the call, is called "covered" call writing. In the context of the Treasury bond futures option, a covered call write involves being short one call and long one futures contract.

The profit/loss profile for only the underlying long Treasury bond futures contract, priced initially at 70, is shown in Exhibit 2. It has unlimited upside potential (if the futures price

EXHIBIT 2
Long Futures

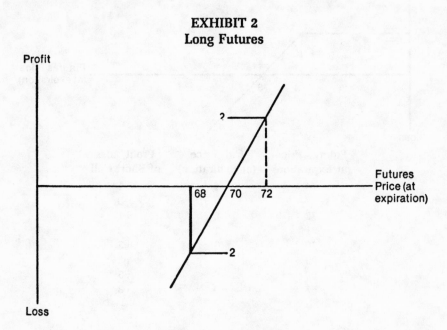

Futures Price	Profit/Loss on Long Futures
74	4
73	3
72	2
71	1
70	0
69	−1
68	−2
67	−3

increases) and unlimited downside potential (if the futures price decreases).

A standard covered write involves a combination of selling one call (a neutral/bear strategy) and buying one futures contract (denoted by 1/1) (a bull strategy), which has a profit/loss profile which is a combination of Exhibits 1 and 2, and is shown in Exhibit 3, along with the profit/loss profile for the underlying long futures contract. As indicated in Exhibit 3, a covered write has a limited profit, the premium, if the

EXHIBIT 3
Covered Call Writing
(Short One Call Against Long One Futures Contract)

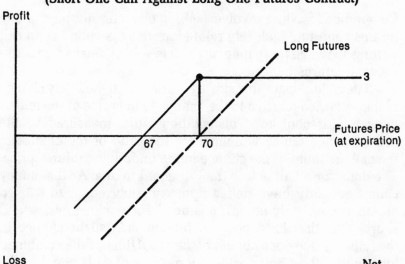

Futures Price (at Expiration)	Call Price (at Expiration)	Profit/Loss on Long Futures	Profit/Loss on Short Call	Net Profit/Loss on Short Call/Long Futures
74	4	4	−1	3
73	3	3	0	3
72	2	2	1	3
71	1	1	2	3
70	0	0	3	3
69	0	−1	3	2
68	0	−2	3	1
67	0	−3	3	0
66	0	−4	3	−1

futures price increases (since the option will be exercised and the call writer will "deliver" the futures contract he holds as cover) and an unlimited loss if the futures price decreases (since the call will expire worthless and there will be a loss equal in value to the difference between the strike price and the final level of the futures contract).[1] Thus, the covered write is obviously a neutral/bull strategy.

The profit/loss possibilities for long futures, short call, and short call/long futures (1/1) strategies are summarized in Exhibit 4.

Ratio Call Writing

Covered call writing involves selling one call and buying one futures contract. A closely related strategy is called ratio call writing, in which more than one call is sold against an underlying long futures contract.

The rationale for this strategy is based on the likely change in the call price relative to the change in the price of the underlying futures contract. This relationship is measured by the call's "delta," which is defined as the ratio of the change in the call premium to the change in the underlying futures price. The delta for a call is less than or equal to one. At-the-money calls frequently have deltas approximately equal to 0.5. To obtain a completely *neutral* position between long futures and short calls, that is, a position for which a slight change in the futures price does not affect the profit/loss of the combined long future/short call position, a number of calls equal to the reciprocal of delta would have to be sold against the futures contract.

A very common strategy, the "ratio write," consists of selling two calls against one long futures contract. This covered write would be neutral if the call's delta were 0.5. Consider the results of a ratio write: the profit/loss profile would be a combination of Exhibit 3, a covered write, and Exhibit

---

[1] Note that the profit/loss profile for a coverd call (1/1) is the same as that for a short put.

EXHIBIT 4

	Futures Price Increases	Futures Price Constant	Futures Price Decreases	Type of Strategy
Long Futures	Profit-Unlimited	No Profit/Loss	Loss-Unlimited	Bull
Short Call (Naked Call Write)	Loss-Unlimited	Profit	Profit-Limited	Neutral/Bear
Short One Call/Long One Futures (Coverd Call Write)	Profit-Limited	Profit	Loss-Unlimited	Neutral/Bull
Short Two Calls/Long One Futures (Ratio (2/1) Call Write)	Loss-Unlimited	Profit	Loss-Unlimited	Neutral

EXHIBIT 5
Ratio Call Writing
(Short Two Calls Against Long One Futures)

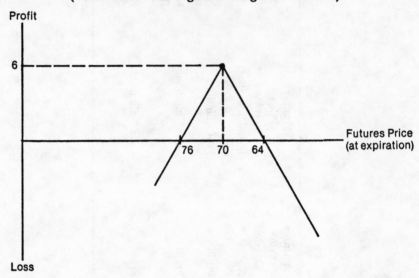

Futures Price (at Expiration)	Call Price (at Expiration)	Profit/Loss on Long Futures	Profit/Loss of Short 2 Calls	Net Profit/Loss of Short 2 Call/Long Futures
77	7	7	−8	−1
76	6	6	−6	0
75	5	5	−4	1
74	4	4	−2	2
73	3	3	0	3
72	2	2	2	4
71	1	1	4	5
70	0	0	6	6
69	0	−1	6	5
68	0	−2	6	4
67	0	−3	6	3
66	0	−4	6	2
65	0	−5	6	1
64	0	−6	6	0
63	0	−7	6	−1

1, an additional short call, and is shown in Exhibit 5. Since two calls are sold instead of one, the premium collected is twice as great (six rather than three) as for a covered write. In either case, the amount of premium collected is equal to the maximum profit, which occurs when the underlying price at expiration equals the strike price.

Since the standard covered write (1/1) has unlimited loss potential if futures prices decrease, and a naked short call has unlimited loss potential if the futures price increases, this ratio write, which is a combination of these two, has unlimited loss potential for either increasing or decreasing prices, but twice the profit potential (which is limited) as a covered call for stable prices. As shown in Exhibit 5, in this example, losses occur outside the futures price range from 64 to 76. Thus, this ratio write strategy is a neutral strategy, that is, it profits with stable prices, with unlimited loss potential for either price increases or decreases.[2] Thus, while a short call is a bear strategy, and a covered write is a bull strategy, a ratio write is a neutral strategy.

Writing two calls against one futures contract is a basic theme in ratio call writing. An important variation on this theme is now considered.

Delta Neutral Call Writing

One for one and two for one covered writing strategies have been considered. As indicated above, if the reciprocal of the delta of the call is used as the number of calls sold, a neutral or completely offset covered call write—at least initially—will result. This is called a delta neutral, or just neutral covered write. In this case, *small* changes in the futures price will cause completely offsetting profits and losses in the futures position and the call positions, and there will be no net profit or loss on the net position.

---

[2] Note that the profit/loss profile for a ratio write is the same as that for a sell straddle, which is a combination in which both puts and calls are sold. See Chapter 5.

For example, if the delta of an at-the-money June 70 call on a futures contract is 0.67 (1/0.67 = 1.5), then 15 calls would be sold against 10 futures contracts for a delta neutral covered write. If the futures price then increased from 70 to 71, the profit on the long futures position would be $1,000 times 10 contracts for a total profit of $10,000.[3] The short calls would then decline in value by 0.67 (since the futures increased by 1.0 and the call's delta is 0.67). So, the total loss on the short calls would be 15 × 0.67 times $1,000 for a total loss of $10,000. Therefore, the net profit/loss would be zero—this is a neutral position.[4]

However, for large increases or decreases in the futures price, this position would not remain neutral. Why? Because, for significant futures price increases or decreases, the call's delta increases or decreases, respectively. Specifically, if the futures price increases, the call becomes more in-the-money and its delta increases (toward 1.0 for deep-in-the-money calls). If the futures price decreases, the call becomes more out of the money and its delta decreases (toward zero for deep out-of-the-money calls). Thus, the initial weight of 15, based on the initial delta of 0.67, would be too low or high, after the futures price increased or decreased, respectively, by a significant amount.

Consider the example summarized in Exhibit 6. The delta of a call at the initial futures price of 70 is 0.67. For small (by assumption) increases or decreases in the futures price, say to 71 or 69, there is no incremental profit or loss on the overall position—profits or losses on the long futures are offset by equal losses or profits on the short calls.

However, if larger changes in the futures price occur, the call's delta will change, increasing as the futures price increases and vice versa. If the hedge ratio of 15, based on the original delta, 0.67, is used, it will then be inappropriate

---

[3] Each 1.0 price change in the Treasury bond futures contract is worth $1,000.

[4] In practice, the delta would not remain constant with 1.0 moves from 70 to 69 or 71 in the underlying futures price, but this example assumes that the delta remains constant over this range to keep the arithmetic simple.

EXHIBIT 6
Futures Price Change, Delta and Profit/Loss Position

	Futures Price	Delta	Hedge Ratio	Profit/ Loss on Future	Profit/ Loss on Call	Net Profit/ Loss
Initial	70	0.67	15	—	—	—
Small	69	0.67	15	-10	+10	0
Change	71	0.67	15	+10	-10	0
Large	60	0.60	16.67	-100	+90*	-10
Change	80	0.80	12.50	+100	-120**	-20

*(.6 × 15 × 10)
**(.8 × 15 × 10)

for significant futures price changes in either direction. And, in either case, as shown in Exhibit 6, there will be an incremental loss in the long 10 futures/short 15 call position.

Thus, the maximum profit occurs at the initial futures price, and small futures price changes do not affect the profit. But, significant futures price changes in either direction cause incremental losses in the position.

Thus, to keep the position neutral against price changes, the number of calls held short will have to be continually changed as the futures price increases or decreases and the delta increases or decreases. That is, to maintain neutrality as the futures price increases, some calls will have to be liquidated; and if the futures price decreases, additional calls will have to be sold. The frequency of the adjustments of the positions must, of course, recognize transactions costs. The management of delta neutral call writes is considered in a later section.

In view of this discussion, it can be observed that a routine 2/1 covered write might be slightly bullish, slightly bearish, or neutral depending on the initial value of the delta of the call written.

Variable Ratio Write (Trapezoidal Hedge)

Typically in covered, ratio, or neutral call writes, at-the-money calls are sold, because at-the-money calls have the greatest time value. This is an obvious choice when the futures price is close to a call strike price. However, when the futures price is between call strike prices, there are advantages to, instead of writing calls on either the nearest in-the-money or nearest out-of-the-money calls, to write calls on a combination of each, thereby straddling the futures price with call strike prices.

Consider the following example of a covered call write. Assume that the June Treasury bond futures contract price is 71; the June 70 call is priced at four and the June 72 call is priced at 3.5 (or $3\frac{32}{64}$, since call premiums are expressed in 64ths), written 3–32. Consider two cases:

(a) A portfolio manager sells two June 70 calls against one June futures contract;
(b) A portfolio manager sells two June 72 calls against one June futures contract.

Exhibits 7 and 8 provide the calculation of profit/loss profiles for these two covered writes. Note the equations for calculating the maximum profit and the downside and upside break-even points in the notes to Exhibits 7 and 8. The profit/loss

EXHIBIT 7
2/1 Write with June 70 Call

Futures Price at Expiration	Call Price at Expiration	Profit: Long 1 Futures (@ 71)	Profit: Short 2 Calls(70 @ 4)	Net Profit: Long 1 Futures/ Short 2 Calls
78	8	7	$2 \times (-4) = -8$	−1
77(Up)	7	6	$2 \times (-3) = -6$	0
76	6	5	$2 \times (-2) = -4$	1
75	5	4	$2 \times (-1) = -2$	2
74	4	3	$2 \times 0 = 0$	3
73	3	2	$2 \times 1 = 2$	4
72	2	1	$2 \times 2 = 4$	5
71	1	0	$2 \times 3 = 6$	6
70(Max)	0	−1	$2 \times 4 = 8$	7
69	0	−2	$2 \times 4 = 8$	6
68	0	−3	8	5
67	0	−4	8	4
66	0	−5	8	3
65	0	−6	8	2
64	0	−7	8	1
63(Down)	0	−8	8	0
62	0	−9	8	−1

Notes

Maximum Profit = Strike Price − Futures Price + 2 × Call Price
= 70 − 71 + 2(4)
= −1 + 8 = 7 (Maximum profit occurs at the strike price)
Downside Break-even point = Strike Price − Maximum Profit
= 70 − 7 = 63
Upside Break-even Point = Strike Price + Maximum Profit
= 70 + 7 = 77

EXHIBIT 8
2/1 Write with June 72 Call

Futures Price at Expiration	Call Price at Expiration	Profit: Long 1 Futures (271)	Profit: Short 2 Calls(72 @ 3.5)	Net Profit Long 1 Futures Short 2 Calls
81	9	10	$2 \times (-5.5) = -11$	−1
80(Up)	8	9	$2 \times (-4.5) = -9$	0
79	7	8	$2 \times (-3.5) = -7$	1
78	6	7	$2 \times (-2.5) = -5$	2
77	5	6	$2 \times (-1.5) = -3$	3
76	4	5	$2 \times (-.5) = -1$	4
75	3	4	$2 \times .5 = 1$	5
74	2	3	$2 \times 1.5 = 3$	6
73	1	2	$2 \times 2.5 = 5$	7
72(Max)	0	1	$2 \times 3.5 = 7$	8
71	0	0	7	7
70	0	−1	7	6
69	0	−2	7	5
68	0	−3	7	4
67	0	−4	7	3
66	0	−5	7	2
65	0	−6	7	1
64(Down)	0	−7	7	0
63	0	−8	7	−1
62	0	−9	7	−2

Notes

Maximum Profit = Strike Price − Futures Price + 2 × Call Price
          = 72 − 71 + 2(3.5)
          = +1 + 7 = *8* (Maximum profit occurs at the strike price)
Downside Break-even Point = Strike Price − Maximum Profit
          = 72 − 8 = 64
Upside Break-even Point = Strike Price + Maximum Profit
          = 72 + 8 = 80

profiles are shown in Exhibit 9, and the critical parameters of these profiles are summarized in Exhibit 10.

Given the initial futures price of 71, when writing the two in-the-money calls (70 strike price), the maximum profit is seven (at the strike price of 70) and the range of profitability is from 63 to 77, from eight below, to six above the initial futures price. Thus, this strategy is slightly bearish since its

EXHIBIT 9
Profit/Loss Profiles for 2/1 Covered Writes
(Initial Futures Price = 71)

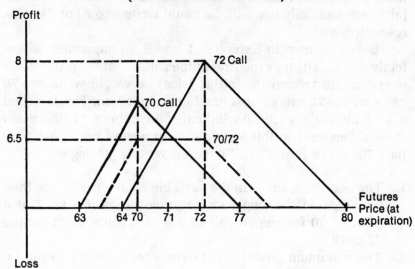

profit range extends further on the downside than on the upside.

On the other hand, when writing two of the out-of-the-money calls (72 strike price) the maximum profit is eight (at the strike price) and the range of profitability is from 64 to 80, from seven below, to nine above the initial futures price. This strategy is, thus, slightly bullish since its profit range extends further on the upside.

EXHIBIT 10
Critical Parameters

	(70 Call @ 4) Case (a)	(72 Call @ 3.5) Case (b)
Maximum Profit	7	8
Price of Maximum Profit	70	72
Downside Break-even Price	63(−8)	64(−7)
Upside Break-even Price	77(+6)	80(+9)

Implementing slightly bearish or bullish strategies is appropriate if this is consistent with the investor's outlook. And, if the investor wanted to be somewhat more bearish or bullish (although basically neutral), he could write two 68 or 74 calls, respectively.

But, as shown in Exhibits 11 and 9, to implement a perfectly neutral strategy (neutral in the sense that the profit range is symmetric around the initial price) he would write one 70 call and one 72 call against one futures position. This is called a variable ratio write. As indicated in Exhibit 11, there are three differences in this variable ratio write from either pure June 70 call or June 72 call covered writing strategies:

1. The maximum profit in the variable ratio write is less than for either of the single strike price writes (6.5 vs. 7 at a price of 70 for the 70 call and 8 at a price of 72 for the 72 call);
2. The maximum profit occurs over a range of expiration futures prices (from 70 to 72, the range between the two strike prices), rather than at a single futures price (70 for the 70 call and 72 for the 72 call), and;
3. The range of profitability is symmetrical around the original futures price (from 63.5 to 78.5, 7.5 below and above the original futures price of 71), making this ratio covered write perfectly a neutral strategy in this sense.

Overview

Call writing against a long position in the underlying instrument can be done in a variety of different ways giving a variety of different profit/loss profiles. The selection of the number of calls sold, and the choice of the call strike prices used are important decisions in implementing the strategy consistent with the investors' investment needs and view of the market. And, continually managing these positions is also important, as discussed later in this chapter.

EXHIBIT 11
2/1 Write with One June 70 and One June 72 Call

Futures Price at Expiration	70 Call Price at Expiration	72 Call Price at Expiration	Profit/ Loss Long 1 Futures	Profit/ Loss on Short 1 70 Call	Profit/ Loss on Short 1 72 Call	Net Profit/ Loss
79	9	7	8	−5	−3.5	−0.5
78(Up)	8	6	7	−4	−2.5	+0.5
77	7	5	6	−3	−1.5	+1.5
76	6	4	5	−2	−0.5	+2.5
75	5	3	4	−1	+0.5	+3.5
74	4	2	3	0	+1.5	+4.5
73	3	1	2	1	+2.5	+5.5
72[Max]	2	0	1	2	+3.5	+6.5
71[Max]	1	0	0	3	+3.5	+6.5
70[Max]	0	0	−1	4	+3.5	+6.5
69	0	0	−2	4	+3.5	+5.5
68	0	0	−3	4	+3.5	+4.5
67	0	0	−4	4	+3.5	+3.5
66	0	0	−5	4	+3.5	+2.5
65	0	0	−6	4	+3.5	+1.5
64	0	0	−7	4	+3.5	+0.5
63(Down)	0	0	−8	4	+3.5	−0.5

WRITING TREASURY BOND FUTURES CALLS AGAINST TREASURY BONDS

Basics

The discussion in the previous section considers writing Treasury bond futures calls against the actual underlying of the option, the Treasury bond futures contract. But portfolio managers are more likely to write such calls against actual Treasury bonds, bonds which may or may not be deliverable on the Treasury bond futures contract, or other closely related bonds, such as corporate or mortgage related bonds.

This section considers writing options on the Treasury bond futures options contract against actual Treasury bonds. Writing calls against other types of bonds is very similar. In this application, there are three instruments involved, directly or indirectly: Treasury bonds, Treasury bond futures contracts, and Treasury bond futures options, as summarized in Exhibit 12.

To effectively implement such call writing strategies requires an understanding of the specifications of the Treasury bond futures options contract and Treasury bond futures contracts. A general summary of the contract specifications follows.

	Treasury Bond Futures Contract	Option on Treasury Bond Futures Contract
Denomination	$100,000	$100,000 (one Treasury Bond Futures Contract)
Deliverable Grade	Treasury Bonds with maturity (or call, if callable) greater than 15 years	Treasury Bond Futures Contract
Months Traded	March, June, September, December	Same as Treasury bond futures trading months (strike prices are in 2 point increments, e.g. 64, 66, etc.)
Trading Unit	1/32 of 1% of par ($31.25)	1/64 of 1% of par ($15.63) (2/64 is valued at $31.25)

	Treasury Bond Futures Contract	Option on Treasury Bond Futures Contract
Last Day of Trading	First Friday (1:00 P.M. EST) preceding by at least five business days the first notice day for the corresponding Treasury bond futures contract. (First notice day is last business day of preceding month.)	Eighth to last business day of delivery month (1:00 P.M. EST)

Options on the Treasury bond futures contracts are based on one Treasury bond futures contract. Upon exercise and assignment, the long call is assigned a long futures position at the call's strike price, and the short call is assigned a short futures position at the strike price. For puts, the long is assigned a short futures position at the strike price, and the short is assigned a long futures position at the strike price.

To effectively write Treasury bond futures calls on actual Treasury bonds requires an adjustment based on the relation between the Treasury bond held and the Treasury bond futures contract. Consider the relationship between deliverable Treasury bonds and the Treasury bond futures contract. The Treasury bond futures contract is based on an eight percent par coupon, 20-year Treasury bond. To adjust the invoice price for the delivery of other coupons (all coupons are deliverable) and other eligible maturities, the invoice price for the delivery

EXHIBIT 12
Options on T-Bond Futures

T-Bonds	T-Bond Futures Contract		T-Bond Futures Options
Dollar for Dollar(1/1)	Factor (F)	1/1	
Write	Net: Factor (F)		
Delta Neutral	Factor (F)		1/Delta
Write	Net: Factor/Delta		

of Treasury bonds is set equal to the futures settlement price times a conversion factor (F) provided by the Chicago Board of Trade.[5]

Thus, as is the common practice in futures hedging, to hedge $100,000 of Treasury bonds, F futures contracts are sold rather than one futures contract. This hedge ratio equates the gains or losses on the Treasury bond with the losses or gains on the futures positions.[6] The appropriate hedge ratio shall be denoted by H.

Since the relation between the Treasury bond and Treasury bond futures contract is determined by this hedge ratio, and the option is based on the futures contract, the number of calls sold on underlying Treasury bonds must also be adjusted by the futures hedge ratio. Thus, if to hedge $100,000 of a specific Treasury bond with Treasury bond futures contracts requires H futures contracts, then H calls should be sold to do a 1/1 covered write on these Treasury bonds. To do a delta neutral covered write on this Treasury bond, a number equal to H/Delta calls would be sold. These relationships are summarized in Exhibit 12.

Effect of Futures Convergence

Since Treasury bond futures options are based on Treasury bond futures contracts, the options premiums respond directly to changes in Treasury bond futures prices. Obviously, Treasury bond futures prices depend on Treasury bond prices (spe-

---

[5] This conversion factor equals the price at which the deliverable bond, with the deliverable bond's coupon and maturity, yields eight percent times .01.

[6] This adjustment applies precisely only to the cheapest deliverable bond on the futures contract. Several Treasury bonds are deliverable on the futures contract, but one is the cheapest to deliver by the short and is usually delivered. For noncheapest deliverable Treasury bonds, the conversion factor must be multiplied by the quotient of the dollar value of the price change due to a one basis point yield change in the bond being hedged divided by the dollar value of the price change due to a one basis point yield change in the cheapest deliverable bond to determine the hedge ratio.

cifically, the price of the cheapest deliverable Treasury bond).
Thus, Treasury bond futures options premiums depend indirectly on Treasury bond prices. However, the relationship between Treasury bond futures prices and Treasury bond
prices—the difference is called the *basis*—must be considered
in writing calls on Treasury bonds.

Treasury bond futures prices relate to Treasury bond
prices as follows:

1. When the Treasury yield curve is upward sloping (long-
    term rates are higher than short-term rates), futures prices
    are less than cash prices and futures prices decrease the
    longer the maturity of the futures contract;
2. When the Treasury yield curve is downward sloping, fu-
    tures prices are greater than cash prices and increase with
    maturity.

These results are shown in Exhibit 13.

At the maturity of a futures contract, the futures price
equals the cash price (the cash price of the cheapest deliverable adjusted for the conversion factor, as specified in the futures invoice price)—this is called *convergence.* Thus, as convergence occurs, Treasury bond futures prices increase

EXHIBIT 13
Futures/Cash Price Relationships

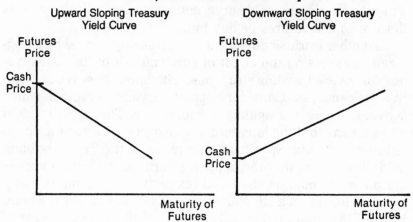

relative to Treasury bond prices with an upward sloping yield curve, and vice versa. Futures price increases cause losses to short futures positions and gains to long futures positions.

Short calls, if exercised, are assigned short futures contracts. Thus, with an upward sloping yield curve, convergence leads to an increase in the call premium and a loss to sellers of calls. Another way to express this phenomenon is that, with an upward sloping yield curve, if cash prices remain constant, futures prices increase and, thus, call premiums increase, causing a loss to writers of calls.

This is an important result for call writers. The convergence that occurs between Treasury bonds and Treasury bond futures (with an upward sloping yield curve) causes premium increases and as a result losses to covered call writers. Such losses tend to offset the profits that accrue to the call writers (sellers), due to the decrease in time value.

With an upward sloping yield curve, convergence also causes losses in the two common forms of hedging or insuring fixed income securities, selling futures and buying puts. Thus, with an upward sloping yield curve, convergence works against the three common forms of hedging, insuring or generating income from a fixed income portfolio.

Of course, with a negatively sloped yield curve, futures prices decrease relative to cash prices due to convergence, causing premium decreases and profits to call writers. With a negatively sloped yield curve, convergence similarly benefits those who sell futures or buy puts.

Another intrinsically related relationship should be recognized in assessing the effect of convergence on the effectiveness of covered writing strategies, with either positive or negative yield curves. Consider a positive yield curve for which convergence works against a call writer. The positive yield curve means that the long-term interest rate exceeds the short-term interest rate. Specifically, in terms of the Treasury bond held, this means that the coupon return on the bond exceeds the financing cost on the bond (explicit or opportunity cost), which is based on a short-term rate. Thus, the longer the bond is held, the greater the dollar value of the excess return of the coupon return over the financing cost. And this increasing return countervails the negative effect of convergence on the short call; and, in fact, these two effects have the same antecedent. The positive yield curve causes both the convergence, which causes the loss to the short call, and the generation of an excess of coupon return over financing cost; and these two results tend to offset each other.[7]

In a 1/1 covered writing strategy (on the cheapest deliverable Treasury bond), if the futures contract were accurately priced (on the basis of carry), these two factors would exactly offset each other, and the profit on a covered write would be due only to the compression of time value of the call premium. However, for a covered writing strategy for which more than one call is sold, there will be a greater negative effect from convergence than positive effect from carrying the bond. There will, thus, be an offset to the premium compression of the short calls.

This discussion applies in the opposite direction with a negative yield curve. But, in general, a negative yield curve causes convergence which benefits a call writer, but leads to a loss from carrying the bond, since the carry cost will be greater than the coupon return.

The effect of cash-futures convergence on covered writing strategies should be recognized. A system which gives quantitative analysis of the effects of convergence on covered writing strategies is provided below.

One other theoretical consideration should be recognized. While most theories have limitations, the theory for pricing options on stocks and other underlying instruments is generally thought to be accurate. However, a widely accepted theory for determining the price relationship between an underlying and an option and the future on the underlying, has not yet

---

[7] Of course the futures contract convergence depends on the relationship between the coupon return and the financing cost of the cheapest deliverable bond, while the actual dollar gain from carrying the Treasury bond depends on the relationship between the coupon return and financing cost of the bond actually held, and these two will not necessarily be exactly the same.

been developed. Thus, there may be more uncertainty in the
delta used for delta neutral writing of calls on Treasury bond
futures contracts on underlying Treasury bonds than for delta
neutral call writing on stocks or other underlying instruments
directly. This adds a risk to the covered call writing strategies
discussed in this chapter.

Applications

1. Assessment of Potential Outcomes

The previous section discusses the profit/loss profiles of various types of covered writes with various numbers of calls
sold against the underlying. Before choosing a specific strategy
and transacting it, it is essential to be able to very conve-
niently, quickly, and precisely, analyze the profit/loss profiles
of the strategies being considered.

A system which provides this type of information is illustrated in this section. Exhibits 14, 15 and 16 show profit/loss
profiles provided by this system for three different types of
call writes on the 12 percent Treasury bond of 8/15/13: a 1/
1 covered write (Exhibit 14); a 2/1 covered write (Exhibit 15);
and a delta neutral covered write (Exhibit 16). Parts 1, 2, and
3 of each exhibit show the actual positions held, a graph of
the profit/loss profile, and a table of the profit/loss profiles,
respectively. Note that for each of these covered writes, profit/
loss profiles over two holding periods are given:

(a) A short holding period of one week (seven days);
(b) A long holding period, until the expiration of the option
     (42 days).

Exhibit 14 shows, in effect, a 1/1 write on the 12 percent
Treasury bond. The number of calls sold is 142, since the conversion factor for the 12 percent Treasury bond on the June,
1984 futures contract, referred to above, is 1.42. The hedge
ratio is, thus, of approximately the same value. This call write,
then, represents a 1/1 write. Its profit/loss profile is of the
same type as in Exhibit 3, that for a 1/1 covered write. It is
a neutral/bullish strategy, since it achieves a fixed profit for
stable or increasing prices, but shows an unlimited loss for
price decreases.

EXHIBIT 14
1/1 Covered Write of 12 Percent Treasury Bond

1. *Transaction:*

   Sell 142 June, 1984 66 Calls

   Buy 100 12.00 Percent of 8/15/83 Treasury Bonds

2.

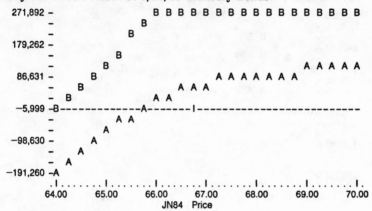

3. Profit/Loss in Dollars

June 84	A	B
64.00	−191,261	−14,147
65.00	−71,792	128,192
66.00	17,778	258,531
67.00	71,039	270,872
68.00	95,081	271,212
69.00	102,802	271,552
70.00	103,142	271,892

Exhibit 15 illustrates a strategy for which 284 (2 × 142) calls are sold against 100 Treasury bonds and represents a 2/1 covered write. It has the same profit/loss profile as Exhibit 5, a 2/1 covered write. It is a neutral strategy, that is, it experiences a profit for stable prices, but losses for either significant price increases or decreases. Since twice as many calls are sold as in Exhibit 15, the maximum profit is greater.

Exhibit 16 shows the profit/loss profile for a delta neutral covered write. In this write, since the delta of the call was .589, 241 calls are sold (142/.589 = 241). Note in Exhibit 16 that small price changes around the initial price do not affect the profit. And, of course, the investor who initiated this delta neutral covered write would not experience the entire profit/

EXHIBIT 15
2/1 Covered Write of 12 Percent Treasury Bond

1. *Transaction:*

    Sell 284 June, 1984 66 Calls

    Buy 100 12.00 Percent of 8/15/83 Treasury Bonds

2.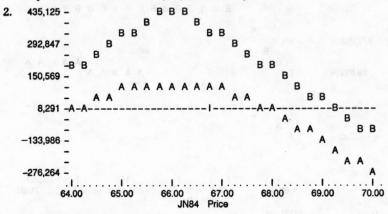

3. Profit/Loss in Dollars

June 84	A	B
64.00	−11,031	174,447
65.00	85,568	316,785
66.00	122,368	435,125
67.00	86,549	317,466
68.00	−7,706	175,806
69.00	−134,604	34,146
70.00	−276,264	−107,514

loss profile shown, since, as the price decreased or increased, he would roll the strike prices down or up, and adjust the hedge ratio to keep the strategy neutral. These adjusted techniques are discussed in the next section (Managing the Covered Write).

An important aspect of these three profit/loss profiles is that the profitability is greater for the long holding period, case B, than for the short holding period, case A. This is the result of the longer time in holding period B, giving the time value in the premium more time to collapse, thus providing a greater return to the seller of the call. And, in these examples, even though the yield curve was positive, the negative effect

EXHIBIT 16
Delta Neutral Covered Write of 12 Percent Treasury Bond

1. *Transaction:*

   Sell 241 June, 1984 66 Calls

   Buy 100 12.00 Percent of 8/15/83 Treasury Bonds

2.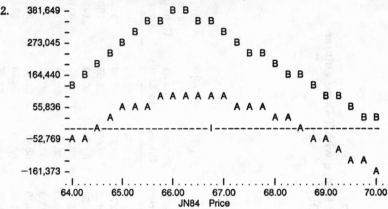

3. Profit/Loss in Dollars

June 84	A	B
64.00	−65,607	117,338
65.00	37,917	259,676
66.00	90,696	321,649
67.00	81,852	303,356
68.00	23,420	204,696
69.00	−62,714	106,037
70.00	−161,373	7,377

of convergence did not dominate the compression of the time value of the premium.

Profit/loss profiles similar to these for any combination of Treasury bonds, Treasury bond futures contracts and Treasury bond futures calls and puts can be constructed by covered call writers.

2. Tracking the Outcome

After implementing a call writing program, it is important to be able to track the outcome of the strategy as the market price of the bond changes. This is particularly important if the strategy is managed and adjusted as discussed in the next

EXHIBIT 17

Results of Delta Neutral Call Write and Hedge with T-Bond Futures Over Several Days

Strategy:

Bought $5,000,000 of 10 3/8s due 11/15/12 at 86.96875

Sold June 70 T-Bond Options on Futures at 1.96875

(1) Date	(2) Cash Price	(3) Option Price	(4) Cash Mark To Market	(5) Options Mark To Market	(6) Daily Market	(7) Futures Prices	(8) Basis in 32nds	(9) Basis Gain or Loss	(10) Adj. Daily Mkt
12/02/83	88.97	1.97	0	0	0	69.75	59.90		
12/05/83	88.41	1.94	− 3125	4344	1219	69.75	57.90	3125	4344
12/06/83	88.91	1.83	− 3125	19547	16422	69.66	61.65	− 2688	13734
12/07/83	88.69	1.70	−14063	36922	22859	69.50	60.89	− 1438	21422
12/08/83	87.97	1.47	−50000	69500	19500	68.91	61.62	− 2313	17188
12/09/83	87.78	1.44	−59375	73844	14469	68.81	59.36	1250	15719
12/12/83	88.00	1.47	−48438	69500	21063	68.97	60.12	0	21063
12/13/83	87.34	1.23	−81250	102078	20828	68.41	61.60	− 2063	18766
12/14/83	87.09	1.16	−93750	112938	19188	68.28	58.59	2688	21875
12/15/83	87.41	1.23	−78125	102078	23953	68.44	62.37	− 3281	20672

12/16/83	87.84	1.47	−36250	69500	13250	68.97	55.12	7813	21063
12/19/83	87.75	1.44	−60938	73844	12906	68.94	53.37	10563	23469
12/20/83	87.78	1.44	−59375	73844	14469	68.88	56.87	5125	19594
12/21/83	88.06	1.45	−45313	71672	26359	69.09	57.12	4625	30984
12/22/83	88.50	1.58	−23438	54297	30859	69.50	54.89	7938	38791
12/23/83	88.44	1.63	−26563	47781	21219	69.44	55.39	7188	28406
12/27/83	88.69	1.75	−14063	30406	16344	69.84	47.16	19875	36219
12/28/83	88.66	1.53	−15625	60813	45188	69.47	61.14	—	43375
12/29/83	88.66	1.59	−15625	52125	36500	69.66	53.65	1813	46313
12/30/83	88.44	1.45	−26563	71672	45109	69.47	54.14	9813	54234
01/03/84	87.91	1.31	−53125	91219	38094	69.25	45.88	9125	60219
01/04/84	88.51	1.50	−22860	65156	42297	69.66	49.02	22125	59344
01/05/84	88.66	1.56	−15625	56469	40844	69.72	51.15	17047	54531
01/06/84	88.59	1.58	−18750	54297	35547	69.78	46.65	13688	56234
01/09/84	88.58	1.63	−19250	47434	28184	69.75	47.58	19250	47434

section. This section illustrates a system for tracking the outcome of a call writing strategy.

Consider a portfolio manager who initiates a delta neutral covered write on $5 million of the 10⅜ percent Treasury bonds of 11/15/12 with the June, 1984 70 Treasury bond futures calls. This bond's factor on the June, 1984 futures contract is 1.25 and at the initial futures price of 69–24 (69.75), the 70 call is slightly out-of-the-money and the call's delta is 0.45. Consequently, 139 (50 × 1.25/0.45) June, 1984 70 calls are written against the Treasury bonds.

Columns 1–6 in Exhibit 17 show the results of this delta neutral call write over several days. Exhibit 18 illustrates the calculations in these columns of Exhibit 17 for the first two days of the strategy. By January 9, 1984, this covered writing program had netted $28,184.

EXHIBIT 18
Notes on Figure 17

A. *Hedge Ratio*

Express all quantities in terms of $100,000 units, the dollar value of one Treasury bond futures contract.

Thus,

$$\frac{\$5,000,000}{\$100,000} = 50,$$

the number of futures contracts for $5,000,000 of Treasury bonds on a dollar for dollar basis.

Factor (12 percent of Treasury bond of 8/15/13 on June, '84 T-bond futures contract): 1.2487

Delta (June, '84 T-bond futures 70 Calls): .449

Hedge Ratio = (50) × (1.2487)/(.449) = 139.05

Thus, 139 Calls are written against $5,000,000 of 12 percent Treasury bonds

B. *Covered Write Results*

1. *Cash Prices* (Column (2))

12/02   88.97 = 88 − 31
12/05   88.91 = 88 − 29
                        −02

(2 32nds) × (31.25/32nd) × 50 units = −$3125 (loss) (Column (4) for 12/05/83)

EXHIBIT 18 (continued)

2. *Options Prices* (Column (3))

    12/02   1.97 = 1 − 62
    12/05   1.94 = 1 − 60
    ────────────────── −02

(2 64th) × (15.625/64th) × (139 contracts) = $4344 (profit) (Column (5)
for 12/05/83)

3. Result of Covered Write

Cash:	−$3125 (loss)	(Column (4) for 12/05/83)
Short Call:	4344 (profit)	(Column (5) for 12/05/83)
Net:	$1219 (profit)	(Column (6) for 12/05/83)

The covered write generates a net profit of $1,219.

C. *Futures Hedge*

If the 12 percent Treasury bond is hedged with futures, 12.5 futures are
sold against each 10 Treasury bonds (each $1,000,000 of Treasury bonds).
The result of this futures hedge is as follows:

	Cash Price (Column (2))	Futures Price (Column (7))	Factored (1.2487) Times Futures Price	Factored Basis	Factored Basis(32nds) (Column (8))
12/02	88 − 31(88.97)	69 − 24(69.75)	87.097	1.873	59.90
12/05	88 − 29(88.91)	69 − 24(69.75)	87.097	1.813	57.90

1.813 in 32nds is (1.813) (32) = 58.02 (Column 8 for 12/05/83)*
((1.873 × (32) = 59.94) (Column (8) for 12/02/83)**
Basis Gain or Loss ($ Value) (Column (9)):

    12/02   59.90
    12/05   57.90
    ──────────────── 2.00 (32nds)

(2 32nds) × (31.25) (50) = $3,125 (Column (9) for 12/05/83)

The factored basis (Cash—Factored Futures) narrowed from 1.873 to
1.813 on one short futures so this is a loss.

D. *Options Covered Write vs. Futures Hedge*

Result of Covered Write:	$1219 profit (Column (6) for 12/05/83)
Result of Futures Hedge:	$3125 loss (Column (9) for 12/05/83)
Advantage of Covered Write:	$4344 (Column (10) for 12/05/83)

* The difference between 58.02 and the number shown in Column 8 for 12/
05/83, 57.90, is due to rounding error.
** Again, the difference is due to rounding error.

Columns 7–9 show the results of having hedged the Treasury bonds with Treasury bond futures contracts (adjusted by the conversion factor F) rather than writing calls against them.

Column 10 shows the difference between columns 6 and 9, that is the difference between the covered write program and the futures hedge over this period.

MANAGING THE COVERED WRITE

Since most covered writing strategies have unlimited risk on both the upside or the downside, it is important to monitor and manage such positions. There are two important ways to manage a covered write: managing the strike price and managing the hedge ratio.

Managing the Strike Price—Rolling Down and Rolling Up

A common method of managing covered writes is rolling the strike price of the calls written down or up. This involves decreasing the strike price of the calls written if the underlying price decreases, or increasing the strike prices of the calls written if the underlying price increases. Rolling is achieved by buying back the calls previously written and selling new calls at lower or higher strike prices.

Consider, for example, the covered write consisting of selling of two June 72 calls at 3.5 and buying a Treasury bond futures contract at 71 discussed earlier in this chapter. To be consistent with this example, consider, again, managing the covered write on a Treasury bond futures contract, rather than on a Treasury bond. The 3.5 premium in this example is entirely time value since the call is out-of-the-money. As indicated in Exhibit 8, at expiration (when there is no time value in the call premium), the maximum profit is eight at a futures price of 72. The downside and upside break-even points are 64 and 80, respectively. Of course, prior to expiration, the call would have some time value left, and the maximum profit would be less than eight and the down and upside break-even points closer together.

Roll Down

Consider the appropriate response to a decrease in the futures price from 71 to 67, as summarized in Exhibit 19. With a break-even range of 64/80, this covered call write is, after the price decrease, close to the downside loss area below 67 and, thus, is at this time a bull strategy. The covered writer may want to reestablish a neutral position, and would accomplish this

EXHIBIT 19
Roll Down of Covered Write

A. *Initial*

Futures Price = 71

72 Calls @ 3.5
(intrinsic value = 0; time value = 3.5)

Sell 2 72 Calls @ 3.5

Maximum Profit = 8 (at 72)
Break-even Points: 64/80

B. *Subsequent*

Futures Price = 67

72 Calls @ 1.0
(intrinsic value = 0; time value = 1.0)

68 Calls @ 2.5
(intrinsic value = 0; time value = 2.5)

Rolldown:

Buy 2 72 Calls @ 1

Sell 2 68 Calls @ 2.5

Profit/Loss on initial covered write:

—Loss on futures = 71 − 67 = 4

—Profit on calls = 2 × (3.5 − 1) = 5

Net Gain (Loss) = −4 + 5 = 1 (profit)

New covered write:

Long 1 Futures

Short 2 68 Calls @ 2.5

Maximum Profit: 6 (at 68) (68 − 67 + 2 × 2.5)

Break-even Points: 62 (68 − 6)/74(68 + 6)

by rolling down to a lower strike price. This is accomplished by buying back (and liquidating) the two 72 calls at an assumed price of one. Two 68 calls would then be sold at an assumed price of 2.5 to roll down to a 2/1 covered write with 68 calls, thereby reestablishing a neutral position.

As shown in Exhibit 19, at the liquidation of the 72 strike price 2/1 covered write, the investor has a profit of one, which is the net of a loss of four on the long futures (from 71 to 67), and a profit of five on the two 72 calls (sold at 3.5 and bought back at one). The decrease in the 72 call premium is due to a decrease in time value, which resulted from the passage of time, and of the call moving from at the money to out of the money.

The investor then sells two 68 calls at 2.5 to reestablish the neutral position. This new covered write has, at expiration, a maximum profit of six (at the price of 68) and break-even points of 62/74, thus being neutral given the current price of 67. While the covered write with the 68 call, with the futures price of 67 provides a break-even range of 62/74, which is slightly bullish, a slightly bearish situation would have resulted from rolling to the 66 strike price instead. A trapezoidal hedge (66/68) could, of course, give a neutral break-even range.

It is important to note that even though the break-even range of the original 72 strike price covered write was 64/80, these break-even points applied to expiration when the 72 call premium had no time value remaining. In the example herein, the futures price had decreased to 67 prior to expiration, and the 72 call premium still had 1.0 time value in it. Thus, at this time prior to expiration, if the futures price had declined to 67, the original covered write would not have been at a break-even as it would have been at expiration, but at a loss of 2.0, as shown below:

Loss on Futures: $64 - 71 = -7$

Gain on 72 Calls: $2 \times (3.5 - 1) = 5$

Net Loss: 2

Thus, prior to expiration, when the time value of the call premium has not completely collapsed, the break-even points are closer to the original futures price than they are at expiration. In this example, at the time prior to expiration considered, the lower break-even point would be 66 rather than 64.

Roll Up

Now consider the management in response to an increase in the futures price from 71 to 75. This roll-up of the initial covered write is summarized in Exhibit 20. When the futures price increases from 71 to 75, the premium of the 72 calls correspondingly increases to four, there is a net profit on the initial position of three as shown below:

Gain on futures position: $75 - 71 = 4$
Loss on 72 Calls: $2 \times (4 - 3.5) = 1$
Net Gain: 3

EXHIBIT 20
Roll Up of Covered Write

A. *Initial*

Futures Price = 71

72 Calls @ 3.5
(intrinsic value = 0; time value = 3.5)

Sell 2 72 Calls @ 3.5

Maximum Profit = 8 (at 72)
Break-even Points: 64/80

B. *Subsequent*

Futures Price = 75

72 Calls @ 4
(intrinsic value = 3; time value = 1.0)

76 Calls @ 2.5
(intrinsic value = 0; time value = 2.5)

Roll Up

Buy 2 72 Calls @ 4
Sell 2 76 Calls @ 2.5

Profit/Loss on initial covered write:
—Gain on futures = $75 - 71 = 4$
—Loss on calls = $2 \times (4 - 3.5) - 1$
Net Gain (Loss) = $4 - 1 = 3$ (gain)

New Covered Write:

Long 1 Futures
Short 2 76 Calls @ 2.5
Maximum Profit 6 (at 76)
$(70 - 75 + 2 \times 2.5)$
Break-even Points: 70(76 − 6)/82 (76 + 6)

But, at a futures price of 75, the 72 covered write strategy is no longer neutral, since its break-even points are 64/80.

To reestablish a neutral position, the writer may liquidate his two 72 calls at 4.0 and sell two 76 calls at 2.5. This new position has break-even points of 70 and 82 and is again approximately neutral. To be exact, it is slightly bullish. Rolling to a 74 strike price instead of the 76 strike price would have provided a slightly bearish covered write position. Again, a trapezoidal hedge (74/76) would provide a neutral break-even range.

The profit from the initial covered write resulted in the decline in time value from 3.5 to 2.5 in the 72 call, which resulted from both the passage of time, and the call moving from at the money to in the money. If the futures price had moved from 71 to 75 in a very short period of time, the premium would not have decreased as much due to the passage of time, and the profit of the initial covered write would have been less. In addition, as discussed for the roll down, even though the break-even points for the initial covered write were 64/80, these break-even points applied to expiration and, thus, since the time at which the futures price was at 75 in this example was assumed to be prior to expiration, the break-even range at this time would be narrower.

To have the potential to roll a covered call down or up before a loss is incurred, it is desirable to have both the next higher and lower strike prices within the profit or break-even range. This is one reason for using a trapezoidal covered write—it broadens the profit range. But, since the break-even points refer to expiration, even if the expiration break-even points include the next higher and lower strike prices, a quick and significant price increase or decrease may provide a price outside the profit range at that time.

The basic philosophy of a covered write is to profit from the reduction in the time premium of a short call, as it decreases over time, while the price of the underlying remains approximately the same. By rolling the strike price of the call down or up as the price of the underlying changes, there are two advantages. First, as indicated above, it allows the covered writer to reestablish a neutral position. But, second, and most importantly, it allows the covered writer to buy back a call that has moved from at the money to either in or out of the money and selling a call that is at the money. This is beneficial for the writer, because at-the-money calls have the maximum time value, that is, have greater time value than in-the-money or out-of-the-money calls. Thus, the covered writer is buying a call that has had its time value decline for this reason, and selling an at-the-money call with greater time value.

Of course, one way to respond to a quick and significant upward or downward move in the underlying price is to liquidate the covered write. This should be done if the basic view has changed, and is now that the underlying price will subsequently be volatile. However, if the basic view is that the underlying price will be stable at the new price, rolling up or down to reestablish a new neutral position may be appropriate.

Another aspect of neutrality, discussed above, concerns the hedge ratio, that is, the number of calls written against the underlying. This, too, can be managed as the price of the underlying changes.

Managing the Hedge Ratio

As discussed above, the neutrality of a hedge is affected by the number of calls sold. An initially neutral covered write is achieved by selling a number of calls equal to the reciprocal of the delta of the call. A 1/1 write is neutral/bullish as discussed above, and selling a large number of calls against one underlying will be neutral to bearish. However, as discussed above, as the underlying price increases or decreases, the delta increases or decreases, respectively, and the initially delta neutral covered write is no longer neutral.

Thus, to maintain neutrality, the delta neutral covered writer should adjust the number of calls written as the underlying price changes. As summarized in Exhibit 21, as the underlying price increases, the delta increases. Thus, the number of calls held short should be decreased relative to the amount

EXHIBIT 21
Delta Neutral Call Writing

In the limit, becomes a 1/1 Write
(Covered Write)

Underlying Price Increase
—Delta Increases
—Hedge Ratio Decreases
(Emphasizes futures/bonds relative
to short calls)
Liquidate (Buy Back) Calls
Buy More Futures/Bonds

Initial Price—Delta Neutral
Underlying Price Decrease
—Delta Decreases
—Hedge Ratio Increases
(Emphasizes short calls relative to
futures/bonds)
Sell More Calls
Sell Futures/Bonds

In the limit, becomes a Naked Write
(Large Number of Calls relative
to futures/bonds held)

of underlying held. To achieve this, calls can be bought (liquidating short calls), or more of the underlying asset purchased. In the limit, for a delta equal to one for deep-in-the-money calls, the writer will have a 1/1 or covered write.

On the other hand, as the underlying price decreases, the delta decreases and the number of calls that should be held short against the underlying should be increased. This can be accomplished by selling more calls or selling some of the underlying. In the limit, as the price decreases toward zero for a deep-out-of-the-money call, the delta approaches zero, the hedge ratio approaches infinity, and the covered write becomes a naked write (with a very large number of calls sold against the amount of the underlying).

The hedge ratio can be changed frequently, by buying or selling calls or the underlying, to adjust to changes in the underlying price. Frequent changes, however, lead to large commissions and may be time consuming. This tradeoff must be considered.

While managing a covered write by rolling the strike price up or down and by delta hedge ratio adjustment have been discussed separately, they are usually done together. In fact, if a writer had an initial delta neutral position and then decided to roll up or down due to underlying price changes, he would use the delta of the new call sold to determine the number of calls at the new strike price to be sold (the hedge ratio). He would, thus, be combining a roll and a hedge ratio adjustment.

While delta adjustments should always be made for a roll for a delta neutral strategy, delta adjustments can be made even without rolling to new strike prices, that is at the same strike price(s). Whether making a hedge ratio adjustment without a strike price roll should be done or not, depends to some extent on the width of the strike price intervals. The smaller the strike price intervals, the less the need for delta adjustment prior to the need for a strike price roll.

Protecting Profits

Protecting profits considers a covered writing strategy which has already accrued profits due to the passage of time and the stability of prices, and the reassessment of the strategy to protect these profits.

Consider the covered writing strategy in Exhibit 7. Originally, two 70 June calls were sold for four when the underlying was priced at 70. The original break-even range was 63/77, and the maximum profit was eight at the strike price of 70. Assume that, as time passes, the underlying price decreases from 71 to 70 and the June 70 call premium declines to two. Thus, there is at this time a profit of four on the position. The writers may wish to protect this profit while still attempting to gain the remaining four of the initial maximum profit of eight. He can do so by considering his present position as an initial position, and initiating a new incremental ratio writing strategy.

At this new initial position, the (incremental) maximum profit will be 4 $(70 - 70 + 2 \times 2 = 4)$ and the break-even points will now be 66 $(70 - 4)/74(70 + 4)$. By considering the new position as an initial position, and then considering only the incremental returns, having already incorporated the profits of four, the incremental maximum profit will be four and the incremental break-even points will be 66/74. The covered write could then be closed out at either of these prices to lock in the previous profit of four.

This example was for a 2/1 ratio write. If the call write had been a delta neutral write, the number of calls written could have been adjusted for the new delta of the call at this time also. If there had been a small change in the underlying price, but there was nevertheless a profit, it may be desirable to roll down or up to a different strike price while using the narrower break-even points, which would lock in the accumulated profit. In addition, it may be desirable to roll back to a more deferred contract with the narrower break-even points. However, since premium collapse accelerates near expiration, it may not be desirable to roll back too soon.

Thus, by using such an adjustment, a manager can consider accumulated profits as if realized while continuing to attempt to realize incremental profits. The manager can continue to bring his break-even points closer together and finally roll into the next expiration series.

Overview of Strategy Management

Call writing is a strategy with many potential types of outcomes, depending on the particular application. Naked call writing is a bearish strategy—it has limited downside profit potential but unlimited upside risk. A (1/1) covered call write combines a short call (bearish) with an equal dollar value of the underlying (bullish) and is net a bullish strategy—it has limited upside potential but unlimited downside risk.

In a (2/1) ratio write, calls are sold with a greater dollar

value than the value of the underlying held, in effect adding
bearish naked calls to a bullish covered call. Ratio writes,
thus, become neutral strategies. Ratio writes have unlimited
upside risk (if exercised, the investor does not own enough
underlying to deliver on the short calls) and unlimited downside risk (unlimited loss potential due to the decline in the
value of underlying). By selling additional calls, the profit of
the call writing strategy if the price remains the same increases.

This observation relates to the fundamental concept of
call writing, profiting from the erosion of the time value of
the call premium if the underlying price remains the same
(and the intrinsic value of the call premium remains the same).
The more calls that are sold, the greater the profit from the
erosion of time value. And it is this concept that dictates that-
at-the-money calls be written because they have the greatest
time value. In addition, at-the-money calls are most neutral
in the sense of a symmetric break-even range. But, by selling
more naked calls, the profit/loss profile of the strategy
changes.

An important aspect of a call writing program is its bull-
ish/bearish sentiment, which relates to the range of profitability with respect to the current price. This is illustrated in Exhibit 22.

There are two factors that determine the bullish/bearish
inclination, the number of calls sold and the strike price(s)

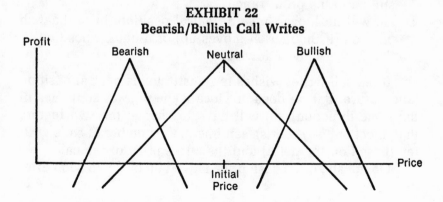

EXHIBIT 22
Bearish/Bullish Call Writes

in the write. Consider the number of calls sold first. Obviously in a ratio write, naked calls, which are bearish, are added to a covered call; so the more calls sold, the more bearish the strategy. Thus, a 3/1 ratio write is more bearish than a 2/1 ratio write. And a ratio write based on the call's delta is neutral, at least at the initial price.

With respect to the choice of the strike price (or prices), the higher the strike price(s) of the call (that is, the more out-of-the-money), the more bullish the strategy. Higher strike prices provide more profit potential on the upside, because they are less likely to be exercised for upward price moves and, if so, only at the higher strike price. However, relative to at-the-money calls, writing out-of-the-money calls provides less premium, because the time values are less.

On the other hand, writing in-the-money calls makes the strategy more bearish, but also provides less income due to time value than at-the-money calls. Thus, the choice of strike prices is an important decision in call writing strategies.

This section provides the basis for the consideration of managing or altering covered writing strategies, as the underlying price increases or decreases. Consider a call writer who initially establishes a delta neutral covered write with the at-the-money strike price call, planning to profit as the time value of the premium erodes. If the market moves up or down, there may be two outcomes:

1. He will not achieve his maximum profit although he *may* still be in his profit range;
2. He will no longer have a neutral position, but a bearish position (if the market moves up) or a bullish position (if the market moves down).

If the call writer wishes to reinstitute his neutral position (and assure that he does not lose if the market continues in the same direction), he will have to change the two factors that affect bullish/bearish sentiment, the number of calls written (based on the delta) and the strike price of the call.

Obviously, if the cash price moved up or down soon after

the covered write is established, there will be little erosion of time value and, thus, little profit in the strategy, if any.

As indicated above, the basic concept of covered call writing is to profit from the erosion of time value of the calls written with stable underlying prices. In this context, the profit/loss profiles throughout this chapter apply to the time of option expiration when the time value had become zero. These profiles, thus, provide the maximum profit, since the time value erosion was at its maximum.

Obviously, for a short holding period, the maximum profit would be much smaller since the time value would not erode completely. And obviously, if the underlying price moved up or down considerably soon after the covered write was established, there may be little profit and, in fact, since the break-even points would be close to the initial price, there may even be a loss.

ANALYSIS OF RATES OF RETURNS ON COVERED WRITING STRATEGIES

In implementing a covered writing strategy, simulations of alternative covered writing strategies being considered are useful to evaluate:

1. The rate of return of covered writes during rising, decreasing and flat markets;
2. The effect of the passage of time (futures convergence and accrued interest) on the rate of return on a covered write;
3. The effect of various in- and out-of-the-money strike prices on the rate of return on a covered write under different price environments; and
4. The effect of various strike prices and hedge ratios on covered writing strategies.

The results of a very flexible program to provide such simulations is demonstrated in this section. The formulas used in this program for calculating the net profit or loss and the rate of return on covered writes with varying strike prices and hedge ratios, in addition to Treasury bonds unhedged and hedged with Treasury bond futures, are provided in the Appendix. The program allows for the specification of:

1. The underlying Treasury bond and its initial price;
2. The initial Treasury bond futures price (which specifies the cash/futures basis);
3. The final Treasury bond price and the final cash/futures basis;
4. The length of the holding period;
5. The strike price of the calls written; and
6. The number of calls written against the Treasury bonds.

Exhibits 23, 24 and 25 show the results of a 1/1 write of call options against $1 million of the 10⅜ percent Treasury bond of 11/15/12 (assumed to be the cheapest deliverable on the futures contract) (which has a factor of 1.25 against the June, '84 futures contract, and so 12.5 calls are written) for the following changes in the Treasury bond price, respectively: (1) two point increase; (2) no change in price, and (3) two point decrease. The dollar value of the profit and loss and the percent rate of return are shown in the bottom two lines of Exhibits 23, 24 and 25. The rate of return results are summarized in Exhibit 26.

Since the initial futures price is 70—29, the 70 and 72 strike prices straddle the initial underlying price and are both near the money. As indicated in column (4) of Exhibit 26, the variation in the rate of return due to changes in the Treasury bond price is least for the Treasury bond hedged by short futures (this variation is due to basis risk), and greatest for unhedged bonds.

Within the call writing categories, across strike prices, the higher the strike price, that is, the more out of the money the call, the greater the potential gain; but also the greater the potential loss, that is, the greater the variance in the return (the greater the "risk"). The lower the strike price, that is,

EXHIBIT 23

Results of a 1/1 Covered Call Strategy Versus a Short T-Bond Futures Strategy; Two Point Increase in Cash Market Price

ASSUMPTIONS:

Date: 1/30/84
Holding period: 19 days
Face value of debt securities: $1 million
T-bond price: 89.18 (10.375% of 11/15/12—cheapest to deliver)
T-bond futures price: 70.29
Basis: 0.30

STRATEGIES:

(1) Short 12.5 June '84 T-bond futures contracts (10.375s have a factor of 1.25 against the futures contract)
(2) Write 12.5 call options (strike prices and premiums assumed below)

MARKET SCENARIO:

Cash price of T-bonds up 2 points to 91.18
Cash/futures basis unchanged

T-Bond Futures Price	Results of: Short Futures	Results of 1/1 covered call strategy					
		Premium: 4.58	2.58	1.04	0.09	0.01	0.01
		Strike: 66	68	70	72	74	76
72.16	79	80	80	2,032	15,508	20,195	20,195
72.17	− 311	− 311	− 311	1,642	15,118	20,195	20,195
72.18	− 702	− 701	− 701	1,252	14,727	20,195	20,195
72.19	−1,093	−1,092	−1,092	861	14,336	20,195	20,195
72.20	−1,483	−1,482	−1,482	471	13,946	20,195	20,195
72.21	−1,874	−1,873	−1,873	80	13,555	20,195	20,195
72.22	−2,264	−2,264	−2,264	− 311	13,165	20,195	20,195
72.23	−2,654	−2,654	−2,654	− 701	12,774	20,195	20,195
72.24	−3,045	−3,045	−3,045	−1,092	12,383	20,195	20,195
Plus accrued interest:	5,416	5,416	5,416	5,416	5,416	5,416	5,416
Net profit/loss:	2,370	2,370	2,370	4,323	17,799	25,611	25,611
Rate of return (%):	4.90	5.25	5.10	9.06	36.84	52.91	52.91
Unhedged rate of return (%):	52.50						

EXHIBIT 24

Results of a 1/1 Covered Call Strategy Versus a Short T-Bond Futures Strategy; No Price Change in Cash Market

ASSUMPTIONS:

Date: 1/30/84

Holiday period: 19 days

Face value of debt securities: $1 million

T-bond price: 89.18 (10.375% of 11/15/12—cheapest to deliver)

T-bond futures price: 70.29

Basis: 0.30

STRATEGIES:

(1) Short 12.5 June '84 T-bond futures contracts (10.375s have a factor of 1.25 against the futures contract)

(2) Write 12.5 call options (strike prices and premiums assumed below)

MARKET SCENARIO:

Cash price of T-bonds unchanged at 89.18

T-bond Futures Price	Results of: Short Futures	Results of 1/1 Covered Call Strategy					
		Premium:	4.58	2.58	1.04	0.09	0.01	0.01
		Strike:	66	68	70	72	74	76
70.29	0		0	0	1953	1,758	195	195
70.30	− 391		− 391	− 391	1,562	1,758	195	195
70.31	− 781		− 781	− 781	1,172	1,758	195	195
71.00	−1,172		−1,172	−1,172	781	1,758	195	195
71.01	−1,562		−1,562	−1,562	391	1,758	195	195
71.02	−1,953		−1,953	−1,953	−0	1,758	195	195
71.03	−2,344		−2,344	−2,344	− 391	1,758	195	195
71.04	−2,734		−2,734	−2,734	− 781	1,758	195	195
71.05	−3,125		−3,125	−3,125	−1,172	1,758	195	195
Plus accrued interest:	5,416		5,416	5,416	5,416	5,416	5,416	5,416
Net profit/loss:	2,290		2,291	2,291	4,244	7,173	5,611	5,611
Rate of return (%):	4.73		5.07	4.93	8.89	14.85	11.59	11.59
Unhedged rate of return (%):	11.19							

EXHIBIT 25

Results of a 1/1 Covered Call Strategy Versus a Short T-Bond Futures Strategy: Two Point Decrease in Cash Market Price

ASSUMPTIONS:
Date: 1/30/84
Holding period: 19 days
Face value of debt securities: $1 million
T-bond price: 89.18 (10.375% of 11/15/12—cheapest to deliver)
T-bond futures price: 70.29
Basis: 0.30

STRATEGIES:
(1) Short 12.5 June '84 T-bond futures contracts (10.375s have a factor of 1.25 against the futures contract)
(2) Write 12.5 call options (strike prices and premiums assumed below)

MARKET SCENARIO:
Cash price of T-bonds down 2 points to 87.18
Cash/futures basis unchanged

T-bond Futures Price	Results of: Short Futures	Results of 1/1 Covered Call Strategy					
		Premium: 4.58	2.58	1.04	0.09	0.01	0.01
		Strike: 66	68	70	72	74	76
69.10	− 80	− 80	− 80	−6,720	−18,242	−19,805	−19,805
69.11	− 471	− 470	− 470	−6,720	−18,242	−19,805	−19,805
69.12	− 861	− 861	− 861	−6,720	−18,242	−19,805	−19,805
69.13	−1,252	−1,252	−1,252	−6,720	−18,242	−19,805	−19,805
69.14	−1,642	−1,642	−1,642	−6,720	−1,8242	−19,805	−19,805
69.15	−2,033	−2,033	−2,033	−6,720	−18,242	−19,805	−19,805
69.16	−2,424	−2,423	−2,424	−6,720	−18,242	−19,805	−19,805
69.17	−2,814	−2,814	−2,814	−4,720	−18,242	−19,805	−19,805
Plus accrued interest:	5,416	5,416	5,416	5,416	5,416	5,416	5,416
Net profit/loss:	2,602	2,602	2,602	−1,304	−12,827	−14,389	−14,389
Rate of return (%):	5.37	5.76	5.60	−2.73	−26.55	−29.73	−29.73
Unhedged rate of return (%):	−30.13						

EXHIBIT 26
Rate of Return (%) of Covered Writing Strategies*

	Initial Premium	Change in Cash Price of 10¾ T-Bond*			Range (Max–Min)
		Up Two Points	Flat	Down Two Points	
Short Futures	—	4.90%	4.73%	5.37%	0.47%
66	4 – 58	5.25%	5.07%	5.76%(Max)	0.51%
68	2 – 58	5.10%	4.93%	5.60%	0.50%
70	1 – 04	9.06%	8.89%	−2.73%	11.79%
72	0 – 09	36.84%	14.85%(Max)	−26.55%	63.39%
74	0 – 01	52.91%	11.59%	−29.73%	82.64%
76	0 – 01	51.91%(Max)	11.59%	−29.73%	82.64%
Unhedged Bond	—	52.50%	11.19%	−30.13%	82.63%

* Initial Cash Price: 89–18
  Initial Futures Price: 70–29

the more in the money the call, the less the upside potential, but the less the downside loss (that is, the less the risk).

The reasons for these results across various call option strike prices are as follows. Writing out-of-the-money calls, for example, the 76 strike price, provides the least premium income (0–01 for the 76 strike price), thus the least profit if the underlying price decreases, and the greatest loss for a downward price move. On the other hand, out-of-the-money calls are less likely to be exercised, and if so, they will be exercised at a higher strike price. Out-of-the-money calls, thus, have the greatest potential gain.

At-the-money calls have smaller premiums (1–04 for 70), and thus have smaller maximum losses if the market moves down. However, they are more likely to be exercised, and if so, at a lower strike price, and thus have smaller maximum profit. However, at-the-money calls have the greatest time value component of their premium, and so have the greatest profit during a stable market. In-the-money calls (low strike prices) have even smaller maximum gains and smaller maximum losses.

Overall, the dollar value of the profit/loss profiles for covered call writes with in-, at-, and out-of-the-money calls are

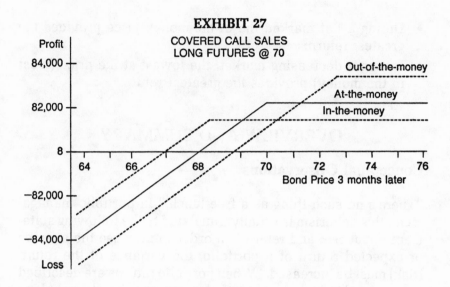

EXHIBIT 27

COVERED CALL SALES
LONG FUTURES @ 70

shown in Exhibit 27. As discussed, the covered write with the in-the-money call is the least aggressive, in that it has the smallest profit if the market moves up, but the smallest loss if the market moves down, due to its greater premium and lower strike price. The out-of-the-money write provides the greatest possible gain if the market moves up, but the greatest loss if the market moves down. The at-the-money call write is between these two extremes for upward or downward moves in the market, but, importantly, note that for a stable market, the profit is the greatest for the at-the-money call, due to its maximum time value.

It is obvious that the selection of the strike price is important in the development of a covered call writing strategy. As discussed above, it relates to the desired bullishness or bearishness of the view with out-of-the-money calls being most bullish and vice versa.

In general:

• During an increasing market, the highest strike price (most out of the money) provides the greatest return;

- During a flat market, the at-the-money price provides the greatest return;
- During a decreasing market, the lowest strike price (most in the money) provides the greatest return.

OVERVIEW AND SUMMARY

Conceptual Observations

"There's no such thing as a free lunch." In portfolio management, this aphorism is usually translated to the following statement about risk and return: "In order to increase the average or expected return of a portfolio, the variance of the return (risk) must be increased." When portfolio returns are described by a normal distribution, portfolios can only be altered along mean-variance lines. However, it has recently been appreciated in stock options that the options markets provide a way to expand the set of investment alternatives by increasing the range of return characteristics the investor can control. "Indeed, the range of returns that can be created through the use of the option markets makes the two-dimensional trade-offs of conventional mean-variance portfolio theory obsolete."[8]

The return distribution for portfolios is generally thought to be symmetric around the mean. But, as options are added to a portfolio, the distribution can be changed into a number of different forms. The upper and lower tails of the distribution can be truncated, leaving the investor with little risk of a loss or little potential for a large gain, or a large portion of the probability distribution centered in a particular range giving a high probability of receiving that range of returns.

Writing call options on a portfolio provides a specific application of these concepts. Exhibit 28 shows the return distribution for a portfolio with calls written at a strike price 15

---

[8] Richard Bookstaber and Roger Clarke, "Options Can Alter Portfolio Return Distributions," *The Journal of Portfolio Management,* Spring, 1981, p. 63.

EXHIBIT 28
Portfolio Covered with
Varying Proportions of
Short Call

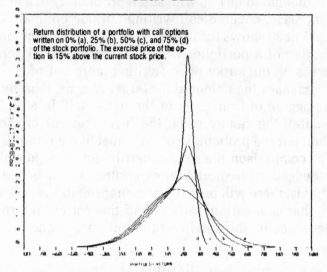

Return distribution of a portfolio with call options
written on 0% (a), 25% (b), 50% (c), and 75% (d)
of the stock portfolio. The exercise price of the option is 15% above the current stock price.

Source: Richard Bookstaber and Roger Clarke, "Options Can Alter Portfolio
Return Distributions," *The Journal of Portfolio Management*, Spring, 1981, p. 66.

percent higher than the current market written on 0, 25, 50
and 75 percent of the portfolio. Writing options on the portfolio
reduces the upward potential of the portfolio, since appreciation is limited to 15 percent before the underlying reaches
the strike price and is called away. The distribution is further
truncated when call options are written on 100 percent of the
portfolio.

There are several important observations that can be
made from Exhibit 28. The usual attraction of a covered writing
program is that it increases the probability of a moderate return, that is, the mode of the return distribution, as measured
by the highest point of the probability distribution, is higher.
But, due to elimination of the potential for high gains, the
mean return for a portfolio covered with short calls is lower.

Thus, a portfolio with short calls has a higher mode, or

most likely return, but a lower mean return due to the elimination of the potential for very high returns, that is, the truncation
of the upper tail of the return distribution. But, if the environment is thought to be one with small probability of a prolonged
price increase, covered call writing may be optimal.

Exhibit 29 shows the effect of the strike price on the return
distribution of a portfolio with calls written on 75 percent of
it. Increasing the strike price (writing more out of the money
calls) increases the potential for larger returns, thereby reducing the degree of truncation of the upper tail. In addition, for
more out-of-the-money calls, the level (return) of the mode
is higher, but the probability of this most likely return is lower.

For comparison the return distribution of a portfolio perfectly hedged with short futures contracts will be a vertical
line, that is, there will be a 100 percent probability of a specific
return, that is, a certain return. And this certain return would
be, theoretically, the risk free rate. Both upper and lower tails

EXHIBIT 29
Portfolio Covered by Short Calls
of Varying Degrees Out of the Money

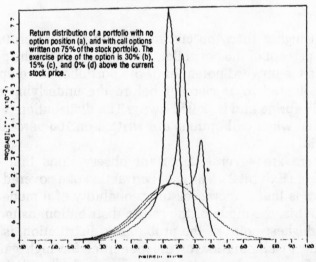

Return distribution of a portfolio with no
option position (a), and with call options
written on 75% of the stock portfolio. The
exercise price of the option is 30% (b),
15% (c), and 0% (d) above the current
stock price.

Source: Richard Bookstaber and Roger Clarke, "Options Can Alter Portfolio
Return Distributions," *The Journal of Portfolio Management,* Spring, 1981, p. 66.

will be truncated; but, in practice, due to basis risk there will be some variation in the return distribution. And, the level and distribution of this return depends on the level of futures price relative to the cash price at the time the hedge is put on.

Thus, the addition of options, in this case covered calls, to a portfolio can significantly alter the return/risk choice pattern usually considered to be confined to normally distributed portfolio returns. But this broader range of choices makes even more important the specification of the portfolio managers' investment goals regarding risk and return.

Overview

Equity managers have been using covered call writing strategies as a means of enhancing the yield on their portfolio and provide a degree of downside protection since the advent of exchange-traded calls on stocks in 1973. With the introduction of options on the liquid Treasury bond futures contract during 1982, fixed income portfolio managers can now accomplish the same objectives.

However, as explained in this chapter, while covered call writing is basically a neutral strategy, its degree of neutrality or bullishness/bearishness can be affected by the number of calls written against the underlying bonds and the strike price(s) of the calls written.

The first section of this chapter discusses some of the fundamental concepts of covered call writing that apply to stock options as well as Treasury bond futures options. The second section discusses the special considerations in using the Treasury bond futures options to write calls on specific Treasury bonds, and relates general covered call writing concepts to writing Treasury bond futures calls on specific Treasury bonds.

The third section discusses the management of covered call writing strategies, which is very important, since all covered writes have unlimited loss potential in at least one market direction, and some in both market directions. The fourth section presents the results of the analysis of the rates of return on alternative covered writes and compares these rates of return of holding Treasury bonds hedged with Treasury bond futures contracts and unhedged.

After the short trading history of the Treasury bond futures option, many fixed income managers are adopting strategies that have been used by equity managers for years. This use is certain to increase.

Before engaging in a covered call writing program, however, the purpose of such a program should be clear. First, negatively, covered call writing should not be done to hedge a bond or a bond portfolio. Short futures and long puts are hedges, in that they limit the maximum loss of a bond or a bond portfolio, although in different ways. Writing calls against a bond or a bond portfolio does not limit the loss—in a declining market, the loss in a covered call portfolio is unlimited.

Rather, covered call writing is a yield enhancement strategy for an expected neutral environment. In rapidly rising markets, covered call writing strategies are not optimal, because the maximum appreciation that can be experienced is determined by the strike price of the calls written (plus the initial time value of the premium). In declining markets, the underlying asset held depreciates in price and, while the loss in the value of the asset held is mitigated by the initial value of the call premium, there is, nevertheless, an unlimited loss on the bond or portfolio.

In stable markets, however, the covered call writer experiences neither the actual loss on his portfolio, due to a declining market, nor the opportunity loss due to not participating to the limit of a rising market, but benefits from the premium received from selling the calls. If the underlying price remains stable, and there is no increase in the volatility of the call, the passage of time will lead to a reduction in the time value of the call premium and a profit in the calls sold. This is the basis for profiting from covered call writing—to realize the profit from the decrease in the time value component of the premium due to the passage of time.

The risks of covered call writing strategies are:

1. An increase in the market price, leading to a loss on the call (and an exercise of the call);
2. A decrease in the market price, leading to a loss on the underlying asset;
3. A significant move in the market price in either direction soon after the covered write is initiated, leading to a loss;
4. An increase in the implied volatility in the call, leading to an increase in the call premium and loss on the calls sold; and
5. The use of a delta in delta neutral covered writing that is too high or low.

As indicated, however, covered call writing can be used as a means of yield enhancement in a stable environment and of reducing the variability of the return on the portfolio, not as a hedge. Now, fixed income managers can use the same mechanism to achieve the yield enhancement/risk reduction results that equity managers have used extensively for at least a decade.

APPENDIX

Rate of Return on Covered Write on Treasury Bond

This appendix provides the method for calculating the rate of return on a covered write with the Treasury bond futures option contract on an actual Treasury bond.

Equations:

$$TI = PC1 + AIP - NO \times OP1$$
$$RCU = (PC2 - PC1) - NO \times IV$$
where
$$IV = \text{Max} ((F.P. - K), 0), \text{ so}$$

$$RCU = (PC2 - PC1) - NO \times Max. ((F.P. - K), 0)$$

$$RR = \frac{RCU + AIE}{TI} \times \frac{360}{ND}$$

Legend:

TI —Total Investment
PC1 —Initial Cash Price
PC2 —Final Cash Price
OP1 —Initial Call Price
OP2 —Final Call Price
FP2 —Futures Price at Expiration of Call
NO —Number of Calls Written
K   —Strike Price of Call
F   —Conversion Factor of Bond
AIP —Accrued Interest Paid (at purchase of bond)
AIE —Accrued Interest Earned (over holding period)
ND —Number of Days in Holding Period
RR —Rate of Return (over holding period)
RCU—Return or Call/Underlying
IV   —Intrinsic Value of Call at Expiration

1. *Out-of-Money (Expires worthless) OP2 = 0:*
$$FP2 < K$$
$$FP2 - K < 0$$
$$Max ((FP2 - K), 0) = 0$$
$$RCU = PC2 - PC1$$
$$RR = \frac{RCU + AIE}{TI} \times \frac{360}{ND}$$
$$= \frac{PC2 - PC1 + AIE}{PC1 + AIP - NO \times OP1} \times \frac{360}{ND}$$

2. *In-the-Money (will be exercised):*
$$FP2 > K$$
$$FP2 - K > 0$$
$$Max((F.P. - K), 0) = FP2 - K$$

(OP2 = FP2 − K, the intrinsic value, at expiration

RCU = PC2 − PC1 − NO × (FP2 − K)

$$RR = \frac{RCU + AIE}{TI} \times \frac{360}{ND}$$

$$= \frac{PC2 - PC1 - NO \times (FP2 - K) + AIE}{PC1 + AIP - NO \times OP1} \times \frac{360}{ND}$$

3. *General:*

RCU = PC2 − PC1 − NO × OP2

where $OP2 = \begin{cases} FP2 - K, \text{ if in the money at expiration} \\ 0, \text{ if out of money at expiration} \end{cases}$

and

$$RR = \frac{PC2 - PC1 + AIE - NO \times OP2}{PC1 + AIP - NO \times OP1}$$

$$= \frac{(PC2 - NO \times OP2) - PC1 + AIE}{PC1 + AIP - NO \times OP1}$$

a) For out-of-money option, OP2 = 0 and

$$RR = \frac{PC2 - PC1 + AIE}{PC1 + AIP - NO \times OP1}$$

For the cheapest deliverable, FP2 = (1/F) × PC2 < K at expiration. Thus PC2 < (F × K) at expiration for the call option to be out of money.

b) For in the money option, OP2 = FP2 − K, and

$$RR = \frac{PC2 - NO \times (FP2 - K) - PC1 + AIE}{PC1 + AIP - NO \times OP1}$$

$$= \frac{PC2 - NO \times FP2 + NO \times K - PC1 + AIE}{PC1 + AIP - NO \times OP1}$$

For a dollar for dollar covered write, NO = F and, since the factored basis (B) is B = PC2 − F × FP2,

$$RR = \frac{B + NO \times K - PC1 + AIE}{PC1 + AIP - NO \times OP1}$$

Observations

1. For *out-of-money* call options at expiration (FP2 < K), the covered writer keeps the entire premium, OP1, that is, he

does not lose due to premium OP2, since OP2 = 0. There may be a capital gain PC2 − PC1 but PC2 can go up no more than to a level that makes the option at-the-money, that is, PC2 = F × K. There may also be an unlimited capital loss.

2. For *in-the-money* call options may have exercise at any time prior to expiration or at expiration. In this case OP2 > 0, so this amount is *subtracted* from the return of the out-of-money result, and thus the overall return may be negative if it ends up sufficiently in the money. At expiration, OP2 equals the intrinsic value (FP2 − K). The AIE refers to the actual period until exercise. At exercise, the covered writer (short call) is assigned NO short futures positions. He will then be short futures/long cash bond. The assumption is then that he liquidates his NO short futures positions (at NO × FP2) and his cash bond (at PC2). It is for this reason that the factored basis appears in the RR equation.

CHAPTER 7

Applications of Debt Options for Banks and Thrifts

John McLean Ezell
Vice President and Manager of Fixed Income Hedge
Products
Merrill Lynch Capital Markets

INTRODUCTION

With the introduction of exchange listed options on fixed income instruments in the fall of 1982, a wide array of new applications for financial intermediaries became available. Initial trading levels have been an impressive indicator of a broad interest in this area, and while most of the early participants actually using these markets have been exploring speculative or trading uses of options, there has been increasing inquiry with regard to true "hedging" or risk management possibilities as well. Continued volatility of interest rates should lead to a very widespread use of the option vehicle for the management of risk, particularly with regard to contingent assets or liabilities or in an insurance-like manner.

Proper management of risk at thrift and banking institutions must involve an awareness of the contingent nature of many of the assets and liabilities in their structure. In most cases, the institutions are effectively shorting options through the nature of their business. For example, gaps arise because depositors have the option to withdraw their money if higher rate opportunities exist. Holding fixed rate mortgages or many mortgage-backed securities is functionally very similar to being short calls due to prepayments on the mortgages underlying the securities. Optional loan commitments such as those given to developers are effectively short put positions. Even if the risk manager at a banking institution chooses not to utilize options in his risk management program, the existence of options markets will give him an excellent perspective on the market's evaluation of the actual levels of risk which are inherent in his position.

The early efforts to apply options in risk management have been primarily of an exploratory nature; and a complete analysis of uses in the bank and thrift industries must await more mature markets, as well as a more widespread knowledge on the part of market participants of the peculiar advantages and flexibilities of fully developed options markets. However, it does not require a great imagination to foresee financial institutions not only utilizing option markets to manage exposure to interest rate shifts in their existing lines of business, but that entire new product areas will be opening up, designed with the intent of placing the bank or thrift more in the role of a middleman, marketing products and servicing clients rather than absorbing the brunt of the risk in interest rate spreads. The use of options in conjunction with other tools of the cash and futures markets will enable the financial institutions of tomorrow the opportunity to maintain much better control over the exposure of their institutions to the vagaries of the market.

However, in most cases to date, these uses remain hypothetical rather than realized. Part of this is due to the natural reluctance of fiduciaries to get involved with new product areas, often for lack of trained personnel. Regulatory and accounting problems still plague many sectors of the business, but in general, seem to be in the process of resolving themselves in a manner somewhat closer to a rational treatment than has been their wont in the past. In sum, the state of the art has probably been reached where it makes sense for banks and thrifts to begin pilot programs, while the business is still in its infancy, and to develop talent for more serious applications in the future. Later, the education will likely prove to be much more expensive for accounts forced to enter the markets in size without adequate preparations of either personnel or systems.

Much has been said and written about the use of options in trading accounts to mitigate risk or enhance returns, but other than some consideration of hedging inventories of securities, that area of application is not the principal concern of this chapter. Instead, concentration will be in the area of managing risk in association with the corpus of the assets or the liabilities of the bank or savings institution. Asset management and liability management are considered separately for clarity and to highlight special applications. This is not intended to suggest that they should be managed separately, although that seems to be the reality of the situation in many institutions. Instead, the mismatch of the assets and liabilities must be weighted and aggregated to develop the nature of that exposure gap, after which they may be managed very much in the same way as a pure asset or liability.

OVERVIEW OF OPTIONS USE

Purchasing puts or calls is the simplest and cleanest use of options, and in many cases the most appropriate application due to the structure of the assets and liabilities of the typical institution. This type of transaction is quite properly viewed in the same light as the purchase of insurance. Calls are purchased to provide protection against falling rates, while puts serve to provide protection against rising rates. And, as insurance premiums decline with an increase in the size of the deductible, so the cost of hedging with long option positions is reduced as incremental interest rate risk is absorbed, that is, as the yield implied by the striking price is farther away from current rates. The principal advantage of hedging with long options is that profit opportunities of favorable rate changes are not foregone.

It is important to note that this type of hedge does have a cost. But, while the cost of hedging in the cash markets or in futures is often obscured by negative carry, convergence costs, or opportunity costs, the option cost is fully reflected in the premium. Another major advantage of this type of risk management is that it is typically less demanding on managers' time and expertise than many other forms of hedging. The lack of margin or collateral flows reduces staffing and systems requirements. Finally, the fact that loss is limited to the premium reduces the need to fine tune basis or yield curve assumptions to protect against environmental changes. These changes can lead to a situation where the position might be overhedged, leading to exposure in what would normally be favorable rate environments.

Selling calls provides some diminution of exposure to rising rates, and selling puts can cushion falling rates; but the risk reduction is limited to the amount of premium received. The main reason for employing this type of hedge is to reduce the risk of the position, without incurring the premium costs of long options, or the convergence costs of futures which reduce the yield on the position. In stable periods, selling options can actually enhance returns. However, there may be opportunity costs associated with any type of risk reduction activity involving the selling of options. For example, a long position offset with short call positions will not fully participate in substantial rallies.

When one examines the cost of hedging with options, as opposed to either cash instruments or futures, they frequently appear to be relatively expensive. In a great many instances, this appearance is due to a failure to take into account hidden cost in the futures or cash hedges. In a positive yield curve environment, for example, futures or forwards will assume a discount structure with respect to cash markets, which represents a significant cost of hedging as the discounted futures or forwards rise to converge with cash markets, producing losses on the overall position. This generally more than offsets any positive carry in the underlying instrument. Similarly, hedging the position with a short position in the cash markets, will incur negative carry. Oddly enough, though puts may look expensive, in most instances the buying of out-of-the-money puts represents the only way to take advantage of a positive yield curve without bearing the large amounts of risk in the event of very sharply increasing rates.

Prior to engaging in any risk management transaction, the option user should first ascertain whether or not he has any attitudes toward either market direction or volatility. Expectations of rate movements favorable with regard to the asset or liability being hedged, suggests less of a need to be hedged, and out-of-the-money options should be bought or sold to minimize costs or increase profit opportunities respectively. On the other hand, if rate movements are expected to move adversely to the item being hedged, at- or in-the-money options should be bought or sold, to minimize costs or to maximize the range of protection respectively. The reason behind this difference is that as the option purchased moves from being an out-of-the-money option, to being an in-the-money option its character alters from being an inexpensive insurance policy with a significant deductible, to that of being very close to a forward sale or purchase with all of the gradations in between.[1] In the case of options being sold, the in-the-money options have a much greater premium level, which provides a greater range of protection, while the out-of-the-money options have lower premiums and less of an opportunity cost if rate movements are favorable.

While the purchase or sale of an option against a position will mitigate risk, a view on the volatility of interest rates is required to take full advantage of the flexibility afforded by options. Assuming that option premium levels reflect volatility in recent markets, options should generally be purchased in a situation where increased market fluctuation is expected, and they should be sold where it is expected that rates will become more stable. Premium expansion or contraction in these events can significantly improve results.

In addition, a perspective on volatility can affect the matu-

---

[1] Alternatively for options model cognescenti, this can be expressed by the fact that as options move from being out-of-the-money to being in-the-money their "deltas" or hedge ratios are increasing.

rity of the option chosen to offset the risk. In most cases when volatility is expected in the near future it is better to buy near term options or sell more distant options. If little volatility is expected, it is preferable to sell nearby options or purchase more distant option maturities. This arises from the fact that the decay of time premium is not a linear function, but progresses much more rapidly in the latter stages of the option's life. Thus, in stable markets, the cost of purchasing a six-month option will be less on a per-day basis than two three-month options purchased sequentially. However, if there is a sharp movement of rates in either direction, then the dollar loss of time premium will be greater in the more distant option. The distinction can be critical when hedging a flow of assets or liabilities, such as a mortgage commitment pipeline, as the longer-term options can be used to cover more than one commitment in the flow if markets are stable, but would serve to protect only what was in the pipeline at the moment in the event of an adverse rate movement. Proper management of this type of flow can result in considerable savings over time.

Finally it is extremely important not to judge the results of each individual hedge. Instead, a program must be allowed to operate over several accounting periods. Savings through hedging occur only during certain periods of the interest rate cycle, and hedging is always suboptimal if it is assumed that interest rates really are predictable. Therefore, those who choose to engage in risk-reducing activities using either futures or options, are often subject to considerable second guessing. Successful programs allow time for the manager to progress along the learning curve, and examine results only after several years of application.

THE NATURE OF THE RISKS TO BE MANAGED

Another key determinant of success in hedging is the choice of markets in which to place the hedges. There are exchange listed markets for a variety of specific Treasury issues, and on some futures contracts. In addition, there are over-the-counter options offered which can be customized to fit almost any scenario. Each of these have their own advantages and related disadvantages, and the correct choice will vary with the type of application. In general, active trading at this date seems to be concentrated in the options on futures, which therefore offer lower transaction costs for actively traded positions, through a narrower bid-ask spread. However, this comes at a cost, in that options on futures by their nature contain yield curve and basis risks which are not present in options on actual securities. An unwillingness to bear or manage this type of risk may cause a shift in the preference of option hedge to one where it is more expensive to make the initial trade, but the management of the position is more easily accomplished. Thus, it is necessary for the manager to be aware precisely of the nature of the risks he is hedging, as well as those which he continues to bear.

These risks can be loosely grouped into five different categories. First and most obvious is *price risk,* or the risk that the overall level of interest rates will change. In most cases, this type of risk is of primary concern, and its order of magnitude much greater than the other types of risk. Consequently, it is the main target of hedging programs and this book, but should not be viewed without concern for other attendant risks.

While it may seem trite, a major portion of the price risk found at many institutions and a significant problem in many hedging programs, arises from lack of precise knowledge of actual exposure. Hedging of any type of loan pipeline is virtually impossible without knowing the status of loans in the process of closing. The increasing movement toward secondary markets and securitization in the real estate loan markets seems likely to spread into other markets. For the middlemen, in particular, who do not have the luxury of burying their mistakes in their portfolios, maintenance of timely reports detailing position exposure is critical.

Yield curve risk arises from a mismatch of maturities be-

tween the asset or liability being hedged and the hedging vehicle. For example, if a portfolio of four-year Treasury notes
is being hedged with an option or future which has the 10-
year note as its underlying instrument, there is exposure to
the sort of snap-up in a positive yield curve which flattens
or inverts the curve in the four- to 10-year sector. While they
are not by any means perfect, options constitute a better type
of hedge than most for dealing with this type of risk, as, in
the face of a steepening curve, the loss is limited to the premium of the put which has been purchased to hedge the position.

A major difference between options on cash securities
and options on either futures or forwards is the yield curve
risk which is inherent in the latter. In a positive yield curve
environment, forward or futures markets generally trade at
discounts to cash with more distant months trading at lower
prices. During the cyclical flattening or inversions of the curve,
the futures or forward market will move to a premium structure, disadvantaging holders of short futures positions; and,
consequently, holders of long puts or short calls based on
the futures. Therefore, during certain segments of the business
cycle, hedgers on the short side of the market should either
prefer options on cash securities, or engage in certain types
of spread transactions which will mitigate any yield curve
risk without significant incremental exposure to price risk, although there may be losses if the curve steepens. The decision
of which method to use is based primarily on the relative
pricing of the various markets.

Basis risk is about the most difficult form of risk to deal
with effectively. It may be defined as the risk of nonparallel
movement between the asset or liability being hedged, and
the instrument or instruments underlying the option or future
which is being used to hedge the position. Managing the basis
risk between two highly diverse financial assets is extremely
difficult, particularly with regard to entirely different sectors
of the market, such as Treasuries and municipal obligations.
However, it can also lead to very attractive opportunities in
the market, when spreads are at historical highs or lows. For

example, if the yield spread between Treasury bills and CDs is extremely tight, and the curve is relatively flat, it might become very attractive to issue longer-term CDs and hedge any resulting gap with the purchase of T-bill calls, assuming reasonable premium levels. If the spread widens, either financing was achieved at a favorable rate, or there is a good probability of profit on the calls. Falling rates result in profits on the calls, reducing borrowing costs; and with rising rates the borrowing was achieved at favorable rates.

Unfortunately, the clear-cut cases where the basis relationships must work for the trade are relatively scarce, and an element of judgment must enter into the picture. For this reason, the more esoteric applications of hedging theory will remain more of an art than a science. Attempts to reduce complicated relationships between diverse securities to rules of thumb or simple regression equations, are doomed to failure unless tempered with a healthy dose of common sense and an intimate knowledge of what is going on, not only in the derivative option or futures market, but also in the underlying Treasury market and the market for the item being hedged. Since a detailed analysis of all of the various factors which make the difference between success and disaster in cross-hedging programs would require an extensive digression into the various cash market relationships, only two points will be made at this juncture. First, any simple estimates based on regression analysis should be taken with a grain of salt, particularly if between two relatively diverse types of securities such as mortgage-backed vehicles against Treasuries. Second, with access to a competent advisor as to these matters or an experienced trader, the savings will probably outweigh any incremental commission costs or advisory fees.

Volatility risk arises from the tendency of option premiums to expand when markets are moving up and/or down rapidly. Unfortunately, most novices reach their decision to begin a hedging program immediately following a very sharp movement in interest rates. Invariably, this sudden increase in interest rate movements coincides with both increased speculative activity and hedging on the same side of the market as the novice. Model afficianados will also enhance their estimates of the values of the premiums, based on their perception of increased volatility. Therefore, purchase of options are made at levels which a few days earlier would have seemed preposterous, and the poor results which tend to follow these episodes are blamed on problems in the markets rather than on the judgment of whoever decided to place the hedge after the losses were virtually predestined. The start of a hedging program should always be based on a well thought out strategy, not a knee-jerk reaction to adverse events. A well planned program, where purchases of options are made to lock in positive spreads at low premium levels is likely to provide better results, than belated purchases at inflated premium levels.

Finally, and second perhaps only to price risk in importance, is *credit risk*. As many participants in the old over-the-counter put and call market for equities and the standby markets for mortgages found, to their chagrin, a contract is only as good as the obligator on the other side of the transaction. Riskless transactions do not exist where a significant move in your favor raises spectors of bankruptcy for the opposite side of the trade. For this reason, option market participants should prefer to deal in listed markets, where the clearing corporations effectively interpose themselves between the two parties of a trade; the rules governing the transaction are very clearly spelled out, and neutral arbiters are generally readily available if disputes arise. Over-the-counter options may be of considerable use for particular circumstances, but transactions should be undertaken with established, well-capitalized firms. Saving a 32nd will seem insignificant if the principal is lost.

USE OF OPTIONS IN
ASSET MANAGEMENT

Options applications by banks and thrifts boils down to the basics of uses versus assets, and uses versus liabilities, although many different portions of an individual bank or thrift may be involved. Techniques for the application of options against the bank's portfolio are not dissimilar to techniques for applications in the trust department, although there may be significant variations in the levels of risk tolerance or leverage. Similarly, the methods for dealing with assets repricing before liabilities, closely parallel methods for dealing with liabilities repricing before assets.

The first use of options by thrifts or banks on the asset side is generally to "hedge," or more properly, to reduce the risk of a portfolio extension through the sale of calls or, less frequently, the purchase of puts. For example, when rates of interest payable to depositors were deregulated, many institutions attempted to maintain their traditional spreads either by downgrading the quality of their portfolio investments, or by extending out on a positively sloped yield curve. Since the futures markets were sharply discounted from the spot markets, the only risk reduction method which was available and did not reduce current yields, was to sell calls against the position. This proved effective during a period of time when premium levels were rather high with regard to the volatility actually experienced. They fared poorly relative to short-term investments when the market dropped sharply, though they still provided a return several hundred basis points above an unoptioned position in the underlying securities. This illustrates the use of call sales as a hedging device, which enables the manager to achieve risk/reward configurations between either a fully hedged position or a pure long position. Very fine gradations can be achieved through the use of in-the-money options (closer to a hedged position), at-the-money options (maximizing current returns), and out-of-the-money options (closer to pure positions, but with higher current returns). (See Exhibit 1.) The maturity structure of options is also incorporated into producing lower current returns, but with risk reduced commensurately.

Note that there is no particular reason that the calls must be written against the precise deliverable instrument; they may be applied to any security or loan which can be expected to vary proportionately in yield with the vehicle underlying

EXHIBIT 1
Returns Selling Calls vs. Assets

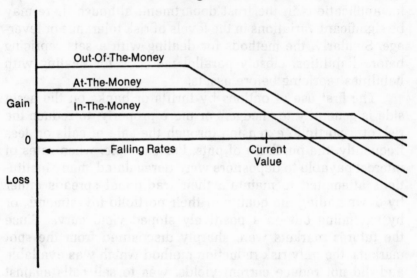

the option, assuming a degree of comfort with the basis risk. However, in practice, this sort of macro-hedging of bank portfolios seems to be more of a theoretical exercise than anything actually done, and particular positions are more often the target of hedges. This seems likely to remain the case, until there is a greater degree of economic rationality introduced into the accounting and management of portfolios carried at historic cost. Until then, there will probably be some well justified reluctance to sell calls against a historically valued portfolio, particularly one which is under water, as there is a likelihood that the prices will run up causing losses to be recognized in the option position without offsetting gains being recognized in the portfolio. Consequently, most early applications of call selling are in portfolios where gains can be recognized in the event of a rally, or which are kept on mark-to-the-market accounting.

In situations where a hedged asset position cannot afford a rally, a put hedge is generally preferable to either selling calls or futures. This might occur because of the accounting reasons cited above, or because of an inability to meet the cash flow requirements of a futures or cash hedge. The maximum loss or cash flow requirement for a put hedge is limited to the premium which is paid at the time of purchase. Another extremely useful application for put hedges occurs in cross-hedge situations, where a rally or yield curve shift would cause the Treasury underlying the hedge vehicle to outperform the issue or loan being hedged. For example, if options or futures on long-term Treasuries were being used to hedge mortgage-backed issues, a sustained rally would cause losses on futures or short call risk adjustment techniques, as the prepayment assumptions cause the mortgage-backed securities to lag the Treasuries. A put hedge in this instance would provide downside protection without exposing the position to large losses on the upside. This application should be particularly noted by thrifts with significant mortgage banking activity, as there have been several problems involving thrifts attempting to hedge mortgage obligations in the Treasury and bond futures market.

The one-sided risk feature also benefits banks, which typically are holding shorter-term securities than the 10- and 30-year Treasuries upon which the futures and options markets are based. Not only will some relief be provided from situations where the yield curve is flattening, but also from the yield distortions which may develop around supply and demand factors in the two sectors. While most of this type of situation is rapidly self-correcting, the margin flows and paper losses can prove temporarily embarrassing.

Another good application is the hedging of prime rate loans. The purchase of bill puts, perhaps in conjunction with a T-bill/CD futures spread, will provide protection against rising interest rates, and will also prove advantageous over other types of hedging methods when the prime rate adjustments in falling rate markets are somewhat sticky with regard to the rates on short-term securities.

As opposed to selling calls against a position which in-

creases the current yield on the hedged position,[2] the purchase
of puts will reduce the return being earned on the asset, and
in this sense probably produces the purest manifestation of
the cost of hedging available. The amount of the yield reduction is dependent on the time value in the put at the time of
purchase. The greatest reduction in yield comes with at-the-
money puts where the time value is maximized, while there
is less reduction for either in-the-money or out-of-the-money
puts, either of which have less time value. In return for this
reduction in yield, a hedge is provided which still enables
the investment to appreciate in the event of falling rates. The
appreciation potential for any asset is reduced by an opportunity cost equal to the size of the premium paid for the put.
Thus, an in-the-money-put hedge of an asset will cause a lesser
decline in the yield of the hedged asset than an at-the-money-
put hedge, but the overall position will be less responsive in
the event of a rally. Similarly, the opportunity cost of purchasing out-of-the-money puts is less in a rally than at-the-money
puts, but there will be a greater loss on the position if rates
rise. (See Exhibit 2.)

The purchase of out-of-the-money puts to hedge assets
can be likened in many ways to the purchase of insurance
against rising interest rates. Premiums are lower if the client
is willing to absorb some of the risk; that is, to purchase out-
of-the-money options, or the insurance policy with the larger
deductible.[3] The purchase of in-the-money puts is generally

---

[2] This is not necessarily true for European style options which can
be exercised only at maturity. All exchange listed options on cash securities
are at this time of a predominantly American option style which can be
exercised at any time. Options on futures are a hybrid in that they can
be exercised at any time; but, since the deliverable item is a futures contract,
the perversities of European options pricing can occur where a distant option
may be priced at less than its intrinsic value, thereby producing situations
where selling calls can reduce current yield or the purchase of puts could
enhance current yield over the life of the option. Pricing of cash options
can be at a discount only when cost of carry considerations and delayed
settlement cause them to trade very slightly below their intrinsic value.

[3] It is ironic to contemplate the number of asset managers who would
never consider using a small fraction of their assets to purchase puts. Most
own fire insurance on their house and would never complain if the house
didn't burn down.

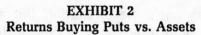

EXHIBIT 2
Returns Buying Puts vs. Assets

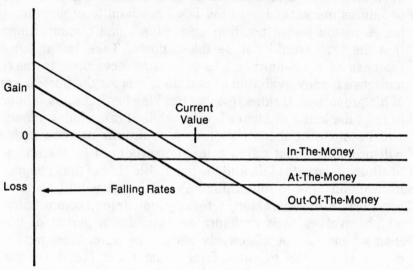

the best method for putting a floor under the rates which will be earned, while still retaining the ability to participate in large rallies.

While most asset managers limit their options activity to the purchase of puts or the sale of calls against the assets actually in portfolio, there are applications on the other side of these transactions. The purchase of calls can be used to set floors on the rate of return on floating-rate securities. For example, the purchase of three calls on T-bills with expirations out three, six, and nine months effectively, would set a floor on the rate of return of a one-year security floating quarterly off three-month Treasury bill rates. The sale of puts with the intention of acquiring the securities will generally outperform anticipatory "hedges" in long futures in all except sharply rising markets, due to the reduction of cost by the put premium received.

Another set of applications revolve around what might be called contingent assets, or, in other words, assets which may or may not come into being. For example, a loan commitment which may not come to fruition, but which has either been funded or sold in advance is difficult to hedge in cash or futures markets, due to the large probability of sustaining losses in the hedge position under the same circumstances that the loan would not be taken down. Take for instance the case of a commitment to a housing developer to make mortgage money available at certain levels for the purchasers of his properties. If rates rise, the banking institution will have to fund the loans at higher levels, while if rates fall, no loans will be made at the higher levels. A futures or cash hedge will protect against rising rates, but produces losses on the position when rates fall, and the profitable side of the "hedged" transaction fails to materialize. A put hedge would be more appropriate. In general terms, for any loan or loan commitment, which involves caps or floors on rates for a period of less than a year, can be effectively hedged by purchasing puts to cap rates or calls to put a floor under them. For those that extend beyond a year in the term of their cap or floor, pure hedging transactions are precluded by the maturities available on the options and futures exchanges. While the listed option maturities can be extended by stacking maturities in a manner similar to that practiced in the shorter-term futures markets, this will require considerably more managerial time, carries more risk, and should be priced accordingly.

Hedging of gap risk, where there is exposure resulting from liabilities repricing before related assets, is done in a manner very similar to straight asset hedging. For instance, if a six-month Treasury bill were funded through 90-day deposits, then the purchase of a T-bill put with an expiration date 90 days hence would protect against a rise in rates, as long as the rate paid on the deposits bore some reasonable relationship to the 90-day bill rates. Note that if rates fall, then the lower rates paid on deposits will allow a higher spread between rates, and that the price of the put should be taken into account in the original spread assumptions. Selling calls, probably out of the money, with an expiration near the beginning of the gap, will mitigate the risk somewhat; and if exercised near the expiration date would effectively eliminate the gap. However, the selling of calls provides protection against rising rates only to the extent of the premium received.

In any type of gap hedging it is wise to compare the cost of hedging with an option versus a future. In the short-term markets, this is a fairly straightforward process, involving a comparison of the discount (or premium) in the futures market to the premium of the option. The situation is somewhat more complex in the longer-term markets where there are a number of deliverable issues, and the markets track 8 percent coupons by convention, but the principles are the same. Often what looks like an expensive put turns out to be a bargain against a sharply discounted futures position, or a low-priced call is less of a value than it might appear.

USE OF OPTIONS IN LIABILITY MANAGEMENT

The use of options on the liability side of thrift or bank management is in most respects quite similar to the applications on the asset side, except they tend to be on the opposite side of the markets and tend to be more oriented toward the short-term sector securities. Many of the applications in the options markets are quite similar to those found in futures markets in terms of optimizing issuance of CDs using strip yields in the futures market instead of the actual cash markets. For example, the purchase of a 90-day bill and a strip of three successive bill futures contracts is a substitute for investment in a year bill, or issuing one-year CDs and purchasing a strip of three bill futures, effectively reduces the maturity of the issuance to 90 days. It is not unusual to find profit opportunities on one side or the other of this market, and if there is an inclination to use some of the gains from synthetic issuance or purchases to allow greater profitability, then calls can be purchased in place of the long futures position, or puts purchased in place of the short futures position. In fact, when the market structure is such that there is a sharp premium or discount structure in the T-bill, domestic CD, or Eurodollar futures, it is not unusual to find that the corresponding options position will represent relative value when the premium or discount on the futures is compared with the premium level on the option.

Hedging floating-rate liabilities or the issuance of short-term CDs is fairly straightforward, except that there are no listed options on CDs which forces one into the T-bill options, whose movements do not necessarily parallel exactly those of the CD market. Consequently, measures should be taken to control the basis risk inherent in the position. To ratio the trade based on rules of thumb, or more recently on regression analysis, is common; but, in most cases, it seems easier and perhaps safer, simply to hedge the basis risk through a spread of T-bill futures versus the domestic CD futures market. In any event, the CD/T-bill relationship should be closely monitored, as well as the relationship of the hedging bank's paper to the prime paper which is deliverable against the contracts. As in asset hedging, in situations where the basis is expected to move adversely, it may be advisable to substitute an options hedge for a futures or cash hedge. For example, the prime rate is frequently sticky in rising rate environments. The purchase of puts on T-bills should provide some relief in this type of situation, as the T-bill market tends to be a good deal more fluid in its response to rising rates. This type of anticipatory strategy is particularly appropriate when the stickiness of the prime is likely to be associated with an increased loan demand.

Hedging the issuance of longer-term debt is an area where the use of options can at times be of particular benefit, in that it allows the actual issuance of the debt to be done at times when the markets are not crowded. When rates are generally expected to fall, investors and Wall Street will tend to trade government and nongovernment debt at very tight spreads, and will devote more attention to the few issuers who do come to market. In this type of scenario, the bank or thrift is in a position to extend the maturity of their liabilities, including long-term debt, and to purchase calls. If the expected decline in rates materializes, the profits on the calls can be applied to reduce the effective cost of the borrowing; while, if the decline does not occur, the institution will have benefited by extending the structure of their liabilities at the low rates in the marketplace. The only real caveat is that the cost of borrowing has been increased by a small amount, if rates remain flat.

Hedging gap risk, where there is exposure resulting from assets repricing before liabilities, is similar to the hedging of pure liabilities. For a simplified example, consider the case of a three-month T-bill funded by six-month deposits. The gap could be hedged either through the purchase of a bill future three months forward, or the purchase of a call. The purchase of the call allows greater profitability, in the event of sharply rising rates, which may fit the overall risk structure of the bank better than the futures hedge which effectively locks in a rate. Again, as in all hedging, the institution should remain very conscious of basis risk and the stages of the interest rate cycle.

SUMMARY

As the financial options markets develop, and an appreciation grows for their usefulness in the management of contingent risk, increased use by banks and thrifts can be expected. The phenomenal growth in the financial futures markets demonstrates the economic viability of risk transfer mechanisms. While they do not remove the necessity of making judgments, the advent of listed options on financial instruments will broaden hedging opportunities, and allow a much closer correlation with the types of risks actually incurred by banking institutions. If the swings in interest rates continue, it is likely that the use of these and other risk management tools will prove to be critical in the plans of profitable thrifts and banks.

CHAPTER 8

Fixed Income Options as Risk Management Tools for Life Insurance Companies

James A. Tilley, Ph.D., F.S.A.
Vice President
Morgan Stanley & Co., Inc.

David P. Jacob
Senior Research Analyst
Morgan Stanley & Co., Inc.

INTRODUCTION

The combination of interest rate volatility and the options granted by life insurers to their policyholders and to the corporations to whom the insurers lend money, has left insurers exposed to the risk of financial loss, against which no simple static maturity or duration matching strategy will provide protection. For instance, both the policyholder "option" to withdraw funds at book value (or at least book value less a modest surrender charge) essentially on demand, and the option to take policy loans at below market rates, expose the insurer who has "written" these options, to severe disintermediation, should interest rates rise. A long maturity strategy would lead to losses in rising rate environments as the policyholders exercise their options. A short maturity strategy would likely not enable the company to profitably offer a competitive crediting rate in a level or falling interest rate environment.

An example of this kind of option-related risk in falling rate environments is the reinvestment risk arising from bonds being called, or mortgages prepaid, and the risk that a larger amount of funds than expected will be contributed by policyholders under "guaranteed rate" arrangements. The latter situation can arise in a universal life policy that establishes for inforce policies a guaranteed floor interest rate for the balance of the calendar year—the policyholder has the option to continue premium payments, or to increase his coverage (and hence his premium), at the guaranteed interest rate. This rate is generally of greater value than insurers take into account when establishing the guaranteed rate.

In some cases, insurers knowingly grant such underpriced options through the design and pricing of their products, but state law (e.g., nonforfeiture laws in the case of book value cash out), often constrain them from doing otherwise.

Thus, the dilemma faced by insurers is how to control their exposure to the type of interest rate risk described above, and still price their products in a way to be simultaneously competitive and profitable. In this chapter, some constructive solutions to asset management problems posed by interest sensitive products are discussed. Although the focus will be on investment aspects of the "challenge," product design and pricing aspects will also be considered, because the three areas cannot really be separated.

The remainder of this chapter is outlined as follows. Two specific applications are considered. The first is an example of hedging the disintermediation risk of a single premium deferred annuity (SPDA) product. The second shows how options might be used to price an escalator feature in a thrift plan guaranteed interest contract (GIC). This will be followed by a brief discussion about why the currently available exchange-traded options may not be appropriate for many of an insurance company's hedging needs. A useful alternative will be discussed briefly. The chapter will conclude with several other suggested areas of application.

HEDGING DISINTERMEDIATION RISK

In this example we will focus on a single premium deferred annuity (SPDA) product, but many of the comments and techniques apply with equal force to the disintermediation problem for traditional whole life and universal life products and to the cash flow antiselection problem of thrift plan GICs.

The SPDA design problem has been caused by marketers who have tried to satisfy customer demand for an "ideal" product by including in it several options. Customers want their account balances maintained on a book value basis, and they want to have immediate access to their funds without a rear-end load. From their viewpoint the SPDA should also carry interest rate floor and escalator provisions. Unfortunately, since bond issuers generally do not like to grant options, long-term bonds with coupons adjustable upward but not downward, and always "puttable" to the issuer at par, cannot be found in the marketplace. Without the use of fixed income options to undo the options granted to policyholders, the asset /liability matching problem for SPDAs is not easily solvable.

This example considers the situation of an insurer who experienced severe disintermediation from its SPDA product during 1980–1982. The insurer wants to continue offering the product and wants to retain the bail-out feature that allows the customer to redeem funds without a rear-end load if the crediting rate is dropped below a certain level. The supporting investments are five-year to eight-year par bonds.

The problem posed by the SPDA is that the competitive marketplace demands a crediting rate which reflects *current* intermediate term rates. The product typically allows the policyholder to withdraw his funds at book value less surrender charges, which may reflect the upfront expenses of the product, but almost never take into account declines in market value of the supporting assets due to increases in interest rates. This example illustrates how put options can be used to hedge the risk that heavy cash surrenders will occur after a sharp rise in interest rates.

On January 1, 1983 the insurer's inforce SPDA business had the following characteristics:

Assets

Book value	= $101.7 million
Market value	= $ 96.8 million
Average maturity	= 6.41 years
Average coupon	= 12.35%

Liabilities

Account balances	= $100.0 million
Average surrender charge	= 5.24%
Average credited rate	= 11.20%
Current competitive SPDA rate	= 12.00%

The characteristics indicate that while the business is currently solvent—assets exceed liabilities—the company's average crediting rate is below competitive rates. After analyzing recent experience and considering the product's distribution system and the policyholder profile, the insurer estimates lapse rates as a function of the difference between current competitive SPDA rates and the company's credited rate on new money. The lapse rate expresses the percent of business that will choose to cash out. The following table shows the estimated lapse rate for various increases in the difference between the company's new money rate and competitive rates over a six-month period, and the corresponding loss to the company that needs to be offset.

Interest Rate Increase	Lapse Rate	Loss Experience to be Hedged
0.0%	0.0%	$ 0
0.5	0.0	0
1.0	0.0	0
1.5	7.5	170,282
2.0	15.0	609,101
2.5	20.0	1,160,882

Interest Rate Increase	Lapse Rate	Loss Experience to be Hedged
3.0	25.0	1,875,759
3.5	27.5	2,518,415
4.0	30.0	3,231,063
4.5	30.0	3,702,389
5.0	30.0	4,161,702

Lapses begin to occur only when rates on competitive SPDAs exceed those on the company's currently offered SPDAs by 150 basis points. Lapses level off at 30 percent after the interest rate increase reaches 400 basis points. The losses needed to be offset by gains from the hedging transaction are equal to the difference between the market values of the assets and the cash surrender values. Cash surrender values have been calculated by bringing the book value account balances forward over the six-month period at the average credited rate and applying an average surrender charge. It is assumed that a pro rata portion of assets is used to fund cash surrenders.

The hedging strategy consists of purchasing deep out-of-the-money put options on fixed income instruments. Out-of-the-money options are used because there is the 150 basis point threshold. If one were using the options on Treasury bond futures, the following types of calculations and assumptions would be used to determine the number of options to buy.

In determining the correct strike yield, it is necessary to estimate the relative yield volatility between the security underlying the futures contract and the target rate from which new SPDA rates are set. In this example, it was assumed that for each 100 basis points move in long Treasury bond yields, five-year corporate bond yields would move by 108 basis points. This would imply that lapses of any consequence would begin only when the yield on the long Treasury bond increases by at least 139 basis points (150 ÷ 1.08). Thus, the strike yield of the put ought to be the long Treasury bond yield plus 139 basis points. Unfortunately, the deepest out-of-the-money put option on the Treasury bond futures that might have been available at the beginning of 1983, would have had a strike yield at least 35 basis points less than necessary. A reasonable hedge strategy using exchange-traded options would have been to purchase 215 Chicago Board of Trade September 70 puts on Treasury bond futures at an estimated premium of 1–30 (recall that the premiums for options on futures are quoted in 64ths), for a total cost of $315,781. The choice of 215 options leads to mild overprotection against expected disintermediation for rate changes under 3 percent and underprotection for rate changes over 3 percent. Exhibit 1 shows the expected results of the hedging transaction.

Since this type of hedge would have to be repeated every six months to provide continuous protection, the option premium should be amortized over that period. For this example, the crediting-rate adjustment (as a level percent of liabilities) needed to cover the option premium is 63 basis points, assuming no lapses until the middle of the year. It should be noted that in following this strategy, the cost of option protection is not fully determined at the outset, because it is unknown what the option protection will cost at each of the renewal dates.

Instead of choosing to hedge as described above, the insurer might only be interested in some kind of stop-loss protection. For example, it might be willing to sustain losses up to $500,000. In this case, it would choose an even deeper out-of-the-money option with an obviously lower premium. Modeling the lapse rate is important in deciding upon the type of desired protection.

To summarize the strategy, the adverse financial consequences of disintermediation can be contained by purchasing interest rate put options in combination with intermediate- and long-term bonds and mortgages. The bonds and mortgages provide the necessary earnings rate to support the liabilities in stable and falling interest rate environments. The put options protect the fixed income assets against principal erosion in rising rate environments, effectively turning them into duration zero instruments, or "cash," to match the demand-deposit

EXHIBIT 1
Hedging Disintermediation Risk

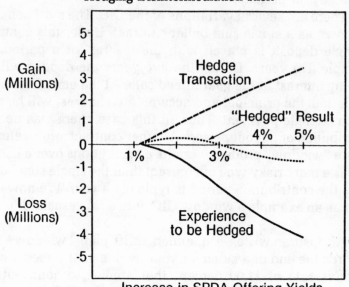

Increase in SPDA Offering Yields

nature of the liabilities. It should be pointed out that a strategy consisting of an intermediate- to long-term bond position combined with a *static* (unrebalanced) short futures position would *not* hedge the disintermediation risk.

GIC WITH ESCALATOR OPTION

Guaranteed interest contracts (GICs) are unique to the life insurance industry. A short description of some of the contracts' features would aid in understanding the risk that these contracts can pose for the insurer. Under these agreements, the insurer guarantees the contract holder a specified rate of return on his deposits for the term of the contract. The guarantee is backed by the insurer's general account.

There are three relevant time periods for a GIC. First is the contribution period during which funds may be deposited at the guaranteed rate. Next is the accumulation or holding period during which interest is being credited; and finally there is the payout period.

There are several variations of the GIC. The most common is known as a single sum bullet contract. Under this contract, a single deposit is placed with the insurer for a period, for example five years. During the five years the deposit will be earning interest at the guaranteed rate. At the end of the holding period, the principal and accumulated interest will be paid out in a single payment. Thus, in this case, there was no real contribution or payout *period*. Another contract, often referred to as a "window" product, permits contributions over a period. This is a more risky type of contract than the single sum bullet, since the contribution period is typically a year. We now consider as an example a window GIC with a rate escalator provision.

An insurer writes a qualified thrift plan "window" GIC towards the end of a calendar year, with a guaranteed annual effective rate of 11.00 percent that applies to contributions received throughout the following year. The GIC then has a four-year holding period followed by a bullet payout (all principal and accumulated interest). In order to make its product more competitive, the insurer considers giving its customers partial protection against a possible rise in rates. The new product design calls for raising the guaranteed rate, if rates offered on new similar GICs rise during the window period. The adjustment to the guaranteed rate is determined at the midpoint of the year and applies only to funds received during the second half of the window period. The interest rate adjustment is equal to the amount, if any, by which interest rates have risen in excess of some threshold level, such as 100 basis points.

Recent experience for the plan has shown that a total of $5 million to $7 million in contributions can be expected fairly uniformly over the year. Also, because of the design of the plan, the total amount of the contributions is not expected to vary much as rates change. To match the expected inflows, the insurer schedules the circling of private placements at a rate of $500,000 each month, based on total expected deposits of $6 million for the year. The insurer is at risk, because it has guaranteed 11.00 percent, but will not receive funds until the following year. To hedge the risk of a possible decline in rates, the insurer can purchase futures contracts on U.S. Treasury bonds using a duration-matching hedge ratio model to determine the necessary number of contracts. Exhibit 2 illustrates, for the second six-months' expected deposits, the gain /loss pattern for the hedged and unhedged strategies assuming *no escalator feature.* The yield on the security underlying the futures contract on the date that the hedge is initiated, is denoted by i_0, and i is the yield on that security at the midpoint of the GIC window period when the escalator, if offered, will go into effect. If the insurer does not hedge, it would benefit if rates are higher during the contribution period than they were when the guaranteed rate was set at 11.00 percent, because it would be able to invest the contributions at higher rates. On the other hand, if rates are lower the insurer would lose money if it had not hedged, because it would have to invest funds at rates below those on which the guaranteed

EXHIBIT 2
Hedging a Window GIC without Rate Escalator

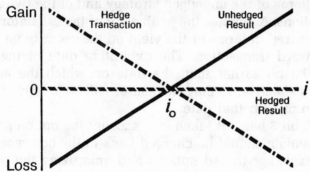

━Unhedged Result: Acquire investments as GIC cash flow is received

▪━Hedge Transaction: On date GIC is sold, buy Treasury notes in the forward or futures market

━▾Hedged Result: Sum of unhedged result and hedge transaction

rate was set. This two-sided risk is offset by the futures hedging transaction.

The escalator feature alters the gain /loss pattern attributable to the funds expected to be received during the second half of the window period, because the gain that will otherwise be realized if rates rise more than the escalator threshold, is now passed through to the plan participants in the form of a higher guaranteed rate. This will result in a loss for the insurer if no additional hedging action is taken, because losses will continue to build on the futures contracts as rates continue to raise above the escalator threshold. The escalator creates a one-sided risk for the insurer. The forward transaction hedges the loss if rates fall; on the other hand, the insurer begins to experience losses only if rates rise above the escalator threshold. This suggests that on the date the GIC is written, the insurer should purchase a put option with a strike yield set so that the option will be out of the money to the extent of the escalator threshold. Stated differently, the intrinsic value of the option should be zero, as long as the new GIC rate is not more than 100 basis points above the old rate. This additional hedging transaction provides the needed gains to offset the cost of the escalator feature. Exhibit 3 shows the gain/ loss patterns of the unhedged strategy and of the two hedging transactions. Δ denotes the equivalent of the escalator threshold measured in terms of the yield on the security underlying the forward transaction. The expiration date of the option should be no earlier than the date on which the escalator becomes effective, so that the insurer will be protected if rates spike on or near that date.

Exhibit 3 has not taken into account the option premium. This premium should be charged back to the contract holder. Using exchange-traded options and amortizing the premium over the lifetime of the GIC on a break-even basis, against total expected GIC deposits under the contract, generally require a 25–35 basis point reduction from the guaranteed rate for the corresponding GIC, without the escalator. In today's extremely competitive GIC market, it is unlikely that contract holders would be willing to pay the cost of such an option.

EXHIBIT 3
Hedging a Window GIC with Rate Escalator

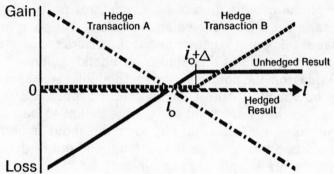

——Unhedged Result: Acquire investments as GIC cash flow is received

•—Hedge Transaction A: On date GIC is sold, buy Treasury notes in the
forward or futures market

••••Hedge Transaction B: On date GIC is sold, buy put option at strike yield
$i_0 + \Delta$ to expire at mid-point of window period

•—•Hedged Result: Sum of unhedged result and hedge transactions A and B

This kind of analysis is nevertheless useful, in that it allows the insurer to price the option, and thus, to decide if it feels the option's perceived value is at least equal to its cost.

PRACTICAL CONSIDERATIONS

Some of the options needed to hedge interest rate risk can be purchased on the exchanges. Some could be purchased in the over-the-counter (OTC) market if state insurance departments so permitted. The legal situation varies by state. For example, in March of 1984, the Superintendent of Insurance for the State of New York issued regulations that prohibit life insurers from using put options. As we have seen from the two preceeding examples, these are precisely the options that are needed to hedge disintermediation, one of the insurance industry's most serious risks. On the other hand, these instruments are permitted in California and Illinois. In New

York State, life insurance companies are now permitted to use *call* options and futures for "bona fide" hedge transactions. Although the combination of a short futures position and the purchase of a call is equivalent to a long put position, it is unclear at this point whether or not the insurance department will permit the use of this kind of synthetic option.

Aside from the possible legal restrictions, there are several other drawbacks to the exchange-traded and OTC options. First, as we have seen, for disintermediation to be realized, rates usually have to increase by some threshold amount. This threshold is often so large that the implied out-of-the-money put options are simply not available. If the available options were used anyway, too much protection would be purchased, with a correspondingly higher premium. These already margin-squeezed products can ill afford unnecessary additional hedging costs. Another disadvantage of listed and OTC options is that insurers typically use corporate bonds and commercial mortgages for their permanent investments and, therefore, would like options to protect those assets. However, the instruments underlying the listed and OTC options are Treasury or Treasury-related instruments. This forces the insurer to bear the basis risk due to spread changes. Moreover, interest-sensitive insurance products require disintermediation protection over their lifetimes, and one cannot currently buy listed options that expire later than nine months from the date of purchase. It may be better to use options with the desired expiration dates, rather than "rolling over" listed options every three, six, or nine months as they expire. These points suggest that a more useful approach is to simulate the option strategy by means of trading between short and long duration bonds as interest rates change.

In a nutshell, put option-like protection for a portfolio can be created by a trading strategy, which decreases the duration of a portfolio as interest rates rise and increases the duration as interest rates fall. The initial and subsequent allocations between short and long duration instruments are determined by the same formulas that are used in option pricing. This type of duration management strategy is exactly what is needed to hedge potential disintermediation, because this risk arises as a result of the dramatic shortening of the duration of the liabilities as interest rates rise. If interest rates rise to high enough levels, the liabilities begin to behave like demand deposits. On the other hand, bonds are not called nor are mortgages prepaid in this environment. Without portfolio rebalancing, a complete mismatch of assets and liabilities results, with cash outflow occurring when rates are high. These observations show why exact matching of assets and liability cash flows for universal life and SPDA products is impossible.

It turns out that systematically shortening the duration of the asset portfolio as interest rates rise, and lengthening it as rates fall, results in a *cost*—in effect, the cost to purchase an asset-side option that "undoes" the liability-side option granted to policyholders. The efficacy of this strategy has been demonstrated mathematically, as well as in practice. Some insurers are in fact already using this approach. There are *no* regulatory constraints on these techniques. The strategy is extremely flexible and can be tailor made in terms of the length of the option protection, as well as the underlying security. (For a full discussion of the technique see Chapter 9).

OTHER APPLICATIONS

Option pricing can help an insurer, and the pricing actuary in particular, to understand the true costs of some of the features of their various products. The *antiselection* problem in thrift plan GICs, where the astute policyholder will likely contribute more to the plan when market rates are less than the guaranteed rate and withdraw or borrow when market rates exceed the guaranteed rate, is better understood in an options framework. The insurer loses if rates move in either direction, and, in effect, has sold an interest rate straddle to the contract holder.

Another example involves the situation of an insurer who desires to retain the business of a client with a maturing GIC. In order to clinch the deal, the insurer offers to set the guaranteed rate today with an option to increase the rate, if rates have risen by the renewal date. The purchase of put options can enable the insurer to do this in a risk-controlled manner.

The option-driven duration management strategy discussed earlier can be used as an integral part of an insurer's asset-liability management program. This will enable the insurer to better handle the problems caused by the policy loan features of a traditional whole life insurance portfolio on the liability side, as well the prepayment problems on the asset side.

There are many more option strategies applicable to the portfolio management problems faced by insurers. It is clear that to be profitable and competitive, insurers will *have* to learn how to use these tools. Options are not without cost, however, and insurers should begin to pass much of the cost to policyholders.

CHAPTER 9

The Use of Synthetic Option Strategies in Fixed Income Portfolios

Robert B. Platt, Ph.D.
Principal and Manager of Fixed Income Research
Morgan Stanley & Company, Inc.

Gary D. Latainer
Senior Research Analyst
Morgan Stanley & Company, Inc.

INTRODUCTION

The early literature on the application of risk control procedures to fixed income portfolios typically emphasized duration or cash flow matching to immunize a portfolio's sensitivity to reinvestment and price risk. These essentially are hedging techniques, that is, two-sided risk control procedures which truncate most of the portfolio's exposure to downside risk, but at the price of also truncating its upside performance potential.

In many portfolio situations, a portfolio manager wishes to leave room for improving performance through active management decisions, but to control systematically the portfolio's exposure on the downside to interest rate related risks. These one-sided risk control strategies require the use of options or option-related techniques.

A typical example of such a strategy would be a portfolio manager interested in taking a long position in the market, but who would like, as well, to truncate the downside risk by also buying a put option which would permit him to sell the portfolio at some stated exercise (or "strike") price. The effect of this strategy would be to alter the variance profile of the underlying portfolio, as illustrated in Exhibit 1. The potential for portfolio loss is truncated, leaving most, but not all, of the upside performance potential. The reduction in the expected return is the cost to the portfolio manager of the put option.

While option strategies are beginning to be employed with increasing frequency in the fixed income markets, their application as a portfolio risk control procedure is still limited by a number of technical and institutional barriers. Firstly, many institutions are precluded by law or internal organizational constraints from participating in the option markets. Secondly, the exchange-traded option markets are not that well developed, and the investor may not be able to find options with the desired characteristics, such as the appropraite expiration date or strike price. Thirdly, over-the-counter options used for portfolio risk control may be inefficiently priced and therefore too expensive for their intended use. Finally, options on portfolios, as opposed to options on individual securities, are not available in general. An option on a portfolio will perform differently from a "basket" of options on the individual securities in the portfolio.

Fortunately for the portfolio manager, it is still possible to achieve the benefits of option-type strategies for his portfolio *without making use directly of actual option instruments*. This involves a technique for achieving downside protection, through the creation of synthetic options by a dynamic process of asset allocation between a particular risky asset, and some particular riskless asset which is used to define the lower acceptable limit of portfolio returns. This approach, which is sometimes called "portfolio insurance," is a very generalized risk control procedure which can be applied to a variety of risky asset classes, and which can achieve a very flexible degree of risk control.

In the next section, we will describe briefly, and in very simple form, the basics of how a synthetic option is created

EXHIBIT 1
VARIANCE PROFILES—LONG VS. LONG PLUS PUT PORTFOLIOS

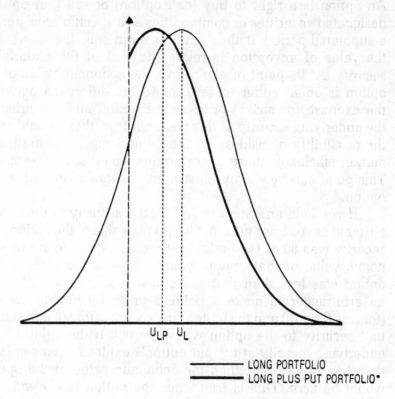

U_L = EXPECTED RETURN ON LONG PORTFOLIO

U_{LP} = EXPECTED RETURN ON LONG PLUS PUT PORTFOLIO**

———— LONG PORTFOLIO
▬▬▬▬ LONG PLUS PUT PORTFOLIO*

*Total probability for long plus put portfolio includes area under curve plus density of dashed line.
**Expected return is equal to expected return on long portfolio, less put premium, plus expected value of enhancement from put.

through dynamic asset allocations. This will be followed, in a subsequent section, by applications which we have made to a variety of portfolio situations which are meant to illustrate the great flexibility that this procedure offers to portfolio managers, for controlling their exposure to interest rate risk.

CREATING SYNTHETIC OPTIONS

An option is a right to buy (call option) or sell (put option)
designated securities or commodities at a specific price during
a stipulated period. It should not be surprising, therefore, that
the value of an option is related to that of the underlying
security. At its point of expiration, the economic value of an
option is equal either to zero, or to the difference between
the exercise (or strike) price of the option and the price of
the underlying security. If this were not true, there would exist
the possibility of riskless profitable arbitrage, and assuming
market efficiency, these opportunities would soon disappear.
This point can be simply illustrated in connection with a put
option.

If you held an option to sell (put) a security to the option
writer at an exercise price of 90, and the value of the underlying
security was 80 at the option's expiration date, then the economic value of that option would be 10. If the price of the
option was less than that amount, it would be possible for
an arbitrageur to make a riskless profit by buying the put
(for less than 10) and the underlying security (for 80) and selling
that security to the option writer (at 90). If the value of the
underlying security at the put option's expiration was greater
than the strike price, then the economic value of the option
would be zero. This is true since the option is a *right*, and
not an *obligation*, to sell the security at the exercise price,
and, therefore, no actual loss need occur on the transaction.
Similar arguments can be made in connection with the pricing
of call options as well.

This arbitrage principle of option valuation leads to an
important insight in modern option pricing theory, viz, that
since the price behavior of an option is related to that of the
underlying security, it is possible to create replicating strategies using that security (in combination with borrowing and
lending) which lead to returns identical to those of an option.
This result was first pointed out in a seminal article on option
pricing by Cox, Ross, and Rubinstein which appeared in 1979.[1]

---

[1] J. E. Cox, S. A. Ross, and M. Rubinstein, "Option Pricing: A Simplified
Approach," *Journal of Financial Economics* (1979), pp. 229–263.

The replicating strategy that produces returns equivalent to a long position in a call option (or alternatively a short put position) involves being long the underlying security and financing some portion of that position with borrowings at some determined rate. For the purpose of option pricing models, this is usually some assumed "riskless" rate such as the return on Treasury securities. The replicating strategy that produces returns equivalent to a long position in a put option (or alternatively a short call position), involves shorting the underlying security and investing in the riskless asset.[2]

For the purpose of illustrating the synthetic option procedure, consider the following set of conditions representing the investment opportunities faced by a portfolio manager interested in purchasing an "at-the-money" put option for one period of time.

Current Price of One Unit of Risky Asset	$50.00
Current Price of One Unit of Riskless Asset	$ 1.00
One Period Return on Riskless Asset	10%
Strike Price of Option	$50.00
Cost of Option	$ 7.00

If we assume, for simplicity, that at the end of the one period of time, the price of the risky asset could be either $30 or $70, then the ending value of the option, and the profit or loss to the portfolio manager on his option position, would be as follows:

Price of Risky Asset	Value of Option	Profit or Loss on Position
$30.00	$20.00	$13.00
$70.00	—0—	−$ 7.00

Of course, in reality, the price of the risky asset may take any one of a number of different values. The full profit profile

---

[2] M. Rubinstein and H. E. Leland, "Replicating Options with Positions in Stock and Cash," *Financial Analysts Journal,* July–August, 1981.

of our put option position would look as in Exhibit 2. The two assumed ending values for the risky asset, $30 and $70, are two of a full continuum of possibilities. The potential profit on the put is limited to $43, since it is assumed that the price of the risky asset cannot fall below zero. Thus, the put position would be worth the strike price of the option less the cost of the option, that is, $7. On the other hand, the downside is limited to the $7 cost of the put.

Viewing the full profit profile of the put position provides some instructive insight on how a synthetic option can be constructed from the underlying cash securities. Clearly, if we are to construct a portfolio of securities whose value will replicate the profit profile of the put option, we would need some asset in the portfolio whose value would rise as the price of the risky asset declines. A short position in the under-

EXHIBIT 2

*Profit Profile of Put Option
End of Period*

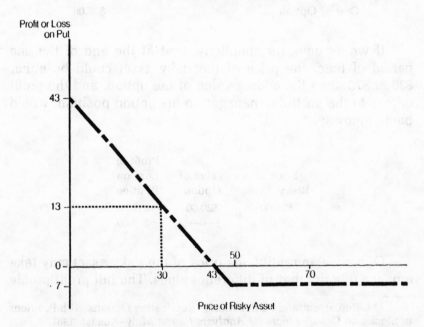

lying asset would have this characteristic. Similarly, in order to truncate the downside loss of the invested position, we would need some riskless asset whose value at the end of the period would be known with certainty, and which would not be affected by the price of the risky asset. The key is to find the number of units of risky assets we must short, and the number of units of riskless assets we must purchase in order to be assured that at the end of the period the value of this portfolio would be the same as the value of the put.

In our simple example, in which the risky asset can take only two values, that is, $30 or $70, this combination can be simply derived algebraically. The replicating portfolio and the cost of the synthetic put would be as follows:

Short One-Half Unit of Risky Asset, Proceeds:	$25.00
Invest in 32 Units of Riskless Asset, Cost:	$32.00
Cost of Option	$ 7.00

That this portfolio indeed replicates the earlier described put option can be illustrated by considering the value of the portfolio at the end of the period for either of the two assumed prices for the risky asset:

Price of Risky Asset	Value of Position	Profit or Loss on Position
$30.00	$-15 + \$1.1\ (32) \cong \$20$	$13.00
$70.00	$-35 + \$1.1\ (32) \cong \$\ 0$	$-$ 7.00

Although this obviously is an oversimplified example, some important insights can still be deduced from it. For one, it shows that the price of the synthetic option is represented by the amount of additional cash that must be utilized to establish the replicating portfolio. In the example shown, this is $7, which is the same as the cost of the replicated put option. Furthermore, it should also be clear from the example, that the units of risky and riskless assets in the replicating portfolio are dependent upon the possible final values of the risky asset. We will come back to this particular point later in this section.

An obvious objection to the implementation of a synthetic put strategy is that it seemingly requires a portfolio manager to short a portion of his portfolio. This is not, in fact, a serious objection, since in many applications the purchase of the synthetic put will be made in connection with an existing long position in the risky asset. In this case, "shorting" is accomplished merely by reducing some portion of one's holding in the risky asset and placing the proceeds in the riskless asset. Another way of saying the same thing is that an allocation of one's portfolio between a risky and riskless asset is the equivalent of holding a long position in the risky asset plus a put option. This can be seen in the following example:

Portfolio = One Unit of Risky Asset + Put

Price of Risky Asset	+	Value of Put	=	Value of Portfolio
$70.00		—0—		$70.00
$30.00		$20.00		$50.00

Replicating Portfolio
One-Half Unit of Risky Asset
+ 32 Units of Riskless Asset

Price of Risky Asset (0.50)	+	Value of Riskless Asset (32)	=	Value of Portfolio
$70.00 (0.50)		$1.1 (32)		$70.00
$30.00 (0.50)		$1.1 (32)		$50.00

The example that we have used was based on a strategy for creating a synthetic put option. It is also possible in practice to construct synthetic call options. As might be expected, since the profit profile of a call option is the mirror image of a put option, the replicating strategy involves borrowing and using the proceeds to buy units of the risky assets, that is, the opposite of the synthetic put strategy. Here too, if used in conjunction with an existing portfolio of riskless assets, the application of the strategy involves merely reducing the number of units of the riskless asset which are owned, i.e., borrowing against the riskless asset, and using the proceeds to buy units of a risky asset. Hence, an allocation of a portfolio between risky and riskless assets can be viewed either as holding a portfolio of risky assets plus a put, or alternatively holding a portfolio of riskless assets with a call on the risky asset.

The previous example of the construction of a synthetic put option is very simplified. The procedure can be generalized. An obvious extension would be to increase the number of possible ending values the risky asset could take, and to increase the number of time periods before the option's expiration. The result of this generalization is that now the possible paths that the price of the risky asset could take in time can be represented by a tree of possible values. This is illustrated in Exhibit 3 which is an extension of our earlier example to two time periods and three possible ending values.

As Exhibit 3 illustrates, this generalization can be viewed as a succession of two possible outcomes, stretched over time, as the path of the risky asset moves along the tree of possible outcomes. The result of this generalization does not, therefore, alter basically the technique for constructing the replicating portfolio for the synthetic option; it merely complicates the mathematics. The important point is that, as the risky asset's price begins to follow one of the branches of the tree of possi-

EXHIBIT 3
"Tree" of Possible Prices
of Risky Asset

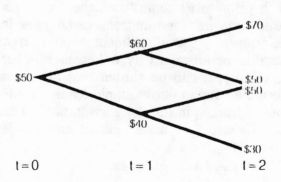

ble outcomes, the initial allocation between risky and riskless assets must change. The asset allocation is *dynamic,* not static. The factors that influence the allocation are the passage of time and the changing value of the risky asset. The replicating strategy is such that, other things being equal, a greater portion of the portfolio is held in risky assets, as risky assets perform well, and a greater portion of the portfolio is held in riskless assets, as risky assets perform poorly.

The example of Exhibit 3 assumes that each event along the statistical tree of possibilities is equally likely. A further generalization of the procedure would be to attach different probabilities to the outcome. If we consider each pair of possible outcomes separately, we might, for example, assign one possible outcome the probability p, where $0 < p < 1$, and the other possible outcome the probability value 1-p.

Those readers with a background in statistics will easily recognize that the attachment of the probabilities p and 1-p to the possible outcomes on each branch leads to the so-called binomial probability distribution. Since this distribution of outcomes defines the economic value of a put in terms of a replicating strategy of investing in risky and riskless assets, it can be used as the basis of a formula to price actual puts. If we extend our example to allow for more possible outcomes, we can reach an interesting conclusion in terms of both option pricing theory and in terms of an underlying replicating strategy of dynamic asset allocation.

If we set t equal to the fixed length of calendar time to the expiration of the put, and n equal to the number of periods of length h prior to its expiration, then $h = t/n$ represents the elapsed time between successive changes in the value of the risky asset. As trading becomes more frequent, h becomes smaller or alternatively n becomes larger. As n approaches infinity, it can be shown that the binomial option pricing formula used in our example leads, as a limiting case of continuous trading in the risky asset, to the familiar Black-Scholes option pricing formula.[3] Furthermore, under this limit-

---

[3] Cox, Ross, and Rubinstein, *op. cit.*

ing case, the proportions of a portfolio in the risky and riskless assets, respectively, necessary to replicate the economic value of the option, are determined directly from the cumulative probabilities calculated as a normal procedure in the application of the Black-Scholes formula.

In developing a practical dynamic asset allocation strategy to replicate a put option, one of two approaches is typically employed. A binomial expansion of outcomes is assumed for a finite number of periods of equal length, often assuming that the outcomes on each branch are equal plus or minus percentage changes in portfolio value. This requires a finite number of asset allocation decisions to replicate the strategy, but limits the protection afforded by the synthetic put to the range of outcomes specified. Alternatively, the Black-Scholes model is used, assuming a lognormal distribution of outcomes for the value of the risky portfolio. This does not require specifying a range of possible outcomes for which put protection is purchased, but does require more frequent asset allocation decisions. In fact, a strict application of this procedure would require that the proportions invested in the risky and riskless assets under the Black-Scholes assumptions be adjusted continuously. In application, however, rule-of-thumb trading procedures are used to limit the frequency of portfolio adjustments.

APPLICATIONS OF PORTFOLIO INSURANCE

In this section, we present two ways in which money managers can use synthetic options. Some of the applications for synthetic options by insurance companies are presented in Chapter 8.

Using Synthetic Options to Obtain Superior Performance in a Fixed Income Portfolio

Consider an active bond manager with the goal of outperforming the Lehman Government/Corporate Bond Index over time.

Managers with this objective will often construct portfolios
that have characteristics quite similar to the Lehman Index
and take moderate duration[4] "bets" against the index. In addition, most of these managers will make some sector and quality
bets, seeking to take advantage of changing yield spreads between various classes of securities. To succeed in this strategy,
the manager must have some ability to forecast interest rates
and spread movements.

Using a synthetic option strategy, a manager can achieve
the above performance goal without having to make any interest rate or yield spread forecast. The key is choosing the correct option strategy in terms of both the level of put option
protection and the risky asset. Typically, in those years in
which interest rates are falling, the manager can outperform
the Lehman Index by holding a more aggressive position than
the index. When rates rise, the manager can usually beat the
index if his return is close to that of a cash portfolio. A correctly
chosen option strategy will therefore combine a risky asset
that is of long enough duration to outperform the Lehman Index
in a falling rate environment, with a minimum return requirement that is high enough to beat the Lehman Index when rates
rise; but not so high that too great a portion of the risky asset
return must be sacrificed when rates fall.

The following synthetic option strategy meets these needs
quite well. Each calendar year, a minimum return on the portfolio of 60 percent of the one-year Treasury bill rate prevailing
at the start of the year is set. For a risky asset, we use the
Long-Term Lehman Government/Corporate Bond Index, and
for a riskless asset, we use the Treasury bill maturing at the
end of the calendar year. Allocations are made between these
two assets in order to replicate the protective put position
on this risky asset. We include transaction costs of ¼ point
on each trade between risky and riskless assets.

The results of this strategy, which are shown in Exhibit
4, are impressive. Returns from the synthetic option strategy

---

[4] Duration is a weighted average maturity when the cash flows are
in terms of present value. The greater the duration of an asset or portfolio,
the greater its interest rate risk.

EXHIBIT 4
Comparative Return of Alternative Investment Strategies

Year	Long-Term Lehman Index Return	One-Year Treasury Bill Return	Total Lehman Index Return	Synthetic Option Strategy Return
1973	1.06%	5.78%	2.28%	2.40%
1974	−6.29	7.40	.17	4.40
1975	16.42	7.32	12.30	10.56
1976	20.55	6.30	15.59	16.86
1977	2.45	4.92	2.98	2.76
1978	−.27	7.10	1.19	4.24
1979	−3.29	12.73	2.28	7.41
1980	−2.70	12.55	3.05	7.12
1981	.08	14.32	7.29	8.46
1982	43.70	14.04	31.10	36.59
1983	6.12	8.86	7.99	5.39
Three-Year Averages				
1973–1975	3.31	6.83	4.79	5.73
1974–1976	9.56	7.00	9.15	10.49
1975–1977	12.87	6.17	10.16	9.91
1976–1978	7.19	6.10	6.40	7.77
1977–1979	−.40	8.20	2.15	4.79
1978–1980	−2.10	10.76	2.17	6.25
1979–1981	−1.98	13.20	4.18	7.66
1980–1982	11.85	13.63	13.17	16.64
1981–1983	15.13	12.38	14.95	16.01
Five-Year Averages				
1973–1977	6.37	6.34	6.49	7.26
1974–1978	6.09	6.60	6.26	7.64
1975–1979	6.76	7.64	6.71	8.25
1976–1980	3.00	8.67	4.89	7.57
1977–1981	−.76	10.26	3.34	5.98
1978–1982	6.18	12.12	8.45	12.18
1979–1983	7.51	12.48	9.87	12.43
Ten-Year Averages				
1973–1982	6.27	9.19	7.47	9.69
1974–1983	6.79	9.50	8.05	10.01
Total	6.26	9.16	7.51	9.29

exceeded returns on the Lehman Index in eight of eleven individual years. Furthermore, the synthetic option strategy outperformed the Lehman Index over all but one three-year holding period, and over each five-year and ten-year holding period (see also Exhibits 5 and 6). For the full eleven years of the Lehman Index, the synthetic option strategy produced returns 178 basis points higher than the index. Significantly, the synthetic option strategy also outperformed one-year Treasury bills over this period, despite the fact that most active bond managers could not do so. These results were all obtained with no value added by the manager in terms of individual bond selection.

Observations can be made regarding the types of years in which the option strategy performs particularly well or poorly. Excellent performance relative to the Lehman Index is usually associated with the long-term bond market doing very well or very poorly, that is, with periods of volatile interest rates. Poor performance relative to the Lehman Index usually occurs when interest rates are stable. In this case, returns are similar among all classes of bonds and the expense of put option protection reduces returns below those of most other bond managers.

Using Synthetic Options as a Decision Tool for Controlling Risk in a Fixed Income Portfolio

As mentioned previously, an option can be replicated by dynamically adjusting a combination of risky and riskless assets. Yet, this is precisely what bond managers do on a regular basis when they adjust the cash positions or durations of their portfolios. The decision to depart from a fully risky position in a portfolio (the maximum duration which a manager would consider holding) involves implicitly purchasing some degree of option protection on the portfolio.

To see this, suppose a manager is actually replicating an option strategy with a 6 percent minimum return target and suppose, further, that the allocation called for between risky and riskless assets at a particular time is 50 percent in each.

EXHIBIT 5

Comparative Three-Year Returns

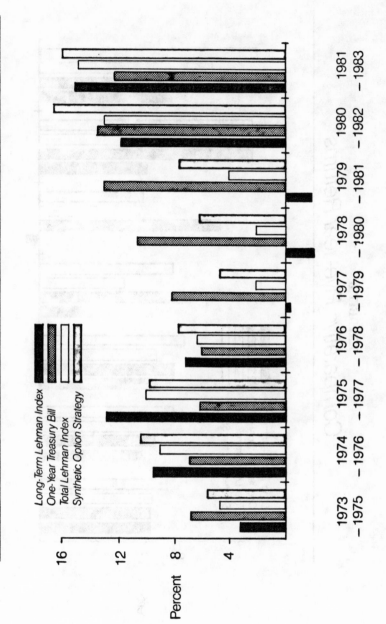

EXHIBIT 6

Comparative Five-Year Returns

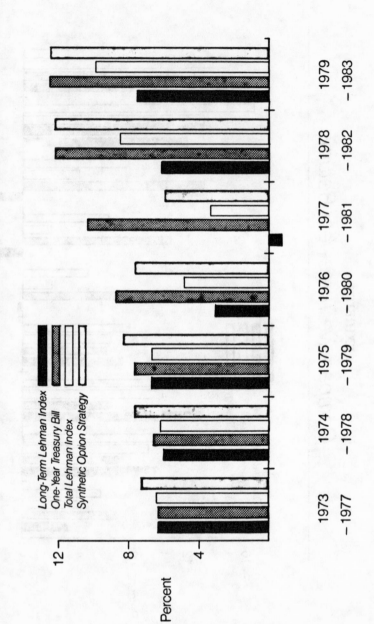

Now consider the same manager, at the same time, not intentionally following an option strategy, but holding a 50 percent cash position in his portfolio. Although he does not intend to follow an option strategy, the manager is holding an equivalent position in his portfolio. The manager is thus implying that, at that point in time, an option with a 6 percent minimum return provides an acceptable degree of protection for the portfolio. Likewise, a manager who would normally hold an eight-year duration portfolio when very bullish on the market, but who is currently holding a four-year duration portfolio, is also maintaining a position equivalent to an option with a particular degree of downside protection.

Exhibits 7 and 8 illustrate these concepts. In Exhibit 7, cash positions ranging between 0 percent (fully risky), and 100 percent (fully riskless), and their associated levels of option protection are shown. Assume a manager is very bullish on the market and would therefore like to be 90 percent invested in long bonds; however, assume the manager would also like to show, if his market outlook is wrong, at least a 7 percent minimum return for his clients. With synthetic option theory, the manager can evaluate this tradeoff in goals using Exhibit 7. The manager decides that the 50 percent cash posi-

EXHIBIT 7
Implied Option Protection of Various
Cash Positions

Percent Cash	Minimum Return of Corresponding Option Strategy
0%	0.36%
10	2.00
20	3.42
30	5.10
40	6.08
50	7.04
60	7.96
70	8.73
80	9.37
90	10.00
100	10.60

EXHIBIT 8
Comparison of Maximum and Actual Durations

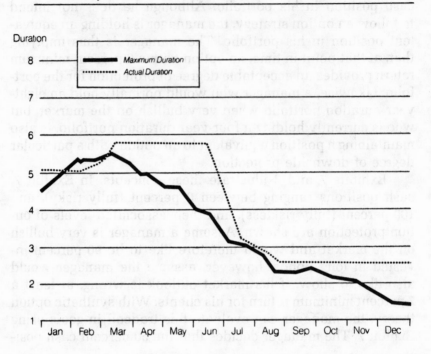

tion associated with a 7 percent minimum return does not leave enough room for upside potential. On the other hand, a 10 percent cash position has an unacceptably low implied option protection of only 2 percent for the year. The manager compromises and selects a 30 percent cash position. This has a reasonable level of downside protection (5 percent minimum return), while retaining a large degree of upside potential (70 percent invested in long bonds).

Exhibit 8 shows how a manager can derive valuable decision information from using synthetic option theory in a duration context. Each week, the manager has plotted the maximum duration that could have been held in his portfolio to achieve a minimum return of 6 percent for the year (a level the manager feels he needs in order to show acceptable performance in a bear market), as well as the actual duration on his portfolio.

The difference in the two lines indicates the manager's risk-taking or risk-avoidance in the portfolio. Whenever the manager departs significantly from the maximum duration, he must ask himself whether he is sufficiently certain about his market outlook to justify his departure. In Exhibit 8, the manager shortened duration considerably in mid-year, deciding that the degree of risk he was taking was not justified. As a further aid, the manager can translate his actual duration into an implied level of option protection, just as he did with the cash proportions of Exhibit 7.

SUMMARY

The two examples presentea in this chapter discussed synthetic option strategies from the view of a performance-oriented bond manager. They are, however, just two of a broad spectrum of potential applications for synthetic option strategies in fixed income portfolios. Synthetic option strategies not only allow investors to structure favorable return distributions that would otherwise be unavailable, but because the replication of an option strategy involves systematic duration management, they are consistent with the activities normally undertaken by bond managers. The ability to better target and quantify duration decisions should make these strategies an important new tool for fixed income managers.

SECTION III

Regulation
and
Taxes

CHAPTER 10

Regulation of Users of Debt Options

Stephen F. Selig, LL.B.
Senior Partner
Baer Marks & Upham

INTRODUCTION

Options on debt instruments are traded both on securities exchanges (e.g., Chicago Board Options Exchange) and futures exchanges (e.g., Chicago Board of Trade). Such options traded on securities exchanges result in the delivery of the actual underlying securities on exercise. That is, if the holder of a long Treasury note call option excercises that option, he will receive the underlying security from the grantor ("short"). On the other hand, options traded on futures exchanges result in the creation of a futures position on exercise. That is, if the holder of a long September 1984 Treasury bond futures call option exercises that option, he will acquire a long September 1984 Treasury bond futures contract at the option strike price, while the holder of the short position (the "grantor") will acquire a short September 1984 futures contract. Conversely, on exercise, the holder of a put option will acquire a short futures contract, and the grantor will acquire a long futures contract.

However, for the typical investor, the technical differences between options on futures and options on physical securities are probably not nearly as significant as is the liquidity of the particular market. Accordingly, this chapter will refer to both types of options as "debt instrument" options.

Options traded on futures exchanges are regulated primarily by the Commodity Futures Trading Commission ("CFTC") and options traded on securities exchanges are regulated primarily by the Securities and Exchange Commission ("SEC"). However, for many types of entities which propose to trade debt instrument options, there are other regulators that are involved. This second layer of regulation comes about because the basic nature of the entity's activities subjects it to substantive supervision by other federal or by state governmental agencies. The entities which are subject to this type of regulation include pension plans, commercial banks, savings and loan associations, credit unions, insurance companies, and common investment vehicles such as mutual funds. These other agencies may limit the extent to which an entity subject to their jurisdiction may use debt instrument options. Indeed, they can—and some do—prohibit an entity from using debt instrument futures altogether.

This chapter attempts to discuss in general terms the scope of such regulation. It will set forth for each category of entity referred to above the name of the regulator, the extent to which that regulator permits the use of debt instrument options, and the conditions which must be satisfied to obtain such permission.

Three preliminary observations are in order. First, exchange trading in debt instrument options commenced only in late 1982. Thus, regulators have had but a limited period to address the utility of these options to the entities whose activities they oversee. Indeed, up until the past few years, options were regarded as improper for such institutions. The regulators took this position because options combine a high degree of volatility with a short life span and thus were regarded as inherently dangerous. Recently, however, many regulators have come to understand that debt instrument options may be used effectively to reduce portfolio risk. This realization in turn has led regulators to replace absolute prohibitions or severe constraints with more objective tests and more reasonable procedural rules.

The second observation flows from the first. This chapter was written in mid 1984. As regulatory authorities become more knowledgeable with respect to debt instrument options, they can be expected to review their regulatory postures.

The third point is that much of the material in this chapter can be presented only in broad general terms. For these reasons, the reader should retain a knowledgeable advisor in order to obtain more detailed and more current information regarding these materials.

PRIVATE PENSION PLANS

Private pension plans ("plans") are subject to the Employee Retirement Income Security Act of 1974 ("ERISA"). ERISA does not talk about the use of options—or, for that matter—any other type of investment. Accordingly, for the most part, to learn whether, and to what extent plans and other deferred compensation plans, such as profit sharing plans, may use debt instrument options, one must look to the general provisions of ERISA.

From the viewpoint of a plan, there are three critical questions: whether, and to what extent the plan may use debt instrument options; whether option premiums and margin deposits are plan assets; and on whom may the plan rely to obtain advice on how to trade debt instrument options.

May a Plan Use Debt Instrument Options?

The basic answer to this question is yes. However, there are limits. ERISA requires that a person making investment decisions for a plan to diversify plan assets "so as to minimize the risk of large losses," and to act "with the care, skill, prudence, and diligence under the circumstances then prevailing;

that a prudent man acting in a like capacity and familiar with such matters, would use in the conduct of an enterprise of a like character and with like aims."

Regulations issued by the Department of Labor ("DOL"), which administers ERISA, provide that this prudence test will be met if the fiduciary gives "appropriate consideration to those facts and circumstances that, given the scope of such fiduciary's investment duties, the fiduciary knows or should know are relevant to the particular investment or investment course of action involved, including the role the investment or investment course of action plays in that portion of the plan's investment portfolio with respect to which the fiduciary has investment duties."

The regulation goes on to define "appropriate consideration" to include:

"(A) a determination by the fiduciary that the particular investment or investment course of action is reasonably designed, as part of the portfolio (or, where applicable, that portion of the plan portfolio with respect to which the fiduciary has investment duties) to further the purposes of the plan, taking into consideration the risk of loss and the opportunity for gain (or other return) associated with the investment or investment course of action, and (B) consideration of the following factors as they relate to such portion of the portfolio:

"(i) the composition of the portfolio with regard to diversification;

"(ii) the liquidity and current return of the portfolio relative to the anticipated cash flow requirements of the plan; and

"(iii) the projected return of the portfolio relative to the funding objectives of the plan."

This DOL rule colloquially is known as the "prudent expert" rule. It is different from and it supersedes the so-called prudent man rule, which governs fiduciaries under state law. Under the prudent man rule, each and every transaction is looked at separately to see if it is a prudent investment. If it is not, and the investment has declined in value, the fiduciary may be charged personally with the loss. However, under the ERISA standard, each investment is looked at as part of the overall portfolio and in connection with the plan's objectives and needs. Thus, an investment, although possibly imprudent if viewed under the prudent man doctrine, may be acceptable under the ERISA standard.

It seems clear that the prudent expert rule should permit a plan to use debt instrument options to hedge its debt portfolio.

For example, if the plan fiduciary holds a portfolio of high quality debt securities, but fears rising interest rates will cause the value of that portfolio to decline, the fiduciary should be able to use debt instrument options as an alternative to using futures contracts or liquidating the portfolio. If the fiduciary buys put options, and the debt instrument underlying the options has a high degree of price correlation to the portfolio, the fiduciary limits his risk of loss to the amount of the option premium, if his market evaluation is correct and may derive a profit (reduced by the amount of the premium), if his analysis is incorrect and the value of the portfolio increases. In contrast, use of futures to hedge may provide greater downside protection, but also will preclude gain if the market rises. Thus, the purchase of puts on debt instruments arguably is more prudent when the fiduciary is less certain about the direction in which the market will move.

The other alternative, liquidating the portfolio and investing in short-term securities, may well have a higher transaction cost and, depending on the size of the portfolio and the liquidity of the individual components, may generate substantial losses.

Use of debt instrument options to effect an anticipatory hedge also may be prudent. If a plan anticipates receiving a substantial cash contribution in three months and would like to be able to invest in debt securities at the present time, because price increases are expected over the next three months, the plan in effect can do so by acquiring a debt instrument call option now. If the plan fiduciary has accurately forecast prices, the cash contribution received in three months, plus the gain on the call, should enable the plan to acquire the securities desired, even though their prices may have risen.

Again, in contrast to futures, if the fiduciary has made a mistake in his assessment of market direction, loss is limited to the premium paid.

Another trading technique, which could be viewed as prudent, is writing covered calls. As explained in Chapter 6, this technique will provide limited price protection in a declining market and will generate additional income in a flat market.

Lastly, since, as noted above, the DOL prudence rule does not prohibit any particular type of transaction, it may be prudent, in light of the overall portfolio of a plan and its investment objectives, to maintain a debt instrument option position with the purpose of generating a profit.

How May a Plan Trade Debt Instrument Options?

ERISA requires all plan assets to be held in trust. In 1982, the DOL issued a regulation providing that registration of securities, in the name of a nominee, does not violate ERISA—provided that the securities are held in the name of a clearing agency, a bank, or an SEC registered broker-dealer.

Prior to the issuance of this regulation, in the case of options on actual securities, a problem had arisen because a previously proposed DOL regulation suggested that if securities were registered in the name of a nominee, ERISA may be violated. Since debt instrument options traded on CBOE and other securities exchanges are reflected by book entry, rather than by physical certificates, they only could be held in nominee name.

In the case of debt instrument options on futures, it generally is assumed that the DOL advisory opinions which were issued in September 1982, relating to futures contracts, also will apply to options on futures. In response to an application by Futures Industry Association, Inc., the national association of futures commission merchants ("FCMs") (the futures equivalent of securities brokers), the DOL issued a series of advisory opinions which, in essence, permit plans to deposit original margin directly with an FCM. The DOL stated that the bundle of rights represented by a futures contract, rather than the amount of margin required to be maintained with respect to that futures contract, constitutes the "plan asset."

Accordingly, a plan now presumably may maintain a debt instrument futures option account directly with an FCM. However, caution still dictates that to avoid extension of credit problems, margin payments by plans should be made promptly and variation margin payments both to and from FCMs should be made promptly.

Who May Make Debt Instrument Option Trading Decisions for a Plan?

Under ERISA, only trustees, fiduciaries named in a plan document, or "investment managers" are permitted to control or manage plan assets. This presents no problem for plans using debt instrument options traded on securities exchanges. However, for plans contemplating debt instrument futures options and other futures contracts, the catch here was that ERISA specifies that only banks, insurance companies, and persons registered with the SEC as an investment adviser, may act as investment managers. This statutory provision excluded FCMs and commodity trading advisors ("CTAs"), who, at this stage of the game, generally may be more knowledgeable about trading futures options than banks, insurance companies, or security advisors. Of course, there are many banks and insurance companies with extensive experience in the type of trading, and the number of such institutions becoming involved in these markets is increasing rapidly.

In any event, the DOL has ruled that if an FCM or a CTA is registered with the SEC as an investment adviser, it may be an investment manager for a plan, even though the advice it gives is solely with respect to futures trading. This provision may be important to plan fiduciaries, because their liability may be reduced to the extent trading decisions are made by an investment manager.

It also is important to keep in mind that a plan may not have an FCM both act as investment manager and execute transactions for the plan. Indeed, a plan may not hire its FCM to give trading advice. However, if the FCM does not charge a separate fee for rendering advice and does not charge commissions greater than those it charges to comparable customers, it may be able to give such trading advice to a plan without running afoul of ERISA.

These restrictions exist because under ERISA a person who, for a fee or other compensation, renders trading advice to a plan or has control of, or discretion with respect to a plan's assets, is a "fiduciary." In general, a plan fiduciary may not effect brokerage transactions for the plan. The securities industry has obtained an exemption from the DOL permitting a fiduciary to act as a securities broker, provided certain conditions are met. However, the DOL has not yet granted a like exemption for fiduciaries seeking to act as an FCM with respect to stock index futures and other futures.

Thus, at this time, a plan fiduciary may not act as an FCM for the plan. However, a person who renders investment advice, but does not receive "a fee or other compensation," is outside the definition of a fiduciary. Accordingly, where the FCM renders advice without charge, and whose commission charges to the plan, do not exceed its charges to comparable customers—it may well be able to render advice and at the same time act as an FCM.

In general terms, the same strictures apply to broker-dealers who effect securities exchange-traded debt instrument options.

COMMERCIAL BANKS

Commercial banks either are national banks, state banks which are members of the Federal Reserve System, or state banks which are members of the Federal Deposit Insurance Corporation ("FDIC"), but not the Federal Reserve System. These commercial banks are subject to regulation as follows:

National banks—U.S. Comptroller of the Currency ("Comptroller");

Member banks of Federal Reserve System—Federal Reserve Board ("FRB") and banking authorities of state of incorporation; and

Member banks of FDIC—FDIC and banking authorities of state of incorporation.

Federal Regulation

The three Federal regulators, the Comptroller, the FRB and the FDIC, have issued a joint policy statement relating to financial instrument futures activities of banks subject to their respective jurisdictions. In contrast, to date, the Comptroller and the FRB each has issued a separate policy statement expressly dealing with options. The FDIC has remained silent.

Accordingly, as a matter of prudence, a bank subject to FDIC jurisdiction which intends to use debt instrument options, should seek confirmation from that regulator that such activity is not prohibited.

In Trust Banking Circular No. 2 (REV) issued in December 1979, the Comptroller expressed the opinion that exchange-traded options are "inherently neither prudent nor imprudent" and concluded that use of such options by trust departments of national banks requires a two-step analysis. First, it must be ascertained whether options may be used by a specific account. If they may be, the next question is whether the proposed use is appropriate for the account.

The circular states that to answer the first question, one must look to the terms of the applicable trust instrument and local law governing trust investments, except that if the trust is governed by ERISA, local law need not be considered, since ERISA supersedes the laws of the several states on this subject. The Comptroller recommends that the bank should obtain an opinion of counsel regarding the legalities of the proposed options transactions before entering into them.

The circular also enumerates several guidelines to be followed by national bank trust departments which seek to effect exchange-traded option transactions. In addition to obtaining the opinion of counsel, the bank's Board of Directors should establish written policies sufficiently specific to spell out permissible strategies. These policies should be reviewed at least annually. In addition, the bank should maintain a record-keeping system which is sufficiently detailed to permit auditors and bank examiners to determine whether trading is being conducted in accordance with the authorized objectives. Such a system should require at least the following entries for each option transaction.

(a) Date.
(b) Quantity, series, class, and type of option (for example, 10 July 20 ATT calls).
(c) Whether an opening or closing trade.
(d) Market price of the option and underlying security.
(e) The purpose of the opening transaction and, if appropriate, the corresponding position in securities held.
(f) The name of the broker executing the trade.
(g) The specific account for which the trade has been made.

The circular goes on to provide that outstanding option positions must be monitored to ensure compliance with Options Clearing Corporation limits, and to make certain that long options are not inadvertently permitted to expire, or short options exercised contrary to the bank's desire.

In January 1973, the FRB issued a letter addressed to the officer in charge of examinations for each federal reserve bank designed to "provide guidance and general standards for Federal Reserve System examiners in those instances where [debt instrument options] are utilized" by trust departments of member banks. In many ways, the FRB letter is similar to the Comptroller's circular discussed above, in that it addresses legality, internal authorizations and controls, and records. However, the FRB goes beyond the Comptroller by specifying those types of option transactions which, in its opinion, are and are not permissible. The FRB states:

(a) Writing covered calls is prudent.
(b) Writing uncovered calls is speculative.
(c) Purchasing call options as an initial investment (as com-

pared to closing out a previously written covered call)
is speculative.
(d) Writing put options to protect existing securities is pru-
     dent.

With respect to debt instrument options, the FRB states:
"Assuming adequate market liquidity, strategies using options
specifying delivery of debt securities may be analyzed in a
similar manner to options on equity securities (discussed previously). However, any uses of options specifying delivery of
futures contracts involve additional considerations. Depending
upon the comparative transactions costs and premium prices,
it could be considered advantageous to utilize options on futures rather than the options markets specifying delivery of
securities for various hedging purposes. This would assume
a substantial correlation in market movements between a security position and a chosen option (on futures) contract position. However, options on futures may involve an additional
risk known as 'basis risk'—the risk that the contract position
would in fact fluctuate in value dissimilarly from the security
position, thereby generating results different from the expected
hedge results. (Basis risk is always present in using futures
contracts to hedge cash positions). It would not appear prudent
to utilize options on futures contracts against futures positions;
activities designed to generate trading profits in derivative
markets appear to involve unacceptable deviations from recognized fiduciary objectives and prudent strategies."

The FRB also expressed some views on plans governed
by ERISA, even though such plans are regulated by the DOL.
The FRB stated that so far as it is concerned, "prudence"
excludes any speculation.

State Regulation

The common denominator of state banking law is that at the
present time there are very few statutes which expressly address the use of debt instrument options by a state chartered
bank. Rather, state laws cover the following range:

(a) Legislation which gives a state bank the same authority as is "authorized or permitted to national banks by an act of Congress." Neither the Comptroller's circular nor the FRB letter described above is an act of Congress and, therefore, it cannot be said with any certainty that a bank chartered in a state which refers to Federal statutes may engage in option transactions.

(b) Legislation permitting a state bank to make "other investments" in some limited fashion (the market basket clause). A bank organized under the laws of such a state arguably could use options. However, the views of the state banking department on whether the market basket clause permits use of debt instrument options should be obtained.

(c) Legislation which permits a state bank to make such additional investments as may be approved by the state official, or department, or other body which administers that state's banking laws.

(d) Legislation which provides that banks have the power to take action reasonably necessary to avoid loss on investments already made. This language seems to permit a bank to hedge with respect to an existing debt portfolio. However, it does appear to permit anticipatory hedging or using options as a substitute for ownership of debt securities.

(e) Legislation which gives a bank authority to undertake such further powers which are incidental to, or necessary for, attaining its business objectives. The Comptroller has expressed the view that the use of debt instrument options is an activity incidental to banking. From this, it could be argued that legislation of this type permits hedging activities.

(f) A few states have adopted a position substantially the same as that of the Comptroller.

The banking authorities of New York and California have expressed the view that commerical banks may use financial instrument markets for hedging. California requires prior written approval and both states require policies and safeguards similar to those contained in the policy statement issued by the Comptroller. It is not clear whether these policies apply to options. Logically, however, there is no reason why, if so requested, the banking authorities of these states would not similarly permit debt instrument option transactions by banks subject to their jurisdiction.

As state legislators and regulators become more familiar with debt instrument options, an increasing number of states can be expected to expressly permit commercial banks, subject to their jurisdiction, to engage in debt instrument option transactions.

SAVINGS AND LOAN ASSOCIATIONS

All savings and loan associations, whether organized under federal or state law, which are insured by the Federal Savings and Loan Corporation, must comply with regulations adopted by the Federal Home Loan Bank Board ("FHLBB"). In September 1982, the FHLBB adopted regulations permitting S&Ls to engage in debt instrument option transactions subject to compliance with certain rules. The regulation covers options traded on an exchange regulated by either the SEC or the CFTC. Under the regulation, insured S&Ls may enter into long positions and short call positions without numerical limit. However, short puts plus forward commitments to purchase securities may not exceed a specified percentage of assets.

Under the regulation, the S&L's Board of Directors must authorize such activity and, in so doing, must establish specific written policies and require the establishment of internal control procedures. In general, debt instrument options may be used to reduce interest-rate risk exposure. The S&L also must adopt internal control procedures which are similar to those required by the Comptroller for national bank trust departments. The Board is required to review positions and unrealized gains or losses at each regular meeting.

An S&L which engages in debt instrument option transactions must notify the District Director—Examinations of the FHLBB district in which it is located, before engaging in such transactions, and must furnish the FHLBB certain information monthly. In addition, there are specified record-keeping requirements.

NATIONAL CREDIT UNIONS

National credit unions are not permitted to use debt instrument options.

INSURANCE COMPANIES

There is no federal legislation or regulation applicable to investments by insurance companies. Accordingly, state law governs the extent to which an insurance company may use debt instrument options. Like state banking laws, state insurance laws are diverse with respect to permitted investments:

(a) Legislation which permits insurance companies to make only those investments which are specifically named in the statute. In such a state, an insurance company will not be permitted to use debt instrument options unless the statute so provides.

(b) Legislation which authorizes specified investments, but does not state that the specified investments are the only ones which may be made. In such a state an insurance company may be able to use debt investment options.

(c) Legislation which enables insurance companies to make, in addition to enumerated investments, "other investments." Here again, it can be argued that debt instrument options may be used, but verification from the relevant state authorities should be obtained.

(d) Legislation which permits an insurance company to make other investments with the prior approval of the relevant regulator (usually the Commissioner of Insurance or Superintendent of Insurance). In such a state, permission will have to be sought and, as noted below, may be difficult to obtain.

(e) Legislation which permits other investments, but only in "good and solvent securities." Debt instrument options probably are not "good and solvent" securities and, thus, may not be utilized by insurance companies in a state with such legislation.

(f) Legislation which expressly permits the writing of

covered calls and/or the purchase and sale of puts and uncovered calls. Approximately 17 states have adopted such legislation.

The fact that both New York and Illinois have adopted legislation permitting insurance companies to use debt instrument options should encourage other states to do the same.

COMMON INVESTMENT VEHICLES

Mutual funds and commodity pools are common investment vehicles designed to enable the small investor to participate in a diverse investment and obtain the advantages of professional management. Mutual funds are subject to regulation by the SEC and, provided requisite disclosure is made, mutual funds may trade debt instrument options traded on securities exchanges. However, the "blue sky" laws of some states place limits on the type and amount of options which a mutual fund may hold. Texas and California are among the more restrictive states.

Mutual funds also may use debt instrument options traded on futures exchanges, although here the restrictions are more onerous. A commodity pool is defined by CFTC regulations as an investment trust, syndicate, or similar form of enterprise operated for the purpose of trading "commodity interests." The term "commodity interests" includes options on futures contracts. Under the Commodity Exchange Act and CFTC regulations, the organizer of a pool must be registered with the CFTC as a commodity pool operator and must file a disclosure document concerning the pool with the CFTC. The CFTC, however, has proposed regulations which will exempt a mutual fund from the registration requirements of the Commodity Exchange Act, if its commodity interest trading is limited to primarily hedging transactions. Under the proposed regulation, a mutual fund seeking an exemption must file a notice with the CFTC and advise shareholders of its intended use of commodity interests.

In addition, mutual funds seeking to trade commodity in-

terests generally have been obtaining SEC exemptions from
Sections 18(f) and 17(f) of the Investment Company Act of
1940, enabling them to do so. Although such exemptions primarily have related to stock index futures and options, the
principles appear to be equally applicable to debt investment
options traded on futures exchanges. The SEC letters generally
have required mutual funds to limit their commodity interest
trading to hedging, and in addition, have required margin to
be held in a separate third party custodial account.

For these reasons, it probably is preferable for mutual
funds to use debt instrument options traded on stock exchanges, if it is practical to do so.

CHAPTER 11

Taxation of Debt Options

Andrew G. Balbus
Associate
Paul, Weiss, Rifkind, Wharton & Garrison

The federal income tax consequences of acquiring, selling, exercising or failing to exercise, options on interest rate futures contracts and options on interest rate sensitive securities (together referred to herein as debt options) are significantly different than the tax consequences of the same transactions with stock options, stock and most other types of property, and thus are important for a prospective debt option investor to be familiar with. While it may come as no surprise that any gains derived from debt options will be taxable, many prospective investors will be surprised to learn that debt options may be taxable at the end of the year, even in the absence of a closing transaction, and that the rate of tax on debt options may be quite lower than the rate of tax on other investments.

The concepts and rules governing the federal income taxation of debt options are among the newest and most complicated in the Internal Revenue Code (the Code). Their historical roots go all the way back to 1981. In that year, in response to the growing use by taxpayers of *straddle* transactions involving commodity futures contracts to defer recognition of

income and to convert short-term capital gain into long-term
capital gain, Congress enacted a number of anti-straddle
provisions.[1] The cornerstones of the new legislation were the
loss deferral rule and an unprecedented new method of taxing
regulated futures contracts that introduced the *mark-to-market
rule* and the *60/40 rule*. In 1982, these provisions were modified
and expanded to cover cash settlement contracts, such as
stock index futures and certain foreign currency contracts.[2]
In 1984, these provisions were amended again, in part to extend the coverage of the anti-straddle rules to options.[3]

This chapter describes and illustrates with examples the
fundamental concepts and rules of debt option taxation. For
several reasons, it begins with a brief description of the transactions that give rise to taxable gain or loss with respect to
interest rate futures contracts. Interest rate futures, options
on interest rate futures and options on interest rate sensitive
securities all fall within the broad statutory category of *section
1256 contracts* and hence are all subject to similar tax
treatment.[4] Also, the rules as applied to interest rate futures
have been established since 1981; prospective investors may
be more familiar with the manner in which interest rate futures
are traded than debt options; and, upon exercise, options on
interest rate futures beget interest rate futures. Next described
are transactions that produce taxable gain or loss with respect
to debt options. This is followed by a description of the rate
of tax that applies to all section 1256 contracts. The second
half of this chapter explains the effect of the anti-straddle
rules on transactions involving debt options which are held
as part of straddles.

The analysis contained herein is based on statutory provisions that are literally brand new, and in many cases, not

[1] Economic Recovery Tax Act of 1981, Pub. L. No. 97–34, 97th Cong.,
1st Sess. (1981).

[2] Technical Corrections Act of 1982, Pub. L. No. 97–448, 97th Cong.,
2nd Sess. (1982)

[3] Tax Reform Act of 1984, Pub. L. No. 98–432, 98th Cong., 2nd Sess.
(1984).

[4] Internal Revenue Code of 1954, as amended, Section ("§") 1256(b).

yet final. In connection with the recent legislation, the Treasury Department is required to issue regulations explaining how the anti-straddle rules work. These regulations may introduce new rules or modify existing rules. Moreover, these forthcoming regulations could take positions, particularly in the area of the taxation of options on interest rate sensitive securities, that are contrary to those expressed in this chapter. Whether any such contrary positions are correct, however, is for the courts to decide. Furthermore, although the description contained herein is quite comprehensive and detailed, it does not consider all of the factors that might affect the taxation of a particular taxpayer. And for simplicity, the effect of transaction costs, such as broker commissions, is not considered.

RECOGNITION OF TAXABLE GAIN OR LOSS

Interest Rate Futures

In general, there are three events that give rise to taxable gain or loss with respect to interest rate futures: (1) sale (also known as a *closing* or *offsetting transaction*); (2) taking or making delivery of the underlying property; and (3) year-end marking-to-market. Under no other circumstances is gain or loss recognized for tax purposes. Thus, any initial margin required to be deposited with a broker to enter into an interest rate futures position, and any *maintenance or variation* margin payments required to be made due to a decrease in the value of the position under the daily mark-to-market system of the exchange on which the futures contract is traded, do not result in taxable loss in the absence of one of the three aforementioned taxable events. Similarly, neither any initial margin received upon entering into an interest rate futures position, nor any maintenance or variation margin received upon an increase in the value of the position is includable in taxable income in the absence of a taxable event.

Example 1: On September 1, 1984, $1 million 90-day U.S.

Treasury Bill futures contracts for delivery in March 1985 are
selling at 88.75, a yield of 11.25 percent.[5] Mike Speculator,
M.D., learns that Congress is going to make a year-end down
payment on the federal deficit. Expecting interest rates to fall
in early 1985, Mike calls his broker and places an order to
buy a $1 million 90-day U.S. Treasury Bill (T-bill) futures con-
tract (a long position). Under the rules of the International
Money Market of the Chicago Mercantile Exchange, the exchange on which the order is placed, Mike deposits initial
margin of approximately $1,500 with his broker to cover ad-
verse price movements with respect to his long T-bill position.
There is no tax consequence to Mike's making the $1,500 de-
posit. Had Mike placed an order to sell a T-bill futures contract
(a short position), he might have been entitled to receive initial
margin (if his account was otherwise adequately collateralized). Still, there would be no tax consequence to Mike's receipt of any initial margin. In October 1984, the price of the
March T-bill futures reaches 89.25. During the previous month,
Mike's long T-bill position had been marked-to-market. Since
Mike's futures contract increased in value, his account was
credited in the amount of the increase—$1,250 [(89.25 − 88.75) ×
100 × $25].[6] If Mike's contract had decreased in value, his ac-
count would have been charged in the amount of the decrease. There is no tax consequence to the flow of maintenance
margin into, or out of, Mike's account in accordance with the
daily marking-to-market of his contract, except at the end of
the year.

The *sale* of an interest rate futures contract is a taxable
event that produces taxable gain or loss in an amount equal
to the difference between the price of the long position on
the date of acquisition, and the price of the offsetting short
position on the date it is entered into, regardless of which
position is entered into first. The amount of gain or loss also

---

[5] Since T-bills are traded on a discount basis, T-bills yielding 11.25
percent on an annualized basis would be sold at 100 − 11.25 = 88.75.

[6] Each .01 basis point represents $25.

equals the sum of the daily mark-to-market adjustments with respect to the position during the taxable year.

Example 2: In November 1984, a further drop in interest rates is anticipated, and the price of Mike's futures contract increases to 89.75. Happy with his killing in the market, Mike sells his long T-bill position by entering into an offsetting short T-bill position. Mike recognizes gain (before commissions) in an amount equal to the difference between the price at which he entered into his short position, and the price at which he entered into his long position—for a gain of $2,500 [(89.75 − 88.75) × 100 × $25]. The result would be the same if the short position had been entered into prior to the long position and the price of the contract had decreased from 89.75 to 88.75.

On the last business day of the taxable year, each interest rate futures position (as well as every other section 1256 contract position) that has not been disposed of by closing transaction or by delivery is marked-to-market and is treated as sold for its fair market value. This is known as the *mark-to-market rule.*[7]

Example 3: Instead of closing out his position in November 1984, Mike, who is a calendar year taxpayer, holds his long T-bill position through the end of 1984. On the last business day of that year, the price of Mike's contract is 89.50. For tax purposes, Mike is treated as if he sold the position at 89.50. Mike recognizes gain in an amount equal to the difference between the year-end price he is considered to have received, and the price at which he acquired his long T-bill position—a gain of $1,875 [(89.50 − 88.75) × 100 × $25].

Gain or loss recognized by a taxpayer with respect to an interest rate futures position under the mark-to-market rule is taken into account in determining gain or loss on the subsequent disposition of the position (whether by means of a closing transaction or by delivery) in the following taxable year.[8] By adjusting the cost basis of a position when it is marked-

---

[7] §1256(a)(1).

[8] §1256(a)(2).

to-market at year-end, increasing the basis by the amount of
any gain recognized or decreasing the basis by the amount
of any loss recognized, gain or loss that is recognized under
the mark-to-market rule is prevented from being recognized
again when the position is disposed of.

Example 4: If Mike *sells* his long T-bill position by entering into an offsetting short T-bill position in February 1985,
when the contract is trading at 89.25, Mike would recognize
a loss of $625 [(89.25 − 89.50) × 100 × $25]. Had Mike not
previously recognized gain of $1,875 with respect to his long
T-bill position at the end of 1984, he would have recognized
a gain of $1,250 pursuant to the sale. The gain would have
been computed by taking the difference between the price
at which Mike entered into his short T-bill position, and the
price at which he acquired his long T-bill position—a gain
of $1,250 [(89.25 − 88.75) × 100 × $25]. Since Mike already
had recognized gain of $1,875 with respect to the long T-bill
position in 1984, a loss of $625 had to be recognized in 1985
to equal the $1,250 economic gain realized during the entire
period Mike held the long T-bill position. To accomplish this,
at the end of 1984 an adjustment was made to the basis of
Mike's long T-bill position, increasing it by the amount of gain
recognized under the mark-to-market rule. As a result, Mike
recognizes a loss of $625 at the time of sale.

The taking or making of delivery of the underlying interest
rate security is a taxable event. In the parlance of the Code,
it is a *termination*. The amount of gain or loss is determined
as if the interest rate futures contract was sold on the date
of delivery.[9]

Example 5: Instead of selling his long T-bill position in
February 1985, Mike takes delivery of the T-bills in March
1985, when the price of the futures contract is 89.75. For tax
purposes, the futures contract is treated as if it was sold on
the date of delivery. Accordingly, Mike recognizes gain in the
amount of $1,250 [(89.75 − 89.50) × 100 × $25].[10] Mike has a

---

[9] §1256(c).

[10] 89.50 represents the original purchase price of 88.75 increased by
the .75 year-end mark-to-market basis adjustment.

cost basis in his T-bills equal to the market price of the T-bills (which is also equal to the futures contract price) on the delivery date.

Debt Options

By and large, the same concepts and rules that govern the taxation of interest rate futures govern the taxation of debt options. They differ significantly, however, from the rules governing the taxation of other types of options, such as stock options.

The four principal events that give rise to taxable gain or loss with respect to debt options, closely parallel the principal taxable events with respect to interest rate futures: (1) sale (also known as a closing or offsetting transaction); (2) lapse; (3) exercise; and (4) year-end marking-to-market. Under no other circumstances is gain or loss recognized for tax purposes. Thus, the cost of acquiring an option to buy or to sell an interest rate sensitive security or an interest rate futures contract, and any margin that might be paid if the option is marked-to-market, do not result in taxable loss to the option holder in the absence of one of four aforementioned taxable events. The cost of acquiring an option, known as the *premium,* is a nondeductible capital expenditure. Similarly, neither the receipt of an option premium by the option writer, also known as the *grantor,* nor the receipt of any margin if the option is marked-to-market, results in taxable income to the option writer in the absence of a taxable event.

The *sale* of an interest rate option is a taxable event that yields taxable gain or loss in an amount equal to difference between the premium paid to acquire the option, and the premium received upon selling the option (usually by entering into a closing transaction). The *lapse* of a debt option is also a taxable event and is treated as a sale of the option on the expiration date.[11] On the lapse of an interest rate option, the writer recognizes gain in the amount of the premium received,

---

[11] §1256(c)(1).

and the holder recognizes loss in the amount of the premium paid.

Example 6: In September 1984, 13 percent Treasury Bonds due November 19, 2014, are auctioned at par. Treasury Bond options covering that issue are introduced with exercise prices (expressed as a percentage of par value) of 98, 100 and 102. Mike Speculator, M.D., acquires a call option with an exercise price of 98. As the holder of that option, Mike has the right at any time during the term of the option, but not the obligation, to buy $100,000 of 13 percent Treasury Bonds due November 19, 2014, for $98,000 [98 percent of $100,000] plus accrued interest. The option premium (also expressed as a percentage of par value) is quoted at $1\frac{1}{32}$, a cost of $1,125 [1⅛ percent of $100,000]. There is no tax consequence to Mike's payment of the option premium and there is no tax consequence to the receipt of the option premium by the writer of the call option. In October 1984, the premium rises to 2, a cost of $2,000 [2 percent of $100,000]. If Mike sells his option, he will recognize gain in an amount equal to the difference between the premium he receives by selling his option, and the premium he paid to acquire his option—a gain of $875 [$2,000 − $1,125]. If, on the other hand, interest rates rise in October and the value of the underlying Treasury Bonds drops to 96, Mike would allow the option to expire. Lapse of the option is treated as a sale. Mike would recognize a loss of $1,125, the total amount of the premium paid for the option. The writer of the option would recognize a gain of $1,125.

Exercise of a debt option is a taxable event.[12] The amount of gain or loss is determined as if the debt option was sold on the exercise date. The interest rate security or future contract underlying the option is treated as having been bought, in the case of a call option, or sold, in the case of a put option, at the prevailing market price.

On the last business day of the taxable year, each debt option that has not been disposed of by way of sale, lapse

---

[12] §1256(c)(1); §1234(c)(1).

or exercise, is marked-to-market and treated as sold for its fair market value.

Capital Gains and Losses and the 60/40 Rule

Interest rate futures and debt options in the hands of virtually all taxpayers are *capital* assets. It makes no difference whether those hands belong to a professional trader who *makes a market* by buying and selling particular interest rate futures or debt options in the course of his business; or to a surgeon who buys and sells according to his instinct as to the direction in which interest rates will move.[13] The one exception is for interest rate futures and options that are used in certain *hedging transactions,* described below.

The taxation of gain or loss from interest rate futures and debt options transactions is quite different from the taxation of gain or loss from the sale of stock. Stock in the hands of most taxpayers is a capital asset. Any gain or loss realized upon the sale of stock is capital gain or loss, but is long-term or short-term depending upon the taxpayer's holding period for the stock. The present long-term holding period is six months.[14]

Long-term capital gains receive preferential treatment under the Code: 60 percent of such gains are deductible by individuals, leaving only 40 percent to be taxed.[15] This results in a maximum rate of tax for individuals on long-term capital gains of 20 percent. An individual's short-term capital gains are taxed in full without deduction at a maximum rate of 50 percent. In contrast, capital losses receive worse treatment

---

[13] *Faroll* v. *Jarecki,* 261 F.2d 281 (7th Cir. 1956). The Tax Reform Act of 1984 confirmed this treatment. In contrast, stock in the hands of a market-maker is ordinary income property, unless the dealer specifically identifies the stock as investment property.

[14] For property acquired after June 22, 1984. The holding period for long-term capital gain (or loss) with respect to property acquired on or before that date is 12 months.

[15] §1202.

under the Code than ordinary losses. Capital losses are deductible in full against capital gains by individuals; however, the excess of any capital losses over capital gains may be deducted against only $3,000 of ordinary income each year, with unlimited carryovers to future years.[16]

In general, any gain or loss recognized with respect to interest rate futures and debt options is capital gain or loss, but is taxed under a special rule. The rule, known as the *60/ 40 rule*, applies to all regulated futures contracts, certain foreign currency contracts, listed nonequity options (including debt options), and listed equity options that are held or written by an options dealer in connection with his business (these instruments are collectively referred to as *section 1256 contracts*).[17] Under the 60/40 rule, 60 percent of the gain or loss with respect to a section 1256 contract is treated as long-term capital gain or loss, and the remaining 40 percent is treated as short-term capital gain or loss.[18]

The 60/40 rule applies without regard to the length of time a taxpayer holds an interest rate futures contract or option and without regard to whether an interest rate futures contract or option is a short or a long position. The maximum rate of federal income tax applicable to interest rate futures, debt options, and all section 1256 contracts, under this rule is 32 percent for individuals, and 35.2 percent for corporate taxpayers.[19]

Example 7: At the end of 1984, Mike's net gain or loss must be recognized and taxed in accordance with the 60/40

---

[16] §1211(b); §1212(b).

[17] §1256(b).

[18] §1256(a)(3).

[19] Individual taxpayers—32 percent: 50 percent maximum rate of tax on the 40 percent of the net gain (or loss) that is treated as short-term capital gain (or loss), plus a 50 percent maximum rate of tax on the 24 percent (taking into account the §1202 deduction) of the remainder of the net gain (or loss) that is treated as long-term capital gain (or loss).

Corporate taxpayers—35.2 percent: 46 percent maximum rate of tax on the 40 percent of the net gain (or loss) that is treated as short-term capital gain (or loss), plus a 28 percent maximum rate of tax on the 60 percent of the net gain (or loss) that is treated as long-term capital gain (or loss).

rule. If, during the year, Mike has recognized no gains from section 1256 contracts other than those described in *Example 3* ($1,875) and *Example 6* (assume $875 gain on sale of the option) his net gain will be $2,750, of which 60 percent, or $1,650, is long-term capital gain and 40 percent, or $1,100, is short-term capital gain. If Mike's income is taxed at the highest marginal rate, the tax due will be $880 [$2,750 x 32 percent].

There are two exceptions under which gain or loss from debt options will not be taxed under the 60/40 rule. The first exception is for gain or loss from debt options that are used in certain *hedging transactions*, described below, which is taxed at ordinary income rates. The second exception is for gain or loss from debt options that are held in specifically identified *mixed straddles*, described below, which may be taxed as short-term capital gain or loss.

Carryovers

If the total of all gains and losses from closing transactions, year-end marking-to-market, delivery, exercise, lapse or other terminations, recognized during the taxable year with respect to interest rate futures, debt options, and all other section 1256 contracts, produces a net loss, and there is insufficient capital gain recognized from other sources to offset such loss, taxpayers other than corporations, trusts, and estates, can elect to carryback this loss—known as the *net section 1256 contracts loss*—to the three previous taxable years and apply it against any *net section 1256 contract gain* recognized during those years.[20]

The precise manner in which the net section 1256 contracts loss is computed, carried back and applied against net section 1256 contract gain is beyond the scope of this chapter (and beyond the patience of most readers).[21] The earliest year to which net section 1256 contracts loss may be carried back is 1981, which is the first year in which a taxpayer could have

---

[20] §1212(c)(1).
[21] *See* §1212(c).

any net section 1256 contract gain against which the loss could be applied. If no net section 1256 contract gain exists in any of the three prior years, the net section 1256 contracts loss can be carried forward indefinitely. Capital losses attributable to assets other than section 1256 contracts do not receive this special three-year carryback treatment.

EFFECT OF THE ANTI-STRADDLE RULES

Straddles—Offsetting Positions

The anti-straddle rules, described below, were designed to prevent taxpayers from deferring the recognition of income and from converting short-term capital gain into long-term capital gain through the use of straddles. The rules may limit or prevent taxpayers from recognizing losses incurred during the taxable year from debt option transactions.

A *straddle* consists of two or more offsetting positions in personal property.[22] In general, a *position* is any interest in personal property, including a futures contract, option, or physical commodity.[23] There is a limited exception for stock and certain stock options.[24] *Personal property* refers to any personal property of a type which is actively traded.[25] Thus, the anti-straddle rules generally apply to interests in all property except stock and real estate. Interest rate futures and debt options are positions to which the anti-straddle rules apply.

In general, positions are *offsetting* when the risk of loss from holding one of the positions is substantially diminished by holding one or more of the other positions.[26] Whether one position offsets another position is a question of fact that can

---

[22] §1092(c)(1).

[23] §1092(d)(2).

[24] §1092(c)(4); §1092(d)(3).

[25] §1092(d)(1).

[26] §1092(c)(2).

be answered only by analyzing the particular positions. However, the Code provides several rebuttable presumptions of situations in which positions will be considered offsetting. If the value of one position ordinarily varies inversely with the value of one or more other positions, even if the value does not *actually* vary inversely, those positions will be presumed to be offsetting and the anti-straddle rules will apply.[27] Mere diversification does not produce offsetting positions, provided the positions are not balanced.

Straddle positions are like two sides of a seesaw: as one side goes up, the other side goes down. As loss is realized on one position, gain is realized on the offsetting position. The most basic straddle consists of a long position and a short position in the same commodity on the same exchange for delivery in different months. Delivery must not be in the same month, otherwise the two positions would cancel each other out. The risk of loss from holding the long position is substantially diminished by holding the short position, because loss on the long position will be offset by gain on the short position and vice versa.

Interest rate futures and debt options are relatively new instruments. The tax laws governing them are also new. Consequently, it is difficult to identify positions that will be considered offsetting with respect to interest rate futures and debt options. Nevertheless, some offsetting positions can be identified. A call and a put option on the same interest rate futures contract or interest rate sensitive security are offsetting positions which comprise a straddle. A long and a short position in the same interest rate futures contract with different delivery months are offsetting positions which comprise a straddle. Additionally, a long position and a short position in different interest rate futures, such as a long bank certificate of deposit futures contract and a short U.S. Treasury Bond futures contract, are offsetting positions, because the value of one position ordinarily varies inversely with the value of the other position, even though the magnitude of those inverse movements may

---

[27] §1092(c)(3).

not be identical. Moreover, straddles can be formed with positions that constitute different interests in the same interest rate sensitive security, such as physical Treasury Bills, Treasury Bill futures, Treasury Bill options and options on Treasury Bill futures, provided the values of such positions ordinarily vary inversely. A put option or a short interest rate futures position and a portfolio of physical T-bills, GNMA certificates, Treasury Bonds, Treasury Notes, or bank certificates of deposit may also comprise a straddle.

In determining whether positions are offsetting, a taxpayer is treated as owning any position held by certain *related persons,* such as a spouse or, in the case of a corporate taxpayer, a corporation that files a consolidated return with the taxpayer. In addition, a taxpayer is treated as owning 100 percent of any position held by a flow-through entity (such as a partnership, S corporation, trust, or regulated investment company) if the taxpayer properly takes into account any gain or loss from the position.[28] Forthcoming Treasury regulations may provide that only the taxpayer's proportionate share of a flow-through entity's position is to be treated as held by the taxpayer. In addition, stock of a corporation that is formed or availed of to take positions which offset positions taken by any shareholder of the corporation, is considered to be a position itself, and is termed *offsetting position stock.*[29] Thus, a straddle can be formed where offsetting positions are held by a taxpayer and a corporation (consolidated or unconsolidated) in which the taxpayer owns stock.

Types of Straddles

Straddles can be composed of positions all of which are section 1256 contracts (section 1256 contract straddles), positions some of which are section 1256 contracts, and some of which are non-section 1256 contracts (*mixed straddles*), or positions all of which are non-section 1256 contracts. Since interest rate

---

[28] §1092(d)(4).
[29] §1092(d)(3)(B)(ii).

futures and debt options are section 1256 contracts, the only straddles that interest rate futures and debt options can be part of are section 1256 contract straddles and mixed straddles. Consequently, the taxation of non-section 1256 contract straddles will not be addressed in this chapter.

Straddles composed of two or more offsetting debt options (or two or more offsetting interest rate futures) constitute section 1256 contract straddles. So do straddles composed of debt options and other offsetting section 1256 contracts, such as interest futures contracts. Section 1256 contract straddles are specifically exempt from the application of the anti-straddle rules (provided such section 1256 contract straddles are not part of larger straddles).[30] Thus, for investors in debt options who hold no interest rate instruments other than section 1256 contracts, the only rules that are likely to apply are the mark-to-market rule and the 60/40 rule. Section 1256 contract straddles are exempt from the application of the anti-straddle rules because the mark-to-market rule is sufficient to prevent the deferral and conversion maneuvers Congress sought to eliminate.

A *mixed straddle* consists of at least one section 1256 contract position and at least one non-section 1256 contract position, provided that the two or more positions are identified in the taxpayer's records as forming a mixed straddle before the close of the day on which the first section 1256 contract position is acquired (or such earlier time as may be prescribed by regulation).[31] The anti-straddle rules apply to mixed straddles.

Anti-Straddle Rules

The most important anti-straddle rule is the *loss deferral rule*. It provides that: *if one of the positions comprising a straddle is closed out at a loss, the loss is recognized in that taxable year only to the extent that the loss exceeds the unrecognized*

---

[30] §1256(a)(4).
[31] §1256(d)(4).

gain in other open offsetting positions. To the extent the loss does not exceed the unrecognized gain, recognition of the loss is postponed until the first succeeding taxable year in which all or part of the loss exceeds the unrecognized gain in offsetting positions.[32]

In the case of a mixed straddle, the section 1256 contract position is subject to the mark-to-market rule at year-end. Any gain is recognized. Any loss from the termination of the non-section 1256 contract position during the taxable year is recognized in full, because there is no unrecognized gain in the open offsetting section 1256 contract position. If, on the other hand, loss is realized on the section 1256 contract position during the taxable year, the loss is deferred to the extent of unrecognized gain in the open offsetting non-section 1256 contract position.

Example 8: In October 1984, Mike Speculator, M.D., purchases a $100,000 Treasury Bond and a put option on a March 1985 Treasury Bond futures contract. Assuming the values of the two positions ordinarily vary inversely, they offset each other and, therefore, comprise a straddle. Since the debt option position is a section 1256 contract but the Treasury Bond position is not, the straddle is a mixed straddle, and Mike identifies it as such on his records before the close of the day. Between October and December interest rates fall. At year-end, the long Treasury Bond position has unrealized gain of $100. That gain is not recognized for tax purposes, however, because physical Treasury Bonds are not subject to the mark-to-market rule. The short debt option position, which is subject to the mark-to-market rule, is treated as sold for its fair market value on the last business day of the taxable year, producing a loss of $120. But, only $20 of that loss is recognized in 1984. Under the loss deferral rule, loss is deferred to the extent of unrecognized gain in open offsetting positions. Here, the amount of unrecognized gain in the open long Treasury Bond position is $100. Thus, $100 of the $120 loss is deferred even though the short debt option is marked-to-market. The remaining $20

---

[32] §1092(a)(1).

of loss is recognized, because the $120 of loss exceeds the
$100 of unrecognized gain in the offsetting long position by
$20. The $20 of recognized loss is taxed under the 60/40 rule.
The $100 of deferred loss is carried over into the succeeding
taxable year subject to the same restriction. If in the succeeding taxable year the long Treasury Bond position is sold, the
$100 of deferred loss would be recognized in full. It should
also be noted that had Mike sold the debt option in 1984 for
a loss of $60, no loss would be recognized in 1984.

Each taxpayer is given the right to make a one-time election for all years to have the mark-to-market rule not apply
to section 1256 contract positions in all mixed straddles.[33] The
election is revocable only with the consent of the Internal
Revenue Service. If the election is made, all mixed straddles
thereafter acquired will become non-section 1256 contract
straddles. The section 1256 contract position will not be subject
to the mark-to-market rule or the 60/40 rule at year-end. If
no straddle position is terminated during a taxable year, no
loss will be realized and, therefore, the loss deferral rule will
be inapplicable. If one of the mixed straddle positions is terminated at a loss, the loss deferral rule will apply: the loss will
be recognized in that taxable year only to the extent that it
exceeds the unrecognized gain in other open offsetting positions. To the extent the loss does not exceed the unrecognized
gain, recognition of the loss will be postponed.

As part of the recent tax legislation, Congress delegated
the Treasury Secretary authority to issue regulations covering
straddles which are to be comparable in application to the
wash sale rule presently covering only stock and securities.
The wash sale rule disallows any loss realized on the sale
of stock or securities where substantially identical stock or
securities are acquired within thirty days before or after the
sale.[34] The rule is designed to prevent taxpayers from realizing
loss on the sale of property when, in actuality, they continue
to hold on to the property. By definition this rule is inapplicable

[33] §1256(d)(1),(2),(3).
[34] §1091.

to most section 1256 contracts, because such contracts are not stock or securities. The forthcoming regulations presumably will cover all positions in mixed straddles (and non-section 1256 contract straddles) and will disallow loss on the sale of an offsetting position where a substantially identical position is acquired within thirty days before or after the sale.

Example 9: On September 1, 1984 Mike Speculator, M.D., enters into a mixed straddle consisting of a put option on physical T-bills and an offsetting amount of physical Treasury Notes. After a month, the short debt option position has unrecognized loss of $20 and the long Treasury Note position has unrecognized gain of $20. Mike sells the short debt option position and replaces it on October 15, 1984 with a comparable short debt option position for delivery in a different month. At year-end, the loss deferral rule will prevent recognition of the $20 loss, provided the values of the long and short straddle positions remain unchanged from October 15 to December 31. On the other hand, if the value of the long Treasury Note position decreases by $20 during that time period, matched by an offsetting increase in value of $20 in the new short debt option position, there would be no offsetting gain in the long Treasury Note position to prevent the recognition of loss. The forthcoming wash sale regulations presumably will prevent such recognition of loss.

Congress also has delegated the Treasury Secretary authority to issue regulations covering straddles that are to be comparable in application to the short sale rules for securities.[35] Presumably, the new regulations will suspend the holding period of a long position upon the acquisition of an offsetting short position. By suspending the holding period of a long position while it is offset by a short position, the regulations will prevent the conversion of short-term capital gain into long-term capital gain. The regulations are also to adopt a rule to prevent the conversion of a long-term capital loss into a short-term capital loss. The present short sale rules apply to *substantially identical property*, which excludes many straddle positions. For example, futures contracts with

---

[35] §1233.

delivery dates in different calendar months are specifically
defined as not being substantially identical. The new regulations are expected to substitute the concept of offsetting position for substantially identical property.

The Treasury Secretary also is required to issue regulations that will recharacterize gains and losses from the disposition of a mixed straddle position where other mixed straddle
positions remain open.[36]

The last of the anti-straddle rules requires the capitalization of interest and carrying costs in the case of straddles.[37]
To the extent that the sum of certain expenses, such as interest
on indebtedness incurred, or continued, to purchase or carry
personal property that is part of a straddle, and carrying costs,
such as insurance, storage, and transportation, that are alloca-
ble to such personal property, exceeds certain income derived
from such personal property, the excess expenses may not
be deducted, but must instead be capitalized as part of the
basis of the personal property. Thus, interest on indebtedness
incurred to purchase T-bills which are held as part of a straddle
with an offsetting short T-bill option position may only be
deductible in part. The balance of the interest expense must
be added to the basis of the T-bills.

Reporting Requirements

Taxpayers must annually report on Form 6781 each position
(whether or not part of a straddle) held at the close of the
taxable year with respect to which there is unrecognized gain
and, in addition, the amount of such unrecognized gain.[38] Pen-
alties may be assessed against the taxpayer for failing to file
the required report where the failure is not due to reasonable
cause. There are exceptions to these reporting requirements
for:

(a)   Positions that are part of certain specifically defined *iden-
      tified straddles;*

[36] §1092(b)(2).
[37] §263(g).
[38] §1092(a)(3)(B).

(b)   Positions that are inventory property;
(c)   Positions that are part of hedging transactions; and
(d)   All positions held during a taxable year if no loss on a
      position has been sustained during the taxable year, or
      if the only loss sustained was on a position described
      in clause (b) or (c).

Many holders of long or short positions in debt options
and interest rate futures will not be required to file reports
because such positions are marked-to-market at year-end.
Since any gain is recognized at year-end under the mark-to-
market rule, there is no unrecognized gain with respect to
such positions to report. But, if physical interest rate securities
are used to offset interest rate futures or options, the physical
interest rate securities positions with unrecognized gain would
have to be reported, unless an exception applied.

Special Rule for Hedging Transactions

A *hedging transaction* is a transaction entered into in the
normal course of a taxpayer's trade or business primarily—

(a)   To reduce the risk of price change or currency fluctuations
      with respect to property which is held or to be held by
      the taxpayer, or
(b)   To reduce the risk of interest rate or price changes, or
      currency fluctuations with respect to borrowings made
      or to be made, or obligations incurred or to be incurred,
      by the taxpayer;
provided, the gain or loss on the transaction is treated as
ordinary income or loss, and the taxpayer clearly identifies
it as a hedging transaction before the close of the day on
which the transaction is entered into (or such earlier time
as may be prescribed by regulations).[39]

Sales of debt options and interest rate futures contracts
by government securities dealers to offset losses anticipated
from the sale of the dealers' government securities inventory

------
[39] §1256(e)(2).

during a period of rising interest rates, and purchases of debt options and interest rate futures contracts by government securities dealers to ensure an inventory supply of government securities for sale to customers during a period of falling interest rates, qualify as hedging transactions. Purchases or sales of debt options, such as T-bill options, to protect a borrower against increased interest expense on a variable rate loan, and purchases or sales of GNMA options to protect a borrower against increased interest expense on a variable rate mortgage, may qualify as hedging transactions. Purchases or sales of interest rate futures by active issuers of debt securities which are designed to minimize the risk of interest rate fluctuations on scheduled debt offerings may also qualify as hedging transactions.

The tax consequences of a hedging transaction are considerable. All gains and losses are ordinary. The maximum tax rate for individuals in 1984 on such gains and losses is 50 percent. The maximum rate for corporations in 1984 is 46 percent. The mark-to-market and 60/40 rules are inapplicable.[40] Thus, there is no recognition of gain or loss at year-end for section 1256 contracts held as part of hedging transactions, unless such contracts are terminated through a closing transaction, delivery, exercise or lapse during the year. Furthermore, the loss deferral rule, any forthcoming wash sale or short sale regulations, and the capitalization of interest and carrying costs rule are all inapplicable to hedging transactions.[41] Thus, a debt option or an interest rate futures contract held as part of a hedging transaction could be closed out at a loss, and that loss would be recognized (and taxed at ordinary income rates) despite the fact that there was unrecognized gain in the taxpayer's offsetting T-bill inventory at the end of the taxable year. If the taxpayer's transaction qualifies as a hedging transaction, but the taxpayer fails to so identify it, the gain or loss will still be ordinary income or loss, but the mark-to-market, loss deferral, wash sale, short sale, and capitalization

---

[40] §1256(e)(1).
[41] s1092(e).

rules will apply. There is a special rule denying hedging transaction treatment to syndicates.[42] In general, syndicates are partnerships in which more than 35 percent of the losses are allocated to the limited partners. In addition, the deductibility by limited partners of ordinary losses from hedging transactions involving debt options and interest rate futures which are entered into by partnerships that are not syndicates is, in general, limited to the taxable income derived from the conduct of the business to which the hedging transaction relates.[43] Any disallowed loss is carried over to the next taxable year, subject to the same limitation on deductibility.

---

[42] §1256(e)(3).
[43] §1256(e)(5).

INDEX

Treasury bonds, writing strategies,
166–206
Treasury bond futures calls against
Treasury bonds, writing of, 166–
168
Treasury bond futures calls, writing
strategies, 150–165
Treasury bond futures contract, writ-
ing strategies, 150–165
Treasury bond futures options con-
tract, writing strategies, 166–206
Treasury bond rate of return on cov-
ered write, 203–206
Treasury Secretary, 295–297
Treasury securities, 25–40
Treasury, *see also* United States
Treasury
Trust Banking Circular No. 2 (REV),
271, 274

U

Underlying security, price of, 67–70
United States Comptroller of the
Currency ("Comptroller"), 271,
274–275
United States Department of the
Treasury, 25
United States Treasury bonds, 11, 12,
150
United States Treasury bond futures
contracts, 150–152
United States Treasury securities,
25–40
auction cycles, 29–32
bank futures, 38–39

United States Treasury securities
(*Cont.*)
cash market, 26–34
categories of, 26–28, 36
coupon securities, 26–32
discount securities, 26–32
futures market, 34–40
note contract, 37–40
secondary market, 39–40
universal life policy, 228–229
use of debt options, 94–112

V

valuation of debt options, *see* pricing
of debt options
variable deliverable, 18–19
variable ratio writing, 160–164
vertical spreads, 136–145
volatility of yields:
fixed income futures, 81–82, 87
fixed income securities, 74–75
volatility risk, banking, 215–216

W

"when-issued market" ("W/I market"), 34
whole life, 105
writing strategies, *see* covered call
writing strategies

Y

yield curve risk, 210, 213, 214